Carol Thatcher was a journalist in Sydney when her mother became Prime Minister. After she returned to London she spent a great deal of time at Number Ten and Chequers.

A freelance journalist, broadcaster and author, she has written two other books, *Diary of an Election* and *Lloyd on Lloyd* with Chris and John Lloyd.

BELOW
THE PARAPET

THE BIOGRAPHY OF
Denis Thatcher

CAROL THATCHER

HarperCollins*Publishers*

HarperCollins*Publishers*
77–85 Fulham Palace Road,
Hammersmith, London W6 8JB

This paperback edition 1997
1 3 5 7 9 8 6 4 2

First published in Great Britain by
HarperCollins*Publishers* 1996

ISBN 0 00 638458 7

Printed and bound in Great Britain by
Caledonian International Book Manufacturing Ltd, Glasgow

CONTENTS

Acknowledgements   vii
Illustrations   ix

1   'She's Done It!'   1
2   The Thatcher Clan   14
3   A Serious Boy   24
4   Major Thatcher   36
5   The First Mrs Thatcher   46
6   Blind Date with a Tory Candidate   56
7   A Distant Dad   69
8   Stress Fractures   83
9   Apprentice Consort   103
10 A Tied Cottage in Downing Street   121
11 Dear Bill   137
12 Two Paces Behind   149
13 Consort Survival: Golf and Gin   162
14 Friends in High Places   175
15 The Falklands   188
16 Back on the Hustings   202
17 Every Minute is Precious   215
18 Love and Loyalty   229
19 Ten Years at Number Ten   246
20 'She's Done For'   261
21 Sir Denis Thatcher   275

Index   293

ACKNOWLEDGEMENTS

IT WAS A U-TURN of mega proportions for Denis to abandon his sacred 'no interviews' policy of Number Ten days and agree to my writing this book with him. I am greatly indebted to Bill Deedes in the first instance who was instrumental in persuading him.

Denis has never kept a letter nor a piece of paper – beyond a cardboard box of recent speeches – so the majority of my work consisted of many oral interviews and the dredging of various archives.

For historical research into Thatcher ancestors in New Zealand I owe an immense thank you to Vivian Morris in the Wanganui Information Centre and, especially, Penny Allen in the Wanganui District Archives who did a fantastic job of unearthing family roots.

To piece together previous generations in Uffington I relied on the work of local historian the late John Little, who had corresponded with Denis, and the Rev John Gawne-Cain, vicar of St Mary's Uffington, who guided me through the church's registers of baptisms and marriages.

Denis's sister Joy Koppier was an invaluable source of information on my grandparents and painted in Denis's childhood and schooldays.

Roger Axworthy profiled Mill Hill School in the days when Denis was a pupil there, while freelance researcher Niamh Dillon left no stone unturned filling in the prep school years and combed the war diaries at the Public Records Office in Kew to trace Denis's war. Ken Crabbe weighed in with some vivid memories to lend Mediterranean colour to their spell in Sicily.

A number of old Atlas employees – Dr Herman Hamburg, Basil Tuck – who'd worked for Denis in the 1950s and 60s (and in the case of Phyllis Kilner and David Roe even for his father) were quite invaluable in helping me reconstruct Denis's business career. Other long-time friends such as Peter Simonis and George Williams took me on through Denis's route to retirement via Castrol and the Burmah Oil Company. I am particularly grateful to the public affairs department at Burmah Castrol Trading Ltd for their efficiency in answering my list of questions.

On Denis's refereeing life Vic and Suzanne Roberts were fabulous and

David Spyer was outstandingly patient with an interviewer who couldn't disguise her female ignorance of the game of rugby football!

Len Whitting and Bill Deedes entertained me with golf and gin anecdotes. Bill was enormously helpful both in his capacity as Denis's closest friend and in communicating the wisdom and judgement I recall from the days when I worked at the *Daily Telegraph* under his editorship.

From the other side of the fence, John Wells regaled me with tales of the 'Dear Bill' letters in *Private Eye*. I am enormously grateful to *Private Eye* for permission to quote excerpts from the column.

When it came to politics, I decided to leave as much as I could in Denis's words because I wanted this book to be HIS reminiscences and the human and humorous side of what it was like to be there in consort's shoes.

A highly enjoyable part of researching *Below the Parapet* was chatting over memories and events with Sir Tim Bell, Cynthia Crawford, Sir Gordon Reece, Joy Robilliard, Caroline Ryder, Lady Wakeham and a number of others who gave me ideas and suggestions. A band of civil servants who'd been in the private office at Number Ten during my mother's eleven and half years there were kind enough to find the time to give me their perspectives of the part Denis played. Sue Goodchild, social secretary at Number Ten, sent me old guest lists and menus and Margaret Hofman accurately and swiftly transcribed hours of tapes.

At HarperCollins I heartily second my father's description of Eddie Bell as 'the best bloody publisher in the world' or 'the best publisher in the world', depending whether or not he's addressing the Archbishop of Canterbury! Val Hudson and Jenny Olivier were saintly at firmly keeping the manuscript on course.

Special thanks to Marco Grass who put up with the author throughout the duration of the project, in our homes in London and Klosters.

LIST OF ILLUSTRATIONS

Thomas Thatcher, Denis's grandfather *(Family collection)*

Madge Thatcher, Denis's New Zealand grandmother *(Family collection)*

Jack Thatcher, Denis's father *(Family collection)*

Kathleen Thatcher, Denis's mother *(Family collection)*

Denis, captain of Holyrood School rugby XV, 1928 *(Family collection)*

Public schoolboy Denis *(Family collection)*

Wartime Denis *(Family collection)*

The first Mrs Thatcher *(Associated Press)*

Margaret Thatcher, the ambitious young Parliamentary candidate Denis met on a blind date *(Evening Standard/Solo Syndication)*

Mark and Carol, aged one *(Family collection)*

New Dad – Denis finds one-year-old twins a handful *(Family collection)*

Denis admires the posters for his wife's election campaign in 1959, while she discusses a speech with her constituency chairman Bertie Blatch *(Desmond O'Neill Features)*

My wife the MP. Family photograph outside the House of Commons *(Family collection)*

Denis and Mark in Lenzerheide, Switzerland, 1962 *(Family collection)*

Mark, Margaret and Denis celebrating Margaret's 1975 Leadership victory *(PA News)*

The Leader of the Opposition and her husband doing a spot of DIY in their holiday flat in Scotney Castle, Kent *(PA News)*

Denis learning the tricks of the trade on his first official overseas trip, India, 1976 *(Family collection)*

Finchley Town Hall, election night, 1979 *(Popperfoto)*

In the line of duty as consort:
Photocall with Beefeater gin Boat Race blondes *(Beefeater Gin)*

Being presented with a momento of his visit to Bahrain race course *(Bahrain Equestrian and Horse Racing Club)*

A rescue 'victim' at the Boat Show *(Srdja Djukanovic)*

Asking intelligent questions about teabags *(Srdja Djukanovic)*

The press conference at Heathrow following Denis's 'rescue mission' when Mark got lost in the Sahara *(Popperfoto)*

Denis and Margaret in the Falklands in January 1983 *(Topham)*

Public Denis: meeting and greeting *(Camera Press/Graham Turner)*

An early cartoon pictures a domesticated Denis armed with a tea towel *(Sunday Extra cartoon, copyright Express Newspapers)*

Private Denis: Sunday papers and a snooze in his favourite armchair at Chequers *(Family photograph)*

Mac cartoon: 'I'm quite happy to go without Christmas pudding this year' *(Daily Mail)*

A disapproving PM watches Denis down a beer in one *(Srdja Djukanovic)*

Mac cartoon: 'It's about the reshuffle, Mr Thatcher' *(Daily Mail)*

A dutiful round of golf with President Bush in Bermuda, despite gales and a tropical downpour *(Associated Press)*

However busy his schedule, Denis always tried to make time for golf *(Rex Features)*

'No heels on the green, please caddie' *(Srdja Djukanovic)*

If you're president or prime minister you shake hands and look serious for the camera but Denis could enjoy a laugh with first ladies Nancy Reagan *(The White House)*, Barbara Bush *(Range/Bettmann/UPI)*, and Raisa Gorbachev *(PA News)*

Denis and his junior fans: signing autographs *(Srdja Djukanovic)*, canvassing the next generation of voters *(Srdja Djukanovic)* and making a guest appearance as grandfather *(Family collection)*

Denis and Margaret at Chequers in the early days *(Srdja Djukanovic)* and just before leaving in November 1990 *(Camera Press/Srdja Djukanovic)*

Denis surrounded by his family at his 80th birthday party. We had a cake made of the infamous *Private Eye* cover featuring him holding a Balthazar of champagne *(Marco Grass)*

Excerpts from the 'Dear Bill' columns reproduced by kind permission of *Private Eye*

BELOW
THE PARAPET

ONE

'SHE'S DONE IT!'

'He had the air of a man who'd just been told his wife had had twins.'

NORMAN TEBBIT

THE GREEN AUDI SEDAN sent white plumes billowing into the cold morning air as it turned out of the garage mews behind Flood Street, Chelsea. Behind the wheel was Denis Thatcher, a grey-haired businessman wearing spectacles, a well-tailored suit, one of his favourite blue and silver striped ties and polished black brogues.

It was barely 7 a.m. but Flood Street had already been cleared of horse-dung after the Household Cavalry's morning exercise. By the time the mounted regiment had reached the end of the street the keener gardeners were outside wielding shovels and scooping up the free fertilizer while it was still steaming.

I was rarely awake to see my father leave for work but I know him to be a creature of habit. He likes his breakfast grapefruit meticulously prepared so that each segment can be lifted easily with a spoon. His marmalade has to have chunky bits of orange and lemon peel and there must be visible cherries in the cherry jam.

He took the same route to work each day, turning left into the King's Road, then joining the M4 heading west towards Heathrow and beyond to Swindon, Wiltshire, and the headquarters of the Burmah Oil Company, where he was divisional director of planning and control.

Denis was approaching his sixtieth birthday and had spent the best part of thirty-five years running companies and keeping share-holders happy, but in less than a hundred days he was due to retire. This abrupt change in lifestyle – which so many men dread – held no fears for him. He was admirably fit, still active and regarded leaving Burmah as a career move rather than a full stop.

'I did have a fixed idea that I might eventually have a boat in the Mediterranean, but the socialists' inflation turned that one into a pipe-dream,' Denis says. As a boy, he had occasionally been taken sailing by his father, Jack Thatcher and, years later, Denis rented a small motor cruiser during one of our holiday fortnights at Seaview on the Isle of Wight. He loved the sea but never did get his own boat.

Unwilling to give up work completely, Denis was looking forward to a balanced routine anchored by a handful of non-executive directorships, loads of golf, lunches with his chums at his club in St James's or at the Savoy; and watching the rugby internationals at Twickenham.

One thing he wouldn't miss was the daily journey from London to Swindon. It was eighty-three miles each way – an hour and a half behind the wheel every morning and, even more loathsome, the return trip every evening after a hard day's work. His long history of slipped discs made driving particularly uncomfortable, but Denis was always stoical about his bad back. 'No one ever died of one,' he told sympathizers.

His standard company Audi didn't run to a radio so Denis drove in silence. On Tuesday 11 February 1975 he needed no reminder of the issue monopolizing the news bulletins and front pages; it had been making headlines for weeks – who would be the next leader of the British Conservative Party?

The Tories had lost two general elections in 1974 – with the October defeat giving the Labour Party and its leader Harold (later Lord) Wilson an overall majority of three seats. This slim victory was enough to sound the deathknell for Edward (later Sir Edward) Heath, who had led the Conservative Party since 1965 and presided over three such losses. 'Even his [Heath's] friends now feel that his three electoral defeats disqualify him from leading the party again,' the *Observer* newspaper announced. Denis agreed: 'The writing was on the wall. It wasn't a question of *if* he would go but *when*.'

Back in the kitchen of 19 Flood Street, Denis had said goodbye to the Rt Hon. Margaret Thatcher, who was on the verge of making history in the second leadership ballot. Victory would make her the first woman to lead a political party in Britain; defeat could possibly condemn her to political oblivion.

As he approached the exit for Swindon and edged into the inside lane, Denis felt calmly detached from these momentous events. He was not a student of the internal machinations and minutiae of party politics and openly admitted his lack of understanding. Margaret's decision to stand had shocked him. Perhaps, like many of his generation, he couldn't imagine a woman leading the Tories and aspiring to lead the country.

The logical candidate to represent the right wing of the party was Keith (later Sir Keith) Joseph, who had advocated a free-market, right-wing agenda in a series of speeches between the two elections in 1974. Margaret was among his strongest supporters and a close friend. Denis, too, admired Keith Joseph enormously. 'I've said – and stuck to it – that I thought he was England's greatest man. He had a big influence on Margaret. He was kind [and] he had total integrity.'

Sadly, Keith Joseph's chance of becoming party leader evaporated after he made a disastrous social policy speech in Edgbaston on 19 October, suggesting that the 'human stock' of society was deteriorating because mothers in the lowest economic classes were having too many babies. It created a media furore and within four weeks he told Margaret, 'I am sorry, I just can't run. Ever since I made that speech, the press have been outside the house. They have been merciless. Helen [his wife] can't take it and I have decided that I just can't stand.'

Margaret understood his reasons but also knew that their views had to be represented. 'Look, Keith, if you're not going to stand, I will,' she said.

It was a massive gamble. She was number two at the Treasury to Robert Carr, the Shadow Chancellor, and only a few rungs short of her greatest ambition – to reach 11 Downing Street. If she stood for the leadership and lost, she risked being thrown out of the Shadow Cabinet for gross disloyalty.

Denis's reaction to the news mirrored that of the mother of the American Presidential hopeful, who asked him, 'President of what, dear?'

I told her I didn't think she could win [he admits]. But she said, 'My friends say this and that,' so I said, 'Well, if your friends say so . . .' Of course, I told her I'd support her all the way – that's what marriage is all about.

I had very grave doubts whether it was possible to win, whether she'd be able to get enough of her colleagues to vote for her . . . I regarded the leadership contest as I did general elections and reshuffles – an occupational hazard of being in politics. Of course, if she wasn't going to win, I had nothing to worry about.

The bookmakers took a similar view and Ladbrokes installed Willie Whitelaw (who hadn't yet entered the race) as 6–4 favourite, Ted Heath at 5–2, Edward (later Sir Edward) du Cann at 5–1 and Margaret the rank outsider at 8–1.

Even so, she made astounding headway in the lead-up to the first ballot and, a fortnight beforehand, the *Daily Mail* wrote: 'Mrs Margaret Thatcher's bid for the Tory Leadership is gathering so much momentum that near panic has broken out among the party's top people. They are worried at the possibility of her beating Mr Heath first time around.' The grandees of the party couldn't bear the thought of being led by a woman, especially a 'suburban house-wife' brought up above a grocer's shop in Grantham – the wrong side of the tracks.

To the amazement of virtually everyone, including my mother, the first count transformed her into a genuine contender. She collected 130 votes – only 31 short of an outright win. A stunned Ted Heath collected 119 votes and resigned within hours.

'I was surprised she beat Heath in the first ballot,' says Denis with typical understatement.

The race was now galvanized. With Heath out of the picture Willie Whitelaw put his name forward for the second ballot and became many people's favourite. However, Margaret's bandwagon was on a roll and just seemed to accelerate.

Neither she nor Denis spent the final few days combing lists of MPs or headcounting. Nor did they discuss the ramifications of victory or defeat. As Denis would say, 'When you're riding over fences, don't worry about the next one, get over the one in front.'

Up until then life in Flood Street had been untouched by the snakes and ladders of national politics. There were piles of *Hansard*s where most families kept their TV guides and, when in government, red boxes here and there, but as far as possible my mother tried to keep her work and family life separate. However, she *was* prone to calling me by her secretaries' names and working through each of them until she got to Carol. This didn't offend me: I was the first to acknowledge that their contribution to the smooth running of her 'show' was greater than mine.

Three miles from the motorway Burmah House came into view. The rather avant-garde low-rise concrete headquarters stood in sixty acres of parkland overlooking the Marlborough Downs.

Parking in his usual spot, Denis proceeded briskly to the main entrance flanked by two massive statues of chinthes, Burma's legendary lion. They had been given to the company by the Burmese government; Denis remembered the meeting when the gift was announced. His had been the lone voice enquiring tactfully just how much it was going to cost to transport the eight-foot-high stone creatures to Britain. 'Silly Thatcher,' thought some of his colleagues, totally enraptured by the generosity of the Burmese government – until the shipping invoice showed up.

This is typical of Denis's approach to business. He is a methodical man with an accountant's mind. Common sense has always been his most valuable asset, along with the pragmatism and homespun logic he inherited from his father. 'Any fool can make it – we've got to sell it,' was a favourite saying or, 'If all else fails, read the instructions.'

Phyllis Kilner had been Denis's secretary for more than thirty years. She had only ever worked for one other man in her entire career and that was Denis's father, Jack Thatcher. The epitome of an old-fashioned career secretary, she wore her hair in a neat bun, was a pillar of the local Girl Guides and was renowned for her loyalty and efficiency. Miraculously, she was also able to decipher my father's handwriting and somehow make sense of his idiosyncratic instructions to amend reports by shifting paragraphs and inserting sentences.

At his desk, Denis turned to tackle the contents of his in-tray.

He sipped a cup of coffee, lit a cigarette and appeared totally untouched by the crucial decisions being taken in the House of Commons. The only thing he could do at that moment was to keep right out of the way.

The real worrying was being done by members of the various campaign teams in a last-ditch muster of their supporters before voting commenced in one of the committee rooms. My mother's campaign was being managed by Airey Neave, MP for Abingdon, who'd become a wartime hero after a daring escape from Colditz. Bill (later Sir William) Shelton, MP for Streatham, who was working with him, recalls: 'After the first ballot we went through the same process again, talking to MPs and canvassing their support. We used to get people who were doubtful to go and see Margaret. We used to meet every evening in one of the committee rooms downstairs and I had a big list of all the members and I kept the details. I did all the paperwork. Airey was a real plotter and sort of handled the PR side. He ran a superb campaign.'

I was twenty-one years old and in the middle of my Law Society exams when the leadership ballot intervened. Margaret, being a barrister, had convinced me that a legal qualification was an asset, or at least better than the general arts degree I had in mind.

The incessantly ringing telephone and constant visitors made study almost impossible, so I escaped and set up camp in a neighbour's house. Sue Mastriforte was a friend of the family and had offered me her spare room. On the morning of the ballot I popped home for a cup of coffee. I went through the back door to avoid meeting any journalists waiting out front.

'What's the matter, darling?' my mother asked, as I sipped a mug of coffee and looked preoccupied.

'Today's exam, Mum.'

'Well, you can't be as nervous as me,' she chided and smiled.

Suddenly my fretting was put into perspective. I could always retake my exam: my mother only had one shot. She looked cautiously optimistic – a mood she often adopted on general election nights. Neither of us went into plans A and B for defeat or victory – there weren't any. For Margaret there was no point in dealing

with a situation until it arrived. She is immensely superstitious and
I knew that there was no champagne on ice because that would be
tempting fate. We Thatchers have spent our entire lives toasting
victory with unchilled champagne or eating Moët-flavoured peas
because someone shoved bottles into the freezer at the last minute
and then forgot about them until the subsequent explosion.

'Good luck,' I said, giving her a hug.

She crossed the fingers on both hands. 'We're not sure if we've
got the numbers.'

I left her, noticing her newly done hair (much debate had taken
place whether the simple act of making the hairdressing appointment might also be tempting fate) and her smart black-and-white
outfit. This image of her is engraved on my memory because she
coordinated perfectly with the tiles on Flood Street's kitchen floor.

Denis lunched as usual in the directors' dining room at Burmah
and at 3 p.m. entered the company boardroom for the weekly
management committee meeting. About a half-dozen senior colleagues sat at a rectangular table overlooked by the bust of Sir John
Cargill, the stern Scottish merchant who founded the Burmah Oil
Company at the turn of the century. Again, no one asked Denis
about the vote and his calmness gave nothing away.

'I was much more optimistic in the second ballot than I was in
the first,' he admits. 'I thought she had a very good chance.'

In Westminster Conservative MPs began filing into a committee
room for the ballot. There were no abstainers among the 276
members, although two papers were spoilt. Phyllis Kilner was
sitting at her desk with her ear tuned to a radio. When the result
was announced, she jotted down the figures on a scrap of paper
and hurried along to the boardroom.

'I wasn't in the habit of bursting into such hallowed ground as
the boardroom without having been summoned,' she remembers,
but then this was different. She knocked softly, edged the door
open and spied her boss sitting near by. She pushed the scrap of
paper onto his blotter and backed out again.

Denis glanced down and read the figures: 'Thatcher, 146;
Whitelaw, 79; Howe, 19; Prior, 19; Peyton, 11.'

'She's done it!' he exclaimed and threw up his arms in the air. Around him, his associates murmured their congratulations and shook his hand. The entire scene was over in less than a minute and then business resumed as normal.

Great events generally provoke great passions in men, but with Denis Thatcher there was no cracking open champagne or instant partying. He was of a generation who rarely 'lost their heads' or displayed their true emotions. Margaret had won an incredible victory and he was profoundly proud of her, but it was *her* victory, not his. Throughout her career he had rarely even visited the side-lines and only occasionally sat in the back row of the grandstand. He had long ago perfected the art of compartmentalizing his life and never permitted his wife's political activities to interfere with his own duties and interests, however minor these might appear in comparison. In truth, he didn't quite comprehend the seismic impact Margaret's victory would have on the Thatcher household and, in particular, on his retirement. Years later he admitted: 'At that very minute, I really didn't understand what it all meant. I don't recall shivers sprinting down my spine – not until I really got involved in the damn thing.'

I heard the result in different circumstances. I was sitting my solicitor's finals in a cavernous hall behind Marble Arch. The Law Society exam had started at 2 p.m. and three hours later I handed my paper to the invigilator.

'Do you know the result of the ballot?' he asked.

My reaction was, 'How on earth could I know?' I'd just spent three hours wrestling with an exam paper.

'Your mother won,' he said and rattled off the figures.

My jaw dropped. Christ, this sort of thing didn't happen to people like us.

'There is a photographer and reporter waiting outside to get your reaction. Would you rather go out the back exit?'

'Yes,' I said without hesitation, feeling dazed. I didn't fancy tackling the press: I had learnt about the dangers when Margaret was the Secretary of State for Education and I was her university student daughter. Even as a child, when occasional family-style

8

photo sessions were called for, I was always trying to wriggle out of the frame while Mark, my twin brother, would make for centre stage.

Finding the back entrance of the hall meant negotiating a maze of corridors and fire escapes until I finally emerged into the dark drizzle of Oxford Street and the anonymity of rush-hour crowds. I remember waiting at a busy pedestrian crossing and sizing up all the commuters, wondering how they'd take the news when they turned on their televisions that night.

I walked home, my mind racing, through Hyde Park and Knightsbridge to the King's Road. I had discovered all the shortcuts when, as a student, I worked as a lift operator at Harrods. The house was empty. Even before I put my key in the back door, I looked through the kitchen window and saw the pyramid of bouquets rising out of the sink. Inside there were more flowers propped in buckets, casseroles and any available container. It looked like a florist's shop.

I tiptoed between the blooms, got a glass of water and immediately left, wandering across to Sue Mastriforte's house. We turned on the news. At the press conference Margaret said: 'To me it is like a dream that the next name on the list after Harold Macmillan, Sir Alec Douglas-Home and Edward Heath is Margaret Thatcher.'

Denis left the office earlier than usual to drive back to London for an impromptu party at the Pimlico home of Bill Shelton. As he registered the first road sign, 'London 83 miles', he gazed at the snake of brakelights ahead and began to contemplate the scale of Margaret's achievement. As a keen amateur historian and voracious reader of political biographies, he knew that rank outsiders often came from the back in leadership battles. He can rattle off examples:

Take Baldwin. No one thought that Baldwin was going to be Prime Minister or Leader of the party. When they won that election the prevailing system meant that the grandees of the party would recommend to the reigning monarch who they wanted as Prime Minister. It is almost certain that they wanted Lord Curzon, but if you read the

9

history it tells you that Curzon hadn't got a telephone, so apparently somehow or other they said they'd have Baldwin.

Bonar Law also came from the back, and I don't think too many people thought Ted Heath would lead the party.

With the M4 and West London behind him, Denis suddenly realized that he'd left Bill Shelton's address in the office. He knew it was in Lupus Street, just off the Embankment, but not the house number. Parking the Audi, he stepped into the rain and ran up the steps of the nearest house. 'So sorry to trouble you,' he said when the door opened. 'Are you giving a party for Margaret Thatcher?' The incredulous occupant shook his head and pointed him further down the street.

When he found the right door, Denis was ushered inside and was immediately struck by the noise. He then made what he calls a 'heart-stopping discovery': 'I think it was a life-changing moment. When I walked into Bill's house and heard the whole room erupt with a roar of "Here! Here! Here!" I suddenly realized SHE was the Leader, and one with an enormous number of friends. Being a non-political person up until then, I suddenly realized that she was enormously important.'

Denis and Margaret did victory laps around the room shaking hands and acknowledging the cheers of a small group of MPs who had been bold enough to back her from the beginning. According to Bill Shelton, Denis gave very little away. 'You couldn't tell much from his face but he smiled very nicely. He was a very controlled man. He came up to Airey and me and said, "Damned well done. Damned well done."'

After only forty minutes at the party Margaret was ready to leave for a working dinner with the Opposition Chief Whip, Humphrey Atkins. She had the job she wanted and couldn't wait to get started. As she left, her constituency secretary Susie Shields spied Mark sitting in the back of a car. Totally overwhelmed by the day's events, Susie grinned at him and babbled excitedly, 'When are they going to move into Number Ten?'

Mark looked dumbstruck. 'Steady on!' he laughed.

Still relatively early in the evening, Denis found himself alone in the Central Lobby of the House of Commons. Norman (later Lord)

Tebbit and his wife Margaret came upon him and recognized a man in need of sustenance and support. They invited him to join them for dinner in the Strangers' Dining Room.

Norman has perfect recall of Denis's reaction to his wife's new celebrity and responsibilities. 'He had the air of a man who'd just been told his wife had had twins. He was adjusting, but he wasn't a political animal – he was far more rational and normal than that.'

Meanwhile I'd gone to bed in Sue's spare room. Around midnight she went next door to tell Margaret that I wanted to see her. I was half-asleep when she knocked on the door and I can't remember exactly what we said to each other. But I do recall that she instantly looked the part: the aura of power about her was almost like a halo. She wished me good luck in my next exam and said good night. I went to sleep knowing that nothing was ever going to be the same again.

All over Fleet Street panic-stricken picture editors were trying to lay their hands on photographs – any photograph – of the new Tory Leader. Most dredged up an image of her seated next to Ted Heath during the opening of the Conservative Party Conference in 1970, wearing a navy and white 'humbug'-style hat and looking very young and serious. As journalists sought reactions to the news from MPs and commentators right across the political spectrum, the general tone was, 'A woman! Fancy that!'

I left the house quite early the next morning, taking the Tube to my last exam. As I sat down, the chap next to me was reading the *Sun* and Margaret was all over the front page. I didn't just read over his shoulder – I practically sat on his lap. Eventually he shut the paper in disgust and put it away to teach me some manners. I half contemplated saying, 'But it's my mum,' but I wasn't ready to start boasting.

The outside world might have been surprised to see Margaret Thatcher emerge as Tory Leader, but she had clearly seen herself in a central role. When the political Polaroid developed into a photograph and confirmed her vision, she was already ahead of the game. I was reminded of the famous scene in the Robert Redford film *The Candidate* where the victorious politician grabs an aide in the loo and barks at him, 'OK, what do we do now?' My mother knew exactly what to do and embraced the leadership as if it had always been her destiny.

The Thatcher law of politics was born on 11 February 1975. 'The unexpected always happens' became the all-encompassing excuse for the turmoil that engulfed the family. Yet Denis's shock absorbers were perfectly attuned and he just carried on as if one's wife becoming Leader of the Opposition was an everyday occurrence. Of course, he had the advantage of being a totally relaxed human being; Margaret, on the other hand, was perhaps the least relaxed person in the world. 'She was a bit frenetic to begin with but we got it better organized,' says Denis, always looking on the bright side.

A meal in the dining room at Flood Street was totally out of the question as every inch of the table became filled by thank-you letters laid out alphabetically: the overall scene was of a patience game played with House of Commons envelopes. Anyone who passed through our coral-wallpapered and mirrored front hall was inveigled into licking and sealing a few. The washing-up was postponed because our kitchen was still jam-packed with bouquets decorated with out-sized blue bows. The walls of Flood Street became as transparent as the florists' cellophane packaging: the Thatchers had splashed down in the goldfish bowl of public life.

There were dozens of photographers and cameramen outside the house next morning. All were looking for the 'morning-after' picture of 'Maggie and hubby' to illustrate the editorials and commentaries. However, they had missed Denis. At 7.30 a.m. he had backed the Audi out of the garage, given it a little more choke, and accelerated along Flood Street towards the M4. Shortly before nine he breezed into his office, said good morning to Phyllis and sat down at his desk. It would never have occurred to him not to go to the office; after all, he had work to do.

In the House of Commons Susie Shields went to collect the mail from the post office in the Central Lobby. She was handed the regular constituency correspondence and an extra armful of telegrams and messages from world leaders and foreign prime ministers not normally in the habit of communicating with the Rt Hon. Member for Finchley and Friern Barnet.

As she sorted through them, Susie suddenly realized that she didn't have a clue where the Leader of the Opposition's office was located. She'd mislaid her boss – quite a blunder for a secretary – but she wasn't the only one. Somewhere during the previous twenty-four hours Denis Thatcher had lost a wife.

TWO

THE THATCHER CLAN

'A man of strong convictions who did not hesitate to
express them.'

Obituary of Thomas Thatcher, published in 1911

ON A HOT JANUARY AFTERNOON in 1995 I stepped out of my
hire car in front of a neat row of single-storey clapboard houses
in Wanganui, New Zealand. Trailers, second-hand cars and
patched-up motorbikes littered the parched front yards, and large
families, some Maori and some white, relaxed in the welcome shade
of their verandahs. The wide suburban verges were studded with
portly, sentry-like pohutukawa trees – New Zealand 'Christmas
trees', as they are popularly known courtesy of the blaze of scarlet
flowers produced in December.

Ignoring my jetlag, I began walking along the street, trying to
picture what it would have looked like a hundred years earlier
when Thomas Thatcher, my great-grandfather, gave it its name. In
1892 he was the chairman of the local Harbour Board in Wanganui
which owned the land, sub-divided it and auctioned off the plots.
Thatcher Street looks square into the sunset over the Tasman Sea
and runs for a third of a mile from Manuka Street, across Bamber,
to the junction with Carson Street, only a few minutes' walk
from the black volcanic sand and driftwood-strewn Castlecliff
beach.

These days the beach is backed by uninspiring cheap holiday
accommodation and fast food outlets, but I tried hard to imagine
what it would have looked like at the turn of the century. Thumbing
through Arthur Bates's book, *A Wanganui Photo Album*, I saw
images of a gentrified playground for family outings: ladies in elaborate hats hitched up their long skirts to paddle in the shallows;
groups tucked into banquet-sized picnics, with rugs draped over the

driftwood for protection against the stiff sea breezes or umbrellas doubling as parasols to provide shade on hotter days.

Until I began researching this book I knew almost nothing of my family's New Zealand connections. Denis freely admits that genealogy has never greatly interested him, and perhaps the only trace of his Kiwi heritage is the passion for rugby inherited from his father. However, if I was to start at the beginning and find the things that influenced Denis's life, it meant making the 12,000 mile journey to Wanganui, a small town low down on the west coast of the North Island, in between New Plymouth and Wellington. Admittedly, I also had more self-indulgent motives. During four sensationally happy years living in Australia in the late 1970s and early 80s I'd never made it across the Tasman to New Zealand. Now I had the chance.

I telephoned the New Zealand High Commission in London for contact numbers for the Wanganui Information Centre. Having faxed through a letter, I woke next morning and found an encouraging reply from the information officer, Vivian Morris. 'I was so interested to receive the fax regarding Sir Denis Thatcher's antecedents,' she wrote, explaining that 'the central business district probably looks much like it did in Sir Denis's grandfather's day, but with better road and pavement surfaces.'

Soon afterwards, Penny Allen of Wanganui District Council Archives began researching and pulling together the pieces of my great-grandfather's life. She sent me birth certificates, speeches, wills and an official photograph of Thomas Thatcher taken during his term as chairman of the Harbour Board.

Meanwhile, I began investigating the family history in England. The Thatcher name is well known around Uffington, near Swindon. Two rows of rectangular and oval plaques to six generations of my forebears are set in the exterior wall of the porch at the south end of St Mary's church. The old registers record baptisms, marriages and burials dating back to 1654. There are a number of references to Thatchers, most of them farmers. Clutching a copy of the family tree, I wandered through the cemetery and found the earliest plaque of a family member. It belonged to Thomas Thatcher, a Berkshire farmer who was born in 1712 and died in 1802.

Five generations later, John Thatcher was born in 1821, and in 1847 he married Elizabeth Ann Belcher, whose family featured in *Tom Brown's Schooldays* by Thomas Hughes, also a village resident. Until recently there was a memorial to her at the entrance to the graveyard in Uffington in the form of a Thatcher Gate, which bore a brass plaque bearing the inscription: 'Erected to the memory of E. A. T. 1903.'

John and Elizabeth had five children. The eldest, Thomas, was born on 10 May 1848 and baptized in St Mary's church. According to Thatcher family legend he sailed to New Zealand to seek his fortune instead of following his father and grandfather onto the land. The exact date of his departure from England is unknown, but in the Heads Row cemetery in Wanganui I found a gravestone with the inscription: 'In affectionate remembrance of E. H. Thatcher, beloved wife of Thomas Thatcher, born 2 April 1856 died 27 December 1881.'

This suggests that Thomas arrived in Wanganui in the 1870s with his first wife, Elizabeth Helen. Her death of pulmonary tuberculosis, at the age of twenty-five, must have been a shattering blow for Thomas, who was left to care for their young daughter Edith in a house on Victoria Avenue, Wanganui's main street.

The first recorded arrival of Europeans is in January 1831 when Joseph Rowe, a whaler and trader on Kapiti Island, organized an expedition to the similar-sounding Whanganui river, hoping to buy or barter for the dried tattooed heads of Maori chieftains. A decade later the first settlers appeared, some of them sailing up from Wellington and others trekking overland. Those who made the journey on foot faced an exhausting five-day hike through wild terrain, much of which was in the possession of hostile Maori tribes.

Once they arrived, the pioneers had no guarantees of safety. They were barely established when simmering tensions with the natives boiled over into bitter and bloody skirmishes which were to rumble on dangerously. However, the infant settlement clung on tenaciously, and by the time Thomas Thatcher arrived Wanganui had the makings of a flourishing little community. When the government offered a section of bush up-country at

Waitotara for sale and settlement, Thomas reverted to his farming roots and purchased land for sheep-farming.

Some time afterwards, he fell in love with a Wanganui-born girl, Margaret Ann Reid, one of nine children of John and Margot Reid, who had emigrated to New Zealand from Antrim in Northern Ireland. Nicknamed Madge, she was nineteen years his junior – a striking, dark-haired girl with distinctive features and an indomitable character. She was also a fearless horsewoman who cut an elegant figure in her formal riding habit. Her father had died when she was only eleven and her pushy mother, a solemn-faced woman who was a practising midwife and devout Catholic, had her sights set on wealthy British settlers for her four daughters.

Widower Thomas was a good catch. A successful grazier, he had twice been chairman of the Wanganui County Council, as well as being appointed to the Harbour Board, where he was known as a rather tyrannical chairman. A portrait of him shows a large, bearded, balding man wearing a severe and purposeful expression.

The newlyweds settled down to life on the farm and in the house on Victoria Avenue. Like so many colonial outposts of this era, Wanganui resembled a little piece of Victoriana transplanted. There were no concessions to climate or environment and men wore heavy wool suits, shirts and ties while the ladies perspired in elaborate long dresses with frills and lace.

The sense of isolation must have been enormous. Victoria Avenue was a dusty strip in the summer and a boggy morass in the winter, and the Land Wars with the Maoris meant that long journeys into the bush were hazardous.

On my second day in town I drove up-river through what is now a popular National Park. The sealed road shadows the meandering river and eventually becomes a gravel track running deep into forests and hills that have scarcely changed. I was overwhelmed by the grandeur of the scenery. The thick bush thinned to a farming landscape of emerald rolling hills, studded with small properties on which sheep and deer grazed peacefully. I photographed the wide hairpin bends in the river, from which rose steep banks densely covered in tropical foliage, and marvelled at those determined and intrepid souls who had tamed the valley. The river road was only opened in 1934 after a thirty-year battle with floods and landslides. Nowadays tourists tear up and down the Whanganui in jetboats that flash past rocks where once the pioneers wedged oars and paddles to keep their boats upright in the swift current.

The domineering Thomas Thatcher made his mark as a businessman. Sheep-farming was the pillar of his business empire and he won fulsome praise from the *Wanganui Herald* for his contribution: 'As a farmer on the Brunswick, he took a great interest in sheep-breeding and for years set himself the task of producing sheep combining the best qualities of mutton and wool.' At various times he also owned a brewery, a malt house and several properties on Victoria Avenue.

He then turned his hand to a new venture: manufacturing sheep dip. His partner in this enterprise was fellow farmer W. T. Owen – another innovator keen to improve the productivity and profitability of bush agriculture. The scourge of all graziers at that time was the dreaded sheep scab and, before each shearing season, the animals had to be submerged in a wash made from tobacco which could be obtained duty free by farmers. The mixture had only limited success so Thomas Thatcher and W. T. Owen set about producing an alternative, arsenic-based concoction. Not only did it work very successfully, but the two wealthy graziers soon realized that arsenic had enormous potential as a wood and skin preservative.

In the archives of the Whanganui Regional Museum I found a meticulous chronicle of the daily life of the sheep farmers – a diary written by another settler, William Caines, from Somerset, who wrote: 'About the year 1890, Mr W. T. Owen commenced the manufacture of Owen's sheep dip. One gallon drums, £1, five gallons, £4.10.

'He also made Atlas Preservative, a preparation for skins and hides and Owen's Railway Preservative for preserving metal and wood. The dip was an arsenic liquid and the railway preservative appeared to be a mixture of tar, pitch and turps.'

The Atlas Preservative Company of Wanganui, New Zealand, was to stay in the Thatcher family for three-quarters of a century.

On 15 October 1885 Thomas 'Jack' Thatcher was born – a son

to carry on the family name and, hopefully, follow in his father's footsteps. Young Jack was always going to find it hard growing up in the shadow of such a domineering man, but he also had to deal with his mother Madge, a snobbish woman and something of a dragon. Later in life he would tell his own son, Denis, nostalgic childhood tales of life on the farm with his half-sister Ede (Edith), but the idyllic days seemed to end when he became a boarder at Wanganui Collegiate School at the age of nine.

The school, on Victoria Avenue, was founded in 1854 to provide an education for the local Maoris and children of European settlers. Nowadays it occupies a site on Liverpool Street, not far away, complete with handsome red-brick buildings and a beautiful chapel.

I contacted the archivist and senior master Russell Goldsworthy, who gave me a guided tour. An outgoing former Sydneysider, Russell took a great interest in the school's history and painted a vivid background to my grandfather's schooldays, helping me to match up the photographs I'd taken from the Thatcher family album with those in the school's museum.

Jack is first mentioned in a roll call of new boys in the *Wanganui Collegian*, the school newsletter, in December 1894. The following year he was a member of the rugby seventh XV – hardly an achievement given that the school only had about 180 pupils. He was in the same XV a year later when, for some reason, his schoolmates had dubbed him 'Jack Scratcher'.

Wanganui Collegiate was a typical clapboard building with a verandah, school-room chapel and headmaster's house. It had a strong British colonial flavour to it, which is hardly surprising considering all the teachers were from England. The National Anthem was sung regularly, along with a pledge of allegiance to the Queen, and at the Easter sports days mothers would dress up as if they were parading the latest fashions at Royal Ascot.

Yet just showing up in the classroom was an enormous feat for some of the pupils. Depending on where they lived, the weather, ambushes in the Land Wars and the tricky river crossing, it could take them a month to reach Wanganui.

Although the regime was strict, the school was quite progressive:

the curriculum included agricultural subjects because many of the boys were the sons of graziers and farmers. Typically, when the school facilities needed expanding the boys rolled up their sleeves and got on with it, at one stage building a cricket pavilion and swimming pool for the school. The indelible message drummed into the boys was of patriotism, duty and loyalty – the prevailing philosophy of the era – and Jack Thatcher absorbed them all.

An early landmark event was the rousing celebration in June 1897 to commemorate the Queen's Reign. In the collection of childhood photographs that my grandfather kept all his life is a picture of the town parade and the Collegiate float which consisted of a dray being pulled by a team of ten bullocks. This was chosen to symbolize the general means of locomotion when the Queen was young. The *Wanganui Collegian* reported: 'Loyalty on a grander scale was doubtless witnessed in London on that eventful day, but the few thousands of Wanganui did their best to make up in quality what they lacked in quantity.'

Appropriately, the August newsletter headed its coverage with a few lines from Rudyard Kipling:

> From East to West the circling song has passed,
> Till West is East beside our land-locked blue;
> From East to West the tested train holds fast,
> The well forged link holds true.

Kipling was something of a demi-god for Jack and his contemporaries. As I flipped through a few of the boys' scrapbooks and diaries in the school museum, I could see how carefully the owners had cut out the latest Kipling poems from the newspaper and glued them in. Jack was only six years old when Kipling visited New Zealand in 1891. The poet was warmly welcomed in Wellington and wrote famously about New Zealand's primeval bush as 'the leafy deep'. In 'The Native Born' he toasted Auckland, writing, 'To the sun that never blisters, To the rain that never chills – To the land of waiting springtime.'

For Jack it was the dawn of a lifelong love affair with Kipling's work, which he would pass on to Denis.

* * *

Ever ambitious and with the preservative business expanding, Thomas Thatcher decided to return to England in 1898 with his wife and children and set up a UK branch to manufacture wood preservative and weed killer. The Atlas Preservative Company was established the following year at Deptford, Kent, on the Thames next to Greenwich – conveniently close to London and its port facilities. Meanwhile, the family returned to Thomas's roots and lived at Uffington in a house called 'The Laurels', named because of the high mature laurel hedge which separated it from the road.

It must have been strange for Jack to arrive in a country that he'd never known yet heard about constantly throughout his life. He was 'English' and almost every painting, picture book and poem from his childhood was English. His father had always referred to England as 'home'. The sense of change was heightened in 1900 when Jack found himself with a new baby sister, Doris.

Although Jack's rugby career at Wanganui Collegiate was hardly distinguished, he brought his love for the game from New Zealand and joined Catford Bridge Rugby Club in Kent. In the 1903–4 season he was vice-captain of the second team, and two years later was promoted to captain. That was the highest level he reached, although he went on to become a committee member of the club. Catford Bridge had the distinction of being one of the first clubs to visit the Continent when it played in Paris in 1898, beating Stade-Français 11–0. It also had a good record in the Kent Cup and Jack graces the 1905–6 team photo, which still hangs in the bar of the clubhouse (now the Bromley Rugby Club).

Like many self-made men, Thomas Thatcher was anxious that his son should follow in his footsteps and join Atlas. Unfortunately, he and Jack had never enjoyed a close relationship and working together didn't improve things. Jack was far more mild mannered and gentle than his father.

After trading for ten years the company was incorporated as a limited company in 1907 and Thomas Thatcher was appointed chairman. He had come halfway round the world to found the business and had bold plans for its future. He sent Jack, aged twenty-five, to America to found a branch of Atlas at Bound Green, near New York.

Ultimately, Thomas always intended to return to New Zealand but this plan was sabotaged by declining health. He suffered a nervous breakdown and was forced to retire. He died on 8 September 1911 in Croydon Mental Hospital, aged sixty-three, with the cause of death given as melancholia, dilation and fatty degeneration of the heart and circulatory failure.

He'd been a fine businessman, with a bullying, despotic nature, but it was his political life that the *Wanganui Chronicle* highlighted in his obituary: 'In local body and Parliamentary elections he also took a prominent part and was a man of strong convictions, and did not hesitate to express them. In this connection old residents will recall a particular election, at which he displayed on the conveyance in which he was bringing voters to the poll several flaring posters with the words: "We eat what we like; we drink what we like; and we don't care a d— for anybody".'

His final will showed that he had, indeed, made his fortune in New Zealand, with considerable land holdings in Wanganui, Palmerston North and Opunake. Having long been a passionate agnostic, he left strict instructions about what was to be done with his body and how his wealth was to be distributed among the family: 'I desire my body to be cremated or buried at the least possible expenses and without any religious or superstitious ceremony and I declare that if any person intended to be benefited by this my Will shall take part in any such ceremony he or she shall forfeit all benefit hereunder.'

As expected, Jack took over Atlas as managing director, inheriting a newish business before he was ready for it and lacking his father's golden commercial touch. Loyalty, duty and honour bound him to the business – a vocation he might not have taken if given the choice. Unfortunately, the economic times were wretched for Jack and the Atlas Preservative Company. The First World War was a serious setback; the main raw materials rose twentyfold in price, the export markets of the world were closed and the finances of the company were stretched to breaking point. Denis puts it in more down-to-earth language, 'It was damn near broke.'

Shortly before his death Thomas Thatcher had employed a new secretary at Atlas, a vivacious South Londoner called Kathleen

Bird, who was in her early twenties. The daughter of a Camberwell horse trader, Thomas Bird, and his wife Louisa Alice, Kathleen was an extrovert red-head with a lively personality. She had borne the brunt of her boss's paranoia during his nervous breakdown when he frequently insisted that she taste the fruit sent up from his country home before he touched it: he was convinced that someone was trying to poison him.

Although she could not have been more different in temperament to the serious Jack, the couple fell in love and were married on 21 May 1912 at Camberwell Register Office.

Madge didn't entirely approve of her son's choice – Denis remembers that she considered he'd married well beneath him – but if opposites attract, then this was a shining example of the rule.

They set up home in an attractive double-fronted Victorian house at 26 Southbrook Road, Lee, Lewisham, and it was here that Denis Thatcher (spelt Dennis on his birth certificate) was born on 10 May 1915.

THREE

A SERIOUS BOY

'At school I was neither successful nor particularly
happy. I didn't like a boarding school environment
very much.'

DENIS THATCHER

'MY EARLIEST MEMORY is walking to a little nursery school
called Miss Garrett's,' Denis says, recalling fondly the quiet, leafy
streets of his childhood in South London.

Like his father, he had a good eye for ball games and Jack
introduced him to cricket in the back garden at Southbrook Road.
'I remember he used to bowl practice balls at me and then patiently
correct every shot,' says Denis. 'Of course, he was mad keen on
rugby football and I can still clearly see the faces of the chaps in a
picture of the 1905 All Blacks team which hung on the wall of my
little bedroom.'

His sister Joy – two years his junior – was a sweet and pretty
child who adored her father and spent much of her first years being
lovingly dandled on his knee. 'My first memory is of my mother
saying, "Jack, would you please put Joy down," as if I was a dog,'
she says, laughing. 'Daddy had been nicknamed Jack Scratcher at
school so he called me Joyscratch.'

The family was completed by Stiffy, a shaggy little Pomeranian,
who was so spoilt by Kathleen that her husband claimed that the
dog came before anyone in her affections.

It was a comfortable, conventional childhood, according to Joy.
'We had a nanny and a normal suburban house, which had five
bedrooms, a garage for two cars, and shiny parquet floor in the
dining room and a drawing room decorated in peach and blue.'

Joy took after her gregarious mother who had a marvellous sense
of humour; Denis was his father's son – quiet, serious and very

24

proper. He would battle against shyness all his life: 'If you're born shy, you're born shy, aren't you,' he says. Family life in Southbrook Road gelled into this distinct gender demarcation.

My mother loved her drink and was very sociable [says Joy]. She didn't really like entertaining at home – she was much keener on going out. No one could be as outgoing as Mum.

I can compare Den with our father in that Daddy was no good with strangers. He was very quiet and didn't mix well, but he still had many great friends. My father's friends were long standing. He did exactly what he wanted – and what he wanted most was to be absolutely besotted with freemasonry.

He had a kind face but was terribly serious, quiet and reserved; he had a good brain in a scholastic way, whereas my mother was terribly astute and completely extrovert.

According to Denis, his father had 'laid down the correct standards by which to live your life ... He was a gentle man and a gentleman. His standards of behaviour and of honour were above reproach and I think I got a lot from him from that point of view.'

At the age of eight Denis was enrolled at Holyrood School in Victoria Drive, Bognor – one of nearly forty private schools in this 'prep school capital' of the South Coast. 'We left by train from Victoria,' recalls Denis. 'There was a whole pile of minute children saying goodbye to their mums and dads and climbing aboard. I don't recall it [the school] being all that bad.'

Holyrood was unusual in that it was purpose-built. It was one of the leading private schools in the town, set in eight acres of grounds in the best part of Bognor, close to the sea. The dormitories were heated by underfloor pipes and each of the seventy-odd boys had his own cubicle. A Board of Education inspection report in the 1920s is glowing in its praise: 'There can be no doubt that the head master has left nothing undone to bring the school into the front rank of preparatory schools. Expenditure on buildings has been of the most generous kind ... the boys are alert and responsive and the instruction given is sound and sensible.'

Denis enjoyed sport and proved to be a reliable left-handed batsman, eventually captaining the first XI in 1928. Many of his boyhood heroes were cricketers. 'I remember names like Jack

Hobbs, Donald Bradman, Herbert Sutcliffe. These were the men that I was brought up with as a kid. One admired them.'

During his final year at Holyrood Denis started to play rugby, a game that became the sporting love of his life, although he exhibited no special prowess on the field. He also learnt to ride, encouraged by his father, who had ridden on the farm in Wanganui from the time he could walk.

On one matter Jack put his foot down: he refused to let either Denis or Joy learn to play a musical instrument. It wasn't that he didn't like music – he was a considerable Gilbert and Sullivan buff – but his younger sister Doris had learned the violin (she later played in orchestras in Johannesburg and Sydney) and Jack just couldn't bear the prospect of his own kids screeching away.

He was something of an absentee father, travelling a great deal to promote the export of Atlas products and then, later, developing a passion for sailing. He even acquired a part-share in a boat named *Thistle*, which was moored in Gosport.

Jack took Denis to his first rugby international at Twickenham – England versus the New Zealand All Blacks – in 1925: it turned out to be a historic clash. 'I remember it well because Cyril Brownlie was sent off,' says Denis, 'which caused an awful scandal at the time because no one had ever been sent off in an international before. My father was thunderstruck and desperately upset that it was an All Black. He always said that both of them should have been sent off and by and large that is probably right today.'

Meanwhile Kathleen had inherited a love of gambling from her father. 'She was very keen on horse racing and dog racing [but] my father disliked it intensely,' says Joy. 'I was a very delicate child and the doctor would often drop round. I was outside – all pale and peaky – and he would pat me on the head. He'd really come to see Mother and to study the form.'

Kathleen liked nothing more than to spend her days at the horses and her evenings at the dogs until her mounting losses became too much for Jack: 'Daddy threw the cheque for her on the table and told her, "You need your brains seen to." From that moment on, she never looked at the horses.'

Instead she turned – with equal addiction – to the stock market, and became quite successful at reading the ups and downs. Joy remembers her mother coming downstairs first thing in the morning, mumbling about not having bought something or sold something. 'God, it's not even seven o'clock in the morning,' Joy told her.

The desire to have a wager never surfaced in Denis. 'I think you're either born with a gambling instinct or you're not,' he says. However he inherited a passion for Rudyard Kipling's poetry: his father 'collected first editions of Kipling bound in red leather – some of the earliest were even written on rice paper'.

Jack eventually joined the Kipling Society, founded in April 1928, and liked nothing more than to share his interpretation of some ambiguous Kipling verse. It was the poet's masonic writings which had provided the catalyst for Jack's interest in freemasonry, on which he spent considerable amounts of time and money as he rose through the hierarchy. In 1919 he founded the Armament Lodge No. 3898, London, formed by freemasons who had worked in the wartime Ministry of Munitions or associated industries. Although Jack returned to New Zealand only once in his lifetime – in 1936 – he still felt a strong link and was a founder member of the New Zealand Lodge No. 5157, London.

The first family car to make an impact on Denis was an old Austin four-seater. 'My mother used to like driving and we used to drive off to Brighton, Bournemouth, Eastbourne and Worthing – all those sort of places – because there wasn't the traffic on the roads in those days.' He also remembers being taken to St Mary's, Uffington, to see his great-grandmother's gravestone in the 'Thatcher corner'.

The children saw a little of their maternal grandmother, Louisa; they called her Lulu and thought her wonderful. Her counterpart, Grandma Thatcher (née Madge Reid), was the first formidable woman Denis ever encountered.

Following her husband's death in 1911, rather than returning to Wanganui she stayed in London to run what Denis describes as a rather upmarket guest house in Nevern Square, Earls Court. Grandma Thatcher had always made it quite plain that she didn't approve of Kathleen. 'They didn't get on at all and never spoke to each other,' says Denis. 'She held the firm view that only very common people went horse racing.'

Kathleen didn't hold it against her and encouraged the relationship between grandmother and grandchildren. Denis and Joy were regularly summoned by the old matriarch to her Edwardian tea parties in Earls Court.

Denis's memories of this dragon-like figure could be lifted out of *Great Expectations*, but the standards she preached became cemented in his psyche and stayed with him all his life:

> We had to wash behind our ears and turn out properly dressed. She was very snobby in a Nancy Mitford sort of a way. She would buy an ordinary pot of decent quality marmalade and then she'd say, 'Of course, I always buy my marmalade from Harrods, they make it especially for me, dear.' That was her to a T.
>
> I remember my Great-aunt Lizzie [married to Archie Elkington] and Grandma talking together and their comments went like this: 'Oh, so-and-so has gone into trade.'
>
> 'Trade?' echoed Lizzie in a disparaging tone.
>
> 'But wholesale, dear, wholesale,' justified Grandma.

Grandma Thatcher terrified Joy, who used to dread being summoned to Nevern Square: 'She looked exactly like Queen Mary. She had a toque and a stick. She wore the toque all the time in the house. She was intimidating but Den was in awe of her. I tell you what sort of person she was, she was extremely strict with us as kids. When we visited, she taught us basic manners like hell – insisted upon them, no question about that. She would always have lunch and tea with her hat on and was tall and elegant and well-dressed.'

Her influence – combined with that of his father – moulded Denis who, according to Joy, was born grown up. 'He was terribly serious when he was young. Mother used to say outrageous things and Den would say, "Mother, must you?" This became a running gag between Mum and me, and whenever she said anything completely over the top we would both imitate Den and chorus, "Mother, must you?" and burst out laughing.'

Despite the teasing, Denis relished his role as the older brother. Joy has an enduring image of him, meticulously turned out in pinstripe trousers and coat, leaning on his stick and fiddling with his leather gloves in the hall as he waited for her to finish getting ready for church. Once there, he knew the hymns and prayer order and would patronizingly hand the books to her open at the correct page to avoid the embarrassment of her flicking through to find her place.

Jack Thatcher was not in his father's league as a go-getting business-man, but he doggedly kept Atlas going through the war and the Depression. He was a fatherly figure – respected by a supportive staff – running an old-fashioned family business producing paint and chemicals in rather ramshackle buildings along a canal in Deptford.

When not at the factory, he devoted himself to freemasonry – which his lively wife resented. Although he sensed his father's disappointment, Denis never evinced an iota of interest in joining a Lodge.

It was freemasonry more than anything else which influenced Jack's choice of public school for Denis. He was enrolled at Mill Hill, set on the Ridgeway amidst impressive gardens on the fringes of North London, in the autumn of 1928. A leading Free Church school, it dated back to 1807 when a group of City Merchants and Ministers set out to provide an educational establishment for religious non-conformists. 'This was the clinching thing from my father's point of view,' says Denis. 'Freemasonry gave him religious comfort.' Jack loathed Roman Catholicism, blaming it for many of the world's ills. 'He would say to me, "You've got to have one prejudice in life without having to defend it."' By sending his son to the leading non-conformist school in the South of England, he sought to make sure that Denis grew up with an open mind.

The new boy found himself in Priestley House – a subdivision of School House. Coming from a prep school with fewer than eighty pupils, where he was at the top, to a public school with 300 pupils where he was at the very bottom – a boy in lower IV – was something of a shock. Sixty years later he described the trepidation he felt that day in a speech in the City of London: 'One moves into one's Public School. There, one is received with neither enthusiasm nor welcome – as befits the junior boys in the school and lowest human beings ever to go there – and for two years is treated as such. This is called character-forming. The only instruction given is, "Keep your mouth shut."'

Sport was prominent at Mill Hill, which suited Denis, and the school prided itself on the quality of its rugby. The international matches in the early 1930s were followed closely because old Mill Hillians regularly featured in the England team.

There is no sense of fondness or nostalgia for those schooldays. 'I was neither successful nor particularly happy there', Denis says of Mill Hill. 'I didn't like a boarding school environment very much. I played hockey, cricket (I was supposed to be a batsman but I was a bit slow), rugby ... all fairly unsuccessfully. I never got into the first eleven or first fifteen. I only ever made the seconds.'

The sporting highlight of his endeavours was to make his house team in 'single-handed hockey', a game unique to Mill Hill, played with cut-down walking sticks, flattened on either side, and a small hard rubber ball hit between goalposts at either end of the playground. He also scored a dogged 51 for the second XI in the Senior House cricket final against Winterstoke. Priestley won the match and, for part of the innings, Denis partnered Bill Murray-Wood, who later won a cricketing blue at Oxford and captained Kent.

When he reached his teens, Denis's shyness became even more debilitating: it inhibited his capacity to expand friendships – the prime defence against the rigours of public school routine. He would turn up at the Debating Society, but never once found the courage to speak for or against a motion, and he hated language classes.

At Priestley House he shared a study with a future long-time friend, Kent Green – although Denis admits they got on better after they'd left Mill Hill. Apparently, their teenage competitiveness kept them from becoming close at school or, as Denis explains perfectly, 'He was cleverer than I.'

In 1929 he watched his first school play, *HMS Pinafore*, which was familiar territory because his father adored Gilbert and Sullivan. When Denis was a little older his father began taking him to see

G & S operas in London's theatreland. 'One summer we attended almost every Gilbert and Sullivan production put on at the Savoy Theatre and enjoyed a beer in the Coal Hole beforehand. As a result I got to like them all,' says Denis.

Jack also impressed upon him the need for caution in matters of finance and investment. Atlas had survived the worst years of the Depression and the family were living a fairly comfortable middle-class existence. According to Denis, 'We didn't go without anything but we couldn't afford to be extravagant.'

However, they could afford an extended family holiday abroad to St Malo in Brittany. Cousins on the New Zealand side of the family joined them, and for Denis and Joy the Jamieson children were exciting holiday companions who told exotic tales of the Far East where their father was in the tin-mining business. The holiday was such a success that it was repeated the following year, but the clan never gathered at Christmas or Easter because Kathleen wasn't fond of entertaining. The family became more geographically scattered when both Jack's sisters, Edith and Doris, married South Africans and made their homes there.

School holidays were normally spent in Lewisham – in 1931 the family moved from Southbrook Road to 46 Lewisham Park – and occasionally the family would stay in a small hotel in Brighton. In addition to sailing, Jack had taken up golf and he and Denis would play together. 'I took it up as a teenager but then left it for years and years,' he explains. 'My father wasn't very good at it.'

When it came to deciding on a career, Denis fleetingly toyed with the idea of becoming a school master – an odd choice, given his lack of enthusiasm for school. 'It was curious – possibly I wasn't very serious about it. I think I discussed it with my father, who naturally wasn't very carried away with the idea. He pointed out there was no money in it, which of course there wasn't.'

Eventually it was a holiday job at Atlas that decided his future direction. Denis found getting on with a job on the factory floor far more 'practical and interesting' than all the classroom theory. In 1930 Atlas moved from Windmill Lane Wharf, Deptford (which an employee called 'a dreary old factory by the side of the Surrey Canal') to spanking new premises in Fraser Road, Erith.

Denis was in his final year at Mill Hill when he was invited to go to the Duke of York's Camp in Southwold. Every summer the Duke sent out invitations to some 400 boys, ranging from apprentices and lads working in the factories to public school pupils, and they all gathered for a week under canvas. The only rule was, 'Play the Game', and there were organized activities from breakfast until bedtime. For Denis, camp life combined his love of male company and sport – and for the first time his leadership qualities surfaced.

> It was run by an organization called the Industrial Welfare Society. All the boys assembled at the Royal Mews in Buckingham Palace Road and went via Liverpool Street to Southwold, where there was a tented camp big enough to take the boys plus staff, and there was a cook house and an enormous entertainment tent. The whole objective was to try and mix young who came from wholly different backgrounds in a competitive and friendly spirit.
>
> We were all divided into sections and there were all sorts of inter-section team games which had all been constructed so that the factory boys had exactly the same chance as the public school boys – the only difference being one of physical fitness.

The experience captivated Denis and for the next three years he returned to help run the camp.

Denis studied conscientiously at Mill Hill and his reward was the satisfaction of passing his School Certificate, although he was disappointed not to have been a monitor or prefect. Initially, he considered going to university to read history. 'I might have got a place because it was a damned sight easier to get in in those days – effectively all you needed was money. My father hadn't got the money and I think he also thought that it wouldn't do me any good.'

Instead Denis did an industrial training course which included a three-month course in shorthand at a Pitman's College – his father's idea. 'My father was absolutely wonderful at shorthand. He used to make notes when he went to masonic dinners and he did it beautifully: thicks and thins with the dots in the right place as Pitman intended – not 150 words a minute or anything like that – about twenty words a minute – but it looked beautiful. He could read his notes back ten years later, whereas the average secretary can have great trouble the following day.'

Joy remembers Denis being less than enthusiastic about mastering the dots and squiggles. 'He practically wrecked the college because he didn't see why he should go and learn bloody silly things like shorthand that only girls did.' Denis admits: 'I buggered off every so often and didn't go. Then I'd sign the little book you had to show your parents to prove you'd attended. I was awfully good at forgery.'

Although mature beyond his years, Denis had to grow up very quickly when Jack suffered a stroke at the age of forty-seven. He carried on working afterwards, although periodic blackouts were frightening reminders of his poor health.

Denis officially joined Atlas in 1933 and thus became the third generation to work in the family business that had been founded in New Zealand nearly forty years earlier. Atlas had just acquired a licence to operate a patented process for the de-greasing of heat-exchanging plant, such as in ships and boilers; it made a huge contribution to the war effort between 1939 and 1945. Eventually it became the Atlas Marine Engineering Service and twenty-four years later was the largest de-greasing and de-scaling service of its kind in the world.

As a raw eighteen-year-old and, more importantly, the boss's son, Denis had to tread carefully at Atlas. David Roe, who'd joined the company as a boy, was given strict instructions by the 'Old Man', as Jack was known, on introducing Denis to the factory floor: 'I don't want him [Denis] to be shown any favouritism or given any special privileges. I want you to start him off on something really difficult, so that he realizes from the beginning that life's not all beer and skittles.'

Phyllis Kilner, Jack's secretary, recalls Denis's first day: 'At eighteen he was already the man he was to become.'

Schooled since birth to be honest, disciplined and honourable, Denis worked hard at Atlas, quickly learning every aspect of the business. When Joy entered the firm as a secretary it became even more of a family business and Denis continued to play the older brother, constantly ribbing his young sister about her chaotic filing.

He was quite merciless when their father called her in to take some dictation and the word 'inventory' turned up as 'infantry'.

As soon as he passed his driving test, Denis's priority was to buy his own set of wheels. 'My first car was a minute Austin Seven. I paid £5 for it, buying it off a mate. It was brown and we painted it mauve/brown at Erith. It wasn't cellulose or anything like that – just oil paint.' David Roe remembers the car far less fondly: 'It's registration number began with EMM, so he called it Little Emma. She didn't always burst into life with the first turn of the starting handle.'

But Little Emma didn't monopolize Denis's attentions. Joy remembers that her girlfriends' mothers warmed to the handsome, serious young man who had such good prospects. She also detected a pattern in Denis's dates. 'They were often called Margaret, funnily enough; Margarets and blondes because my father liked blondes and he said to Denis: "If you brought me the most ravishing brunettes and stood them in front of me it would leave me cold."'

Ill-health limited Jack's work at Atlas and freemasonry occupied his spare hours; he had neither the inclination nor the time to become politically active like his father, although Denis was left in no doubt where he stood: 'He had strong political views – no question about it – they were dyed in the wool conservative.' An imminent polling day would convert this conviction into action. 'We had to address all the damned envelopes for the local Tory candidate,' recalls Denis. 'I think he felt he had a duty. It was my first political duty – and probably my last until Margaret got in the act.'

In 1935 Denis was appointed works manager at Atlas. It wasn't nepotism; he'd earned the promotion. Father and son worked side by side, and away from the office would spend hours talking about rugby. Jack's New Zealand roots meant that he took a particular interest in the touring All Black sides. In 1935 he wrote a frank assessment of the latest team to a friend in Auckland; the letter was published in a New Zealand newspaper: '. . . the All Blacks have a fine set of backs, but their forwards are most disappointing, their displays in line-out work and scrummaging being particularly weak . . . they will have to improve considerably if they are to have any chance of holding the Irish and Scottish forwards.'

Jack made his only return trip to New Zealand in 1936, leaving twenty-year-old Denis to hold the fort at Atlas. Joy and Kathleen accompanied him and, while Jack enjoyed the peace and tranquillity of life at sea, mother and daughter revelled in the social life. 'Daddy and the captain became instant soul mates and they could be found playing chess in the corner,' recalls Joy. 'There was this instant rapport because Atlas supplied products like deck preservative to the ships. Mother was the greatest extrovert in the world and she'd hold what my father called "Snowball Parties". We'd start with a small group and then more and more people would join in while Daddy would be sitting quietly.'

Denis also began to take business trips abroad, mainly short haul to Europe. In 1937 he visited Germany where he saw the Brown Shirts and Hitler Youth marching through the streets: 'I went with a group for a fortnight of factory visits. We went over in a training capacity and then toured around by train and coach doing inspections of engineering factories in cities like Dortmund, Düsseldorf and others. The atmosphere was earnest, completely German. I could see what sort of people they were and I thought they were preparing for war and said so.

'When I got back to England, I said to my father, "It's not a question of if there'll be a war, but when. I might as well go and get trained."'

FOUR

MAJOR THATCHER

> 'I liked the discipline, I liked my brother officers and
> I liked the troops. I owe such success as I've had to
> the army. They taught me to think and they taught
> me the elements of leadership.'
>
> DENIS THATCHER

AT THE AGE OF TWENTY-THREE, a shade under six feet tall
and weighing eleven and a half stone, Denis was commissioned in
October 1938 and became a second lieutenant with the 34th
(Queen's Own Royal West Kent) Searchlight Battalion, Royal
Engineers, based at Blackheath. He wasn't pleased about being
assigned to anti-aircraft. 'I tried like hell to get out of it, but
that is where I was and off we went. At that time there was
the great expansion of the army and the big expansion was in
anti-aircraft.'

He was mobilized before Britain declared war on 3 September
1939, and spent several months in Kent with his eyes trained
skyward, searching for bombers.

> I was a section commander and the system was that we set the
> searchlights up – you had six per section and each light was manned
> by about eight soldiers. There would be a diesel engine generator
> some distance from the searchlight to produce the power. The lamps
> could light an aircraft – if you could find the bloody thing – at about
> 15,000 feet.
>
> Our headquarters were at Robertsbridge, on the Kent–Sussex
> border – which is why I know that part of Kent like the back of my
> hand because I spent so much time going round and round my
> bloody section.

Denis also did a spell as a sapper which, years later, in 1983,
earned him a flattering write-up in the South African *Sapper* magazine: 'Denis Thatcher was one of the Section commanders and I

remember him as a competent young officer [then twenty-five] with decisive personality, business-like and efficient yet with a pleasant manner and a great deal of character.'

Many of the young officers were from the London area and, in common with Londoners at the time, tended to look down on provincials rather as 'bushmen' but I am pleased to state that Denis Thatcher was above this snobbish conception. 'Most of his time was spent in the field looking after his men rather than making frequent calls at Headquarters for social contact – Denis's visits were mainly those carried out as part of his duty which he took very seriously yet he was never dull and possessed a good sense of humour and fun.'

Anti-aircraft may not have been the most glamorous field but Denis warmed to the young airmen he met at the School of Anti-Aircraft Defence at Biggin Hill, Kent. 'It [the school] was run by the RAF except there were always two army officers there to watch in order to make sure that our over-enthusiastic gunners didn't shoot *our* aircraft down. It was fun. We lived with the air force chaps, nearly all of them volunteer flyers, who were super chaps.'

According to Denis, it was on another searchlight instructor's course that he learned how to combat his shyness enough to get to his feet and deliver a lecture or speech:

> The army trains you in any known job and I had to learn the business of being an instructor. We had to give four-minute lecturettes and were taught how to hold the attention of the audience and how to construct a lecture the typical army way – step by step.
>
> For instance, I remember it being drilled into us that if we were using a blackboard then don't toss the chalk from hand to hand and don't say 'Er' if you can help it. It is very difficult standing up and talking to your peers, the people on the course; and, if you were shy like me, hell.

In 1942 Denis spent some time in Cardiff as a staff captain with an Anti-Aircraft Division and it was here that he met a marvellous buoyant showbusiness personality who became a life-long friend. Songwriter Jimmy Kennedy was ten years his senior and overflowed with all the bravado that the shy Denis lacked.

The first time I met him he came into my office and I didn't know who the hell he was. He gave me one of the sloppiest salutes I have ever seen – he nearly waved at me.

I said, 'Who the hell are you?'

He said, 'I'm told I have got to be in here, sir.'

'Don't "sir" me,' I said. 'There's your desk.'

We started working together. He was the Divisional Entertainments Officer, an absolutely incredible fellow but the worst soldier I ever met in my life. We got on terribly well. I was an eager, hard-working officer who was quite ambitious. I wanted to be a colonel – something I never achieved except for a matter of weeks in Marseilles.

On one occasion Jimmy said to me, 'Look, you can't win this war single-handedly.'

I told him, 'Well I'm going to have a damn good try.'

Jimmy was a star and possessed all the charisma and confidence of a true performer. His song-writing hits included 'Red Sails in the Sunset' and the gloriously cheeky lyrics of the wartime classic, 'Hang Out Your Washing on the Siegfried Line', a great patriotic song which allegedly infuriated Hitler.

He spent most of his time swanning around [recalls Denis]. He was fantastic – everyone adored him – and women fell at his feet. He had a wonderful sense of humour but he was so bloody undisciplined.

When we had forty-eight hours' leave we used to go up to London and go to the theatre. He knew everyone and so we could go backstage. I remember going to see Tommy Trinder [the immensely popular brash cockney comic whose catchline was: 'You lucky people!'] at the Palladium. He was a very funny man.

When he wasn't touring showbiz haunts with Jimmy, Denis regularly saw his family, who had moved from a mansion block flat in Notting Hill Gate to the Strand Palace Hotel because the flat was too exposed to bombing raids. The hotel had a restaurant in the basement which doubled as an air raid shelter. The leader of the house band knew that Jack Thatcher was a Gilbert and Sullivan fan so whenever there was an air raid, the band would strike up a G & S tune.

In March 1942 Jack, whose health had deteriorated after another stroke and frequent blackouts, wrote a long, fatalistic letter to a friend – an Atlas agent in New Zealand:

> The trend of war events in recent months has of course added considerably to our anxieties of what may lie in front of you good folk in New Zealand and Australia before the tide begins to turn. This particularly applies to those of us who have numerous friends and relations on your side and especially amongst your young fellows whom we have with us over here and who are in the Middle East.
>
> For the time being it seems to me quite futile to talk on business matters of any kind.
>
> This applies particularly in my case, as the two manufacturing companies with which I am concerned are now, one entirely and the other almost exclusively, engaged on wartime production, and I view with apprehension the prospect in the victorious peacetime to come . . .
>
> It is a long lane that has no turning and in these times the lane does indeed seem to be so long that he is a rash man who will attempt any forecast as to when we can expect to come to that turning.

The challenge of converting Atlas back to profitable peacetime production never fell on Jack's shoulders. He died of a stroke on 24 June 1943, aged fifty-seven. Denis went home on compassionate leave but couldn't attend his father's funeral because he was on standby for an imminent posting to Sicily.

With very little time to mourn, it was a long while before Jack's death had its full impact on his only son. Recalling his father's influence, Denis says, 'He was an honourable man and I think more than anything else, he taught me . . . the clear difference between right and wrong. He loathed untruthfulness and that sort of thing.'

Three days after Jack's death Denis boarded the SS *Ormonde* in Liverpool and sailed for Sicily with the HQ of 73 Anti-Aircraft Brigade. His brigade major, Ken Crabbe, was also aboard and remembers being absolutely staggered at the vast numbers of soldiers piling aboard the ship. 'She was crammed, absolutely crammed – there were bunks everywhere. Denis and I, being staff officers, did have a minute cabin so it was a tiny bit more comfortable than for the other ranks.'

The SS *Ormonde* arrived in Sicily on 19 July and HQ 73 was

briefed to provide anti-aircraft protection for the rear of the 8th Army under the command of General Montgomery. This was part of Operation Husky, a plan to invade Italy drawn up at the Casablanca Conference in January 1943. The landing had begun on 10 July, and the immediate aim was to capture all the ports and airfields up the east coast as far as Catania.

On disembarking, HQ 73 established camp in an olive grove a couple of miles from Augusta. Shortly afterwards they upgraded to a Mediterranean orchard which seemed like paradise. Troops who hadn't seen a piece of citrus fruit for years were now surrounded by ripening oranges and lemons. Even the official war diary was moved to describe it as 'most satisfactory with an abundant running water supply and a pool big enough to allow all ranks good bathing facilities'.

Denis's arrival in Sicily didn't plunge him into the war proper. 'The battle had moved on quite a bit and we were well behind the action. We had full command of the air and I don't suppose we saw more than about half a dozen German aircraft in those first months.'

The sweltering heat was the main cause of discomfort, along with swarms of flies and mosquitoes, which were suspected of carrying malaria. Malaria pills were mandatory: 'We were lined up like school kids and made to swallow them there and then.' The rations were basic: the forces' staple, bully beef, was, however, supplemented by fresh local produce. Even now, Denis cannot bring himself to eat an unskinned tomato because of the memory of flies buzzing around the island's harvested tomatoes.

Liquor supplies were rather parsimonious by Denis's standards: the officers' allowance was a lone bottle of whisky a month. The tobacco situation was also dire, according to Ken Crabbe. 'You got a ration of English cigarettes and you could get an unlimited supply of the alternative, which were Egyptian-made. These weren't every soldier's favourite smoke as this ditty illustrates.

> 'The camel's crop of crumbling crap
> Lay rotting in the sun.
> The camel laughed like anything
> To see what it had done.

Me thinks, he said, this mouldering mass
Will make ten thousand State Express.
Players Please.'

Ken Crabbe is full of praise for the role Denis played in Sicily. 'He was an absolutely marvellous staff officer. The brigade major's job was really to move the troops and tell them where to go. The staff captain's job was to see that they were properly fed and there was plenty of ammunition.

'Denis was extremely accurate. He was very meticulous, his desk was always pretty tidy, it didn't matter if his office was only in a tent.'

By September 1943 Operation Baytown – the second stage of the invasion of mainland Italy – was well under way and life quietened down for Denis. Traditionally, when an army has nothing to do it trains, but one such activity nearly went disastrously wrong. During artillery practice, various soldiers were assigned as 'range officers' – a rather tedious task: the subaltern in charge of several guns would yell out orders identifying the target and the gun crew would wait for the range sergeant to shout out the range. On this occasion, the target was a group of rocks sticking out at three o'clock.

I heard the range sergeant shout out the range and yell, 'Number One gun, fire' [recalls Denis]. Instead of the shell falling on a rock it disappeared over the horizon. I said, 'What range did you give?' and he told me.

Jesus Christ, I thought, my level of worry really rising. I got out my map and saw there was a bit of a village [over the horizon] and I said to him, 'You and I are finished if that bloody shell pitched into the middle.'

I got my driver and we drove over to the place and hoped to God this damned shell hadn't landed on this tiny village. We made some enquiries in our pigeon-Italian and the best we could elicit – which was at least reassuring – was that nobody had been hurt. The Sicilians seemed to be under the impression that a spare German mine had gone off.

Thank Christ for that, I thought, and didn't mention it in my range report.

During the autumn and through Christmas 1943 Denis was based in Taormina, in a magical palace, complete with fountains, vacated by the Germans. The location – wedged on the cliffs below Mount Etna with a precipitous rocky drop into the Mediterranean – was beautiful. Denis wasn't a natural mountaineer but with the best intentions he set out to conquer the summit, flogging upwards towards the crater until he decided, 'Not bloody likely, it was too far. I gave up.'

He was in Taormina until October 1944, when HQ 73 left Sicily for mainland Italy. It was a bumpy trip on the fleet of landing craft across the narrow strip of water which separates Sicily from the toe of Italy. By the time they reached terra firma, many of the troops looked slightly green but recovered to establish a headquarters at Reggio di Calabria.

This stint offered very little in the way of action and Denis remembers that daily life was simply 'dull, very dull'. He and an army pal took a week's leave, borrowed a vehicle and set off to tour Italy.

The scene of the Battle of Monte Cassino (on the plain between Rome and Naples) made a lasting impression. 'It was one of the worst battles and I shall never forget the sight of the little village at the bottom of the hill. There wasn't a brick standing, the whole place was a pile of rubble. The losses were enormous.'

The Italian exercise in boredom came to an abrupt halt when Denis received his next set of orders transferring him to serve with the 7th US Army in Marseilles. He went by boat from Genoa, but 'By the time we got there, there was no battle as far as we were concerned. We were there purely as a British headquarters in Marseilles doing all sorts of funny jobs.'

Although the fighting had ended, the city was a scene of devastation.

Initially, when we got to Marseilles we weren't in the port for the simple reason that the Germans had blown it up. So instead we had our headquarters in a bank and had living quarters for a short time in a pub in Marseilles – damn near in the red light district. I do remember that the owner had a very good stock of Châteauneuf-du-Pape which really was my first taste of getting to know just a little about wine. It was jolly good. Eventually he decided we weren't paying enough for it and said they hadn't got any more.

Denis's time in Marseilles proved to be one of the most enjoyable, hard-working stints of the war for him. A cloak-and-dagger operation to extradite captured Poles from internment in Switzerland was one of his tasks.

What had happened was that when the Poles were captured by the Germans they were put in the German army and then when we captured them we sorted them out as POWs and put them back in the Polish army.

Some of them did a hell of a lot of fighting and didn't know which side they were on or whether they were coming or going. They started fighting for us, got captured, fought for the Germans, got captured by us and started again.

There was this huge camp at Avignon run by the Poles where they re-equipped their chaps and sent them back to the Polish army.

When France fell in 1940 the Second Polish Corps elected to march themselves into Switzerland, where they were promptly interned. 'They stayed in Switzerland and we had a number of people who spoke very good Polish, and when the border opened with France we used to send them through with fair numbers of gold sovereigns. We were buying them back off the Swiss – we didn't advertise it – and there was an undercover element to it. We had lorries on the other side, complete with British uniforms, and we would gather these chaps up, shove them into lorries and beat it down to Avignon.'

Another operation involved conveying the whole of the 5th Canadian Division without the Germans realizing where the reinforcements were headed. 'We didn't keep them in Marseilles very long; the idea was to keep them moving. We were desperate to cover up any give-away clues so we had to collect up any cigarette packets they tossed out because they were different to our brands. We shifted them out on the French railways, which were a bit clapped out. A train never left on time so I'd be tearing my hair out because we wanted it back for the next lot.'

Denis admits that he was disappointed not to have been involved in any proper fighting, but Marseilles had its compensations. 'It was hard work, terribly hard work. Ships were coming from Genoa carrying troops, guns, arms – the whole lot. It was a very interesting job.'

Living accommodation also improved and included a 'very pukka' château within sight of waving palm trees. Unfortunately, the bar stocks had been consumed by the time Denis arrived so there was nothing to drink while admiring the view from the gracious verandah. He and his mates solved the problem by going into gin production.

We learned that you needed to mix juniper juice in with the alcohol. We didn't have any containers so the obvious receptacle was the bath. The mixture was very cloudy and it [the sediment] didn't settle so we had cloudy gin. That was fine but it was practically pure bloody alcohol – the strongest gin in the world. We sampled some of it straight out of the bath and a mouthful of this stuff nearly blew our heads off. That was easily solved – we turned the tap on and watered it down.

It was still terrible stuff and tasted like hell, but it *was* gin. The Americans had fruit juice in their rations – which doesn't go very well with gin either – but it was drinkable. So when our guests came to the château we grandly offered them 'gin and jungle juice', as if it were the most sophisticated cocktail on earth.

Denis was mentioned in dispatches twice and in 1945 was awarded a military MBE. The citation reads:

AT MARSEILLE on 14 February 1945, H.Q. 203 Sub Area assumed responsibility for dealing with the very urgent and large scale operation called 'Goldflake'. The timetable available for preparation was so short that all concerned had to work day and night to ensure adequate arrangements in time. Maj. Thatcher set an outstanding example of energy, initiative and drive. He deserved most of the credit for the very fine message of appreciation which has been conveyed to me from Field Marshal MONTGOMERY as to the excellence of the work done. The operation is still in progrees at the time of writing!

After VE Day in May 1945 Denis found himself setting up a camp on the racecourse at Toulon as holding accommodation where long-serving soldiers from the Middle East and India could be housed while they waited for transport home. 'It consisted of huts – I don't think the racecourse had any stands: the Germans had probably taken them and burned them for firewood. The camp was an absolute disaster because someone selected the wrong place and come the winter the bloody thing flooded.'

Denis didn't vote in the 1945 election, offering the excuse that he was too busy, but he recalls the astonished reaction of one of his senior officers when, after Winston Churchill's defeat, he saw a photograph of the new Labour Cabinet: 'Christ, look – these buggers are wearing suits,' he muttered.

Denis was demobbed and returned home in 1946 to the responsibility of a widowed mother, a sister whose wartime marriage hadn't survived, and the family business.

After six years of war, Denis was thankful for what the army had given him and knew that he had come out better trained and less scathed than many of his friends.

By and large I enjoyed it. Ninety per cent boredom and ten per cent fright was how we described it. Not in my case, because we didn't see any real action, but learned a lot. They taught me discipline, and for all its faults the army was a well-administered organization; everyone knew what they had to do and did it – and if you didn't do it well they moved you on.

The war didn't have a traumatic effect on me but I think I'm an insensitive person.

Fifty years on, he credits the army with being a cornerstone of his life. 'I liked the discipline, I liked my brother officers and I liked the troops. I owe such success as I've had to the army. They taught me to think and they taught me the elements of leadership.'

FIVE

THE FIRST MRS THATCHER

'God guided us both. Neither can one, nor would one
want to rewrite history.'

DENIS THATCHER, on his first marriage

IN FEBRUARY 1976 the *News of the World* began researching
a story about the husband of the then Leader of Her Majesty's
Opposition. They were checking out a tip-off that Denis Thatcher
had been married once before.

When this news reached the ears of Gordon (later Sir Gordon)
Reece, my mother's press secretary, he advised the Thatcher camp
that to prevent the story being sensationalized in an 'unfriendly'
paper, they should give it to a 'friendly' publication such as the
Daily Mail.

In due course the Nigel Dempster column received a telephone
message along the lines of, 'If you look in *Who's Who* you will
find that Denis Thatcher has been married before.' Her marriage
to Denis was recorded within the entry of her second husband,
who was a baronet.

'Are you sure?' queried the diary columnist.

'Yes; her name was also Margaret.'

Immediately interested, Dempster instructed three of his minions
to thumb laboriously through every page of *Who's Who* to find
the reference. They spent several days searching without success.

By mid-week the Thatcher camp was getting edgy. Where was
the *Daily Mail* story? If it wasn't published that week, the *News
of the World*'s scoop for Sunday would be safe. Nigel had to be
helped.

Mail journalist Rod Tyler, who knew Margaret from his days
as an education correspondent when she was Secretary of State,
received a phone call from Alison Ward (later Lady Wakeham),

the Opposition Leader's secretary, who tersely gave him the job of messenger: 'Please tell Nigel Dempster that the relevant information is on page such and such of *Who's Who*.' This meant absolutely nothing to Tyler, but he headed for Nigel's office and delivered the rather cryptic message. Nigel's reaction was less than restrained. 'He was ready to reach across the desk and throttle me,' says Rod.

That night I came home to Flood Street from the solicitor's firm where I was working as an articled clerk to be told by Margaret that a story was about to appear about Denis's first wife. This came completely out of the blue. At twenty-three years of age I had absolutely no idea that he'd been married before. Not once had it been mentioned either by my parents or anyone close to them. Why the secrecy? I wondered. After all, Denis hadn't exactly invented divorce – it happens all the time. Suddenly curious, I tried to discover more.

'Don't mention it to your father,' said Margaret. 'He won't talk about it. It was a wartime thing.'

The following day, Friday 20 February, Dempster's Diary ran a lead item headlined, THE OTHER MRS THATCHER. 'Even the closest friends and family of Denis Thatcher, husband of the Tory Leader, are unaware of a secret he told me yesterday. Margaret Thatcher is his second wife – his first marriage, which took place in wartime, ended in divorce . . .' It went on to quote Denis: 'I can't remember where we met, but we were never able to live together because I was in the army. It ended because I was away, and I can't blame her. The divorce was very amicable . . .'

The *Mail* then despatched star interviewer Lynda Lee-Potter to talk to the lady in question, now Lady Hickman after her marriage to Sir Howard Hickman in 1948. 'Photographs don't do Margot, as she is called, justice because she's a devastatingly attractive woman. She's somehow softer, smaller, slighter than her successor, but there is an uncanny resemblance,' wrote Lee-Potter. 'Their hair might have been chiselled by the same hairdresser, their voices are identical . . .' Lady Hickman admitted, 'Friends do say we look rather alike. I think our tastes are probably similar . . .'

Not surprisingly, Margaret hated these comparisons; she knew how much Denis had been wounded by the divorce and wanted the entire affair consigned to history.

As requested, I didn't mention it to my father and thought little more about Margot until I started researching Denis's life and realized that I couldn't ignore his first marriage. Finding her address, I wrote a letter to Lady Hickman and, on a bitterly cold January day, I drove up to her cottage in a Hertfordshire village.

Arriving mid-morning, I was met by an elegant woman of petite stature, a little younger than Denis, wearing beautiful casual clothes – camel-coloured slacks, a pastel sweater and a row of pearls. In a wonderfully warm voice she invited me inside; two enormous dogs bounded after her. Sitting in front of a cosy fire, she immediately put me at my ease. 'I've got out some things that I wanted to show you,' she told me, and on the coffee table was an assortment of photographs and albums.

Their romance started in 1941, when Denis was based in Cardiff and he and Jimmy Kennedy would hop on the train down to London whenever they had forty-eight hours' leave.

Jimmy knew his way around the remaining bright lights in war-time London's blackout and steered his friend in the direction of an officers' tea dance at the sumptuous Grosvenor House Hotel in Park Lane. He led the way, waving to friends and fans, shaking hands and kissing his following of pretty girls. In the course of the party he introduced Denis to a stunningly beautiful girl in an electric-blue silk dress. Her name was Margot Kempson and Denis fell head over heels in love.

Margot was at the dance with a large party of young people who were determined to enjoy themselves because time off from their various war-time duties was far too precious to be squandered. 'We had a nice time – everyone was laughing and joking,' she said. 'I can't remember whether we went on somewhere to dinner. Everyone was in uniform and that sort of thing. I got on quite well with Denis.'

She flicked through a photograph album, pointing out various pictures. I was struck by how captivating she'd been, with classic, hauntingly beautiful features, luminous skin, blonde hair, a magnetic smile and dancing eyes. She had a fresh and extrovert energy which reminded me of Denis's sister, Joy.

Margot's background and interests were quite different to Denis's. His roots were suburban; she was a country girl from rural Hertfordshire. Her father, Leonard Kempson, designed jewellery, but her passion was horses and she was a natural in the saddle. 'I hunted during the winter months and showjumped in the summer. I loved it. I wasn't a bit academic, I'm afraid.'

She was not only a glamorous party-goer: having danced all night, she would report each morning in uniform and climb behind the wheel of a lorry to transport Mosquito aircraft parts from the factory to dispersal units around the country. The long journeys, often in blackout darkness, had to be undertaken without the aid of road signs.

At that first meeting in the Grosvenor House Denis extracted Margot's telephone number from one of her girlfriends.

> Lo and behold the next day or the day after he rang me and invited me out. From then on we met when we could. It was fun really.
>
> Denis was always charming and awfully sweet. He was a strong character and he was extremely intelligent and very clever at all sorts of things.
>
> He only had just forty-eight hours' leave, sometimes only twenty-four, and we always stayed at the Dorchester, which was lovely. It was *the* place – I mean it was so expensive, £5 a night or something. We used to meet in the little cocktail bar round the side. Denis was always a smoker and he always had a gin and tonic or a beer in his other hand.
>
> He was terribly funny and he was very kind and considerate of other people. He was particularly sweet to my parents and they were very fond of him.

Denis had worn glasses since his schooldays at Mill Hill and Margot remembers teasing him: 'I said to him, "Take your glasses off and let me see what you look like." You know how it is when people who wear glasses all the time take them off and their eyes look rather small. I said, "No, you're much more handsome with your glasses on."'

Denis proposed to Margot just before Christmas 1941 and the

marriage was arranged on Margot's home territory at Monken Hadley, near Barnet. Flicking through the wedding album, I saw a series of photographs that captured the happiness of the wedding day on 28 March 1942. The bridegroom and nearly all the male guests were young and in uniform while Margot, a bride when rationing was in full force, was all in white in a borrowed dress and veil. The reception was held at her parents' home.

Denis's parents and sister were there, along with Jimmy Kennedy and old friends from Atlas, including chemist David Roe. In his book *Standing in the Wings*, Roe recalls an incident involving Jack Thatcher that caused him concern: 'As Denis and his bride pulled away in the car, the Old Man ran after them, throwing confetti. He was panting a little, his face flushed with excitement, and I suddenly realized with a sense of shock he was far from well.'

Denis and Margot borrowed a Morris car from Atlas and spent their week-long honeymoon touring the Thames Valley. 'It was lovely down there,' recalls Margot. 'We spent a few days at the Hindshead at Bray, a timbered traditional pub on the banks of the Thames. In those days mine host had this parrot which sat on the bar. It was super – full of that lovely smell that pubs have when they have masses of beams and wood and open log fires.'

Denis took to husband mode naturally and in several photographs is puffing contentedly on a pipe. However, the war separated the couple immediately after the honeymoon: Denis went back to the army and Margot returned to live with her parents. Married life consisted of lengthy separations punctuated by urgent weekends whenever Denis was on leave.

When he sailed for Sicily in June 1943 they had to make do with writing letters and exchanging photographs. At Christmas 1943 he sent her a photograph of himself inscribed 'To my beloved "Pie"' (he'd always called her Sweetie Pie). 'Denis was a marvellous letter writer,' she says. 'I've still got a lot of his letters. He has such lovely writing – always in fountain pen.'

When Denis was demobbed in 1946 his future looked certain; many of his comrades were returning to confront unemployment, children they didn't know and wives who'd become independent strangers during the previous six years. He had some money saved and the job at Atlas – which gave him the security to buy a house and settle down to normal married life. Sadly, it was not to be. He returned to England to discover that the romance was over.

Margot explains, 'We both fell very much in love to begin with; I think it was the separation really. Well, it was entirely my fault and I regret it a lot; I do. The war was a strange time. You never knew what was going to happen. You grabbed happiness while you could.'

When I mentioned to Denis that I'd been to see Margot, he paused and looked rather misty-eyed. 'Is she still incredibly beautiful?' he asked.

'Yes,' I said and we sat in silence.

I realized then that he would never really open up about what happened. He made only one comment on the woman who'd captivated him so long ago: 'God guided us both. Neither can one, nor would one want to rewrite history.'

Denis was devastated, and after the divorce in 1948 he barely mentioned the marriage even to his closest friends. Kim Coombe, an Old Millhillian, says: 'He came out [of the army] as a sort of gallant, elegant Major – the breakdown of his marriage shattered him totally and he seemed rudderless.'

Hoping to forget, Denis threw himself into business, and relied on the sporting activities of his old school friends to provide his social life. 'I would say we were all demob happy in those days,' says Coombe. 'This is why we all gravitated towards the Old Mill Hillians' club and the rugby club. They were all coming out, captains, majors, all relatively senior – most from a public school background so they all had a shilling or two. There was a tremendous amount of relief and mental escapism from the war so there was a great deal of drinking being done.'

In 1946 Denis became joint general manager of Atlas with a salary of £1,000 a year. The company was in a shambles. Although it had escaped the Luftwaffe bombers, the site on Fraser Road, Erith, was too small for the business, housing an inconvenient jumble of temporary buildings. It had been years since money had been invested in the plant. The year-end profits were about £7,000.

The company had been in war-mode and was in pretty bad shape as a business. It had been making camouflage paint and had been doing quite well in the chemical cleaning business – naval ships and civilian cargo ships. It was ticking over and making a bit of money. There were about thirty people on the payroll.

At the beginning of peacetime the demand for paint was enormous because nothing had been painted for seven years, but we were terribly short of raw materials. Rationing went on for several more years and a black market was in operation. Then inflation started to push the prices up.

In 1947 Denis was appointed managing director and the company's profits rose to £12,000 a year. He urged himself on to 'just build it up' and concentrate on growth despite the inauspicious economic times.

Although he worked tremendously hard, nothing could make Denis love the paint business. He didn't hide the fact; even before the war he had viewed it as 'a lousy industry and a miserable little business'. Even so, he was determined to make it better and to look after his family's investments – his mother and two aunts were the largest shareholders. Denis also actively tried to raise the paint business from its cottage industry status. In 1947 he was elected a member of the Council of the National Paint Federation. The following year he became vice-chairman of the London Association and then succeeded to the chair. 'I formed the opinion that we paid a subscription [to the Federation] and I thought this might do a bit of good for the company. Generally speaking I have always taken the view if you pay a subscription to some trade association you have got to follow your money if you're going to get anything out of it.'

The *Paint Federation Journal* gave him a flattering write-up as chairman of the London Association:

Since the war years when trade association activity was at its peak, there has been some decline in interest and it has been difficult to find individuals who are prepared to take a share in the responsibility of collective organisation.

The London Association was, therefore, delighted to welcome this very likeable young man, who, at the conclusion of hostilities, surprised many meetings by his straight and sensible speeches, his undoubted powers of debate and his ability to form sound judgments. Many of the older members perceived at once a personality calculated to revive the apathetic and a man who would throw his whole interest into any job that he might be called upon to do . . .

In this office [chairman] he has shown commendable foresight and displays a charming personality. His colleagues find that he has a quick grasp of fundamental points and a capable and analytical mind, so that he is sure to take an increasingly important part in Federation affairs.

Denis was also on the committee of the Council of the Paint Materials Trade Association and co-authored a book with the less-than-gripping title, *Accounting and Costing in the Paint Industry*.

We wrote it as a committee. I enjoyed doing it because by that time I had begun to study cost accountancy seriously in between working. I'd never qualified and doing the book taught me a hell of a lot because I had to read copiously and had the advantage of being on a committee of top class accountants.

What we were trying to do was get the industry as a whole – which consisted of hundreds of minute little companies who hadn't got the slightest clue on how to cost their bloody goods – to understand the first principles of costing.

I wrote a lot of my contribution long hand at weekends in the library of the Junior Carlton Club of which I was then a member.

Atlas was export orientated and Denis energetically spearheaded the sales drive with lengthy trips to Africa and other overseas markets.

The first time I ever went to South Africa it was by flying boat in about 1949. It was wonderful, really wonderful. It took four days. On day one we flew from England to Sicily – and landed at Lentini. The day after we flew on down to Khartoum and landed on the Nile. You got off every night and went to a hotel so it was deeply civilized.

Day three was the hop down to Lake Naivasha, one of the Rift Valley lakes in Kenya, and the next day we flew to Victoria Falls and landed on the river above them. They gave us a little trip up the river in the evening.

Then I went on to Johannesburg because in those days we had quite a good business selling paint to the gold mines.

It was the beginning of a love affair with the Dark Continent which would last a lifetime.

Meanwhile at home Denis's interest was captured by another pastime which, like the army, would become a cornerstone of his life:

I make no bones about it, refereeing rugby football is one of the most rewarding things I've ever done. I love the game. I was brought up with it from the age of five.

I got into refereeing because I played a season for the Old Mill Hillians immediately after the war in 1946-47. At that age I was quite useless as a player and thought, 'To hell with this: I'm getting too old to be bashed about.'

There was a junior team and no referee so I volunteered and just enjoyed still being in the game. I took the elementary precaution of looking up the laws of the game. One day someone from the London Society of Rugby Football Union Referees [the oldest and most important society in the world of refereeing] was watching a game when I was in charge. He observed, 'Here we have a referee we can deal with.'

At that time the Old Millhillians' club was expected to provide a representative to the London Society and didn't currently have one so they put my name up and I joined in 1948.

I started at the bottom and was promoted to a better level of game. You always have to have luck. Believe it or not, I was appointed to Finchley RFC and there was a chap there who was a great friend of Cyril Gadney – the greatest referee the world has ever seen.

Word soon reached the society that Denis was quite good and before long he was dispatched to referee Richmond first XV. 'I can't tell you how terrified I was, terrified. On the way there I said to myself, "Thatcher, make a balls of it and you are finished."

'God was good to me, my adrenalin was running and the game went well. It was an easy game to referee; I didn't have any problems and I didn't make too many mistakes.'

This wasn't always the case. Denis once had to referee a match between two schools which both happened to have Field Marshal Montgomery on their board of governors. Denis had briefly met the war hero ('for about thirty seconds') in Sicily. 'I didn't like him. I thought he was a first class ****, although a great soldier.'

That afternoon at St Paul's School in London the illustrious Monty (an Old Boy of the establishment) took it upon himself to march onto the middle of the pitch at half time – in flagrant violation of law 6. 'Without my permission he stamps on the field and he comes over to me. I sharply stand to attention and he then proceeds to talk to both the teams. As the referee, I had the complete authority of rules and regulations to say, "Get the hell off!"'

'Of course I didn't, but you can't just walk onto the field.'

SIX

BLIND DATE WITH A
TORY CANDIDATE

'She stood for Dartford twice and lost twice and the
second time she cried on my shoulder I married her.'
DENIS THATCHER

IT WAS AN INNOCENT enough invitation. Stan Soward, the joint
general manager at Atlas, dropped into Denis's office and found
his boss, shirt sleeves rolled up, hunched over sheaves of figures on
his desk, deep in some complicated calculations. 'Got any plans
for this evening?' he asked.

'No, nothing,' replied Denis, momentarily distracted.

'Good. Then come round for dinner; there's someone I want you
to meet.'

Stanley Soward had joined Atlas in 1912 as a humble office
junior to Denis's father. During the First World War he served as
a sergeant in the Royal Field Artillery in France until wounded and
invalided out in December 1917. His long service with Atlas and
loyalty to Jack Thatcher had imbued him with a fatherly interest
in young Denis and, in particular, his single status.

'He told me he and his wife were having a nice young woman
to dinner who was about to be adopted as the Conservative candidate for Dartford,' recalls Denis.

Before dinner the guests met at the nearby headquarters of the
Dartford Conservative Association. The meeting was already under
way when Denis found a seat and the audience's attention was
trained on a young, very doughty brunette, whose political confidence and determination was tangible. At the tender age of twenty-
three, Margaret Roberts was the youngest candidate standing for
election.

56

Margaret was the second daughter of Alfred Roberts, a grocer from Grantham in Lincolnshire – a stern, authoritarian figure and respected local alderman. She and Muriel – four years her senior – grew up over the shop in Grantham, acquiring from their father a sound knowledge of retail economics as well as the serious, sober virtues he preached from the pulpit of the Finkin Street Methodist church three times every Sunday.

The family finances were tight but Margaret persuaded her father to stretch their meagre resources to pay for Latin lessons – essential for Oxbridge entry in those days – and she duly won a scholarship to Oxford, where she became president of the Oxford University Conservative Association (OUCA) and graduated with a second class degree in chemistry. A year later she got her first job in the research and development section of BX Plastics at Manningtree, just outside Colchester.

Politics were her passion and now she was impatient to get on with the fight against the socialists. 'I was really thrilled to be chosen. I realized it was a very tough seat and I knew I was being given a colossal chance.' Margaret had always been a whizz kid in a hurry. 'I was always much more interested in the conversation of adults than I was in that of my contemporaries and therefore I seemed a little older.'

It was a maturity she needed to make a bid for Dartford. Even if accepted, there was little hope of her winning the seat; the strongly industrial area was one of Labour's safest seats with an impregnable 20,000 majority. Female candidates were something of a rarity in those days; at the previous general election in 1945 there were only 87, 24 of whom got elected to the House of Commons. By 1950 the number of female candidates had increased to 126, although only 21 of them won their seats.

This didn't deter the chairman of the Dartford Conservative Association, John Miller, and his fellow selectors: they were impressed with Margaret and admired her obvious guts and ambition, along with her comprehensive grasp of the issues. Ironically, eighteen months earlier John Miller had approached Denis to ask him if he would consider being the local candidate. Margaret didn't know then and doesn't to this day. 'He came to my office at Erith and asked me to think about it,' recalls Denis. 'I said no without hesitating.'

Denis knew he was no politician in the making. He had already sampled running for office when he stood as a Ratepayers' Association candidate in a Kent County Council election a few years before and wasn't inclined to repeat the experience:

> I don't know what inspired me to stand. The Rotary Club were looking for a candidate to have a go and I'd developed an interest in politics. This was sharpened when I got into business because, as ratepayers, businesses like us were getting clobbered.
>
> I learned the hard way: I didn't do any public speaking, I didn't know the first thing about it; I didn't have a campaign manager or back-up organization; I had sod all.
>
> Eventually, I did a bit of canvassing but didn't take to it – I was too damn shy. I lost. The socialists won. Thank God! [Otherwise] I would have been in politics and not making money.

Margaret's speech that frosty evening in February 1949 took up the Gladstonian theme, urging that 'the government should do what any good housewife would do if money was short – look at their accounts and see what's wrong ... Under the socialists this country will never really pay its way. It will go from one crisis to another and eventually come to such an enormous crash that Britain will go out of existence as Great Britain once and for all.'

These were sentiments that Denis wholly endorsed. He shared completely her hatred of socialism and I grew up listening to him bellow. 'But he's a socialist!' as if describing some common criminal.

Afterwards, the new candidate joined guests at the Soward house for dinner. Denis remembers little of the evening which, not surprisingly, was dominated by politics. Everyone was fascinated by Margaret's perspective on the government and its electoral chances. It never occurred to Denis that there was a match-making dimension to the Soward dinner. He had a reputation around Erith and Dartford as a misogynist – perhaps as a result of his divorce – and although he occasionally dated girls, it was basic courtesy that prompted him to offer Margaret a lift home.

'I said to her, "Miss Roberts, how are you going to get home?"

'"On a train," replied Margaret, who spent a couple of hours each day commuting on trains and public transport. I offered to give her a lift.'

They drove to Liverpool Street station, where Margaret hurried to catch the last train back to her digs in Colchester. 'It wasn't a long drive but enough to find out we had much in common. Denis is an avid reader – he seemed to have read every article in *The Economist* and the *Banker* – and we both enjoyed music; he with his love of opera and mine of choral music.' Their professional interests – his in paint and hers in plastics – also provided common ground for polite conversation, if not for romance. Years later Denis quipped to the wife of a rugby pal who asked him what he'd first found attractive about Margaret, 'Several things; she's got a good pair of legs.'

At nearly thirty-five, and running the family business, Denis seemed mature and worldly. Margaret, twelve years younger, had led a sheltered, rather insular existence in Grantham. Her father was the most dominant figure in her life and Denis recognized this paternal influence; yet their respective fathers had shaped their children in quite different ways. Alfred Roberts preached Methodism, discipline, political and philosophical principles to his daughter, whereas Denis absorbed the New Zealand colonial ethos of Jack Thatcher – in particular, loyalty, duty and patriotism.

Both had some local politics in their genes: Denis's grandfather had been chairman of the Harbour Board in Wanganui and Margaret's father had been mayor of Grantham. During the blackout hours of the war, she and her father would conduct long and exhaustive debates on the evils of Nazism while the whole family sheltered from air raids under the solid dining-room table.

Margaret knew all there was to learn from a textbook about the theory of free market economics. As a candidate, she thumped it home to the voters in her election addresses. Denis's approach to the market place betrayed a stark pragmatism gained from his struggle to rebuild a business in the difficult post-war years.

When they met, Margaret's experience of the outside world was only a fraction of his. She had never been overseas; Denis had travelled extensively. Her family had struggled to make ends meet;

Denis was comparatively wealthy, public school educated, and had worked his way up from the factory floor in his family business. In many ways she was still developing into the formidable person she was destined to become; he was already the man he would always be – adaptable, yes, but not a man to fundamentally change what he believed or the way he conducted himself. He was happy in his own skin and had played with a straight bat since the day he was born.

They met at an extremely fortuitous time in their lives. The age gap was important, and even the chemist in Margaret couldn't have written an equation that balanced more usefully. She was a young workaholic, overflowing with ambition and in the starting blocks of a political career that would dominate her life; Denis was strong, reliable and of independent means. With a flash sports car and his own bachelor flat off the King's Road in Chelsea, he was no mean catch for a girl from provincial Grantham. 'He had a certain style and dash,' says Margaret, '. . . and, being ten years older, simply knew more about the world that I did. He knew at least as much about politics and a good deal more about economics.'

Being so shy, Denis admired how boldly and skilfully Margaret challenged members of the audience who dared to heckle her half-way through a political speech that she'd doubtless been up half the night drafting and redrafting.

It certainly wasn't a whirlwind romance. Years later, when asked whether she'd fallen in love with him at first sight, Margaret gave an answer which was typical of the politician she became: 'No; there were two elections to fight first.' Denis says: 'She stood for Dartford twice and lost twice and the second time she cried on my shoulder I married her.'

Both of them were so busy that it was difficult to find time to be together. Margaret had her job and often spoke at two or three meetings a night. Denis had Atlas to run and his social life revolved around the Old Millhillians' Club, his rugby refereeing every Satur-day, and the regular meetings of the London Society of Rugby Football Union Referees at the Feathers, a popular pub opposite St James's Tube station.

During their two-year courtship they discovered the bistros of Chelsea and Soho, and would accompany each other to political functions or Paint Federation dinners. Margaret was in her element when in earnest discussion; she was less keen on idle chat or small-talk. Denis's friends were impressed with his new girlfriend. David Roe recalls dropping in to Denis's flat in 1950:

> I was very surprised to find that we were greeted by a lovely smiley girl. Denis introduced us and she soon disappeared into the kitchen while he and I sat talking for a few minutes. When she came back she brought some tea and sat on the floor, joining in the conversation. Among other things we talked about public speaking and I expressed the view that women didn't usually make good public speakers. Her name was Margaret Roberts . . . twenty-seven years later she became Prime Minister.

Rationing was still in force but Margaret always managed to look well turned out. Her mother had been a seamstress and had taught her how to sew, so she made many of her own dresses, revamping outfits as the fashions changed. She favoured black and navy and the well-tailored look, and adored elaborate, eye-catching hats – often with a theatrical upturned brim. She always carried gloves and was rarely without a single strand of pearls around her neck.

When the general election was called for 23 February 1950, Margaret quit her job and moved into lodgings in Dartford, where she was taken under the wing of John and Phee Miller.

The mechanics of electioneering were virgin territory to Denis. 'It was the first time I saw an agent at work. I didn't know what the hell an agent did. I remember one of the first public meetings I went to with Margaret. It was on a dark and foggy night in Crayford and someone at the back shouted out, "What have you got that we haven't?"'

'A woman in the front row fired back, "Brains!"'

In the days before TV, campaigns were conducted on a more personal level and the tempo was punishing: every night Margaret was out making speeches, or engaging her Labour opponent Norman Dodds in intensely fought debates that were so popular it was often standing room only.

Mr Dodds made no secret of his enormous respect for the serious and talented Conservative candidate and the energetic way she zoomed in and out of campaign headquarters, doorstepped voters and canvassed massed meetings of factory workers during their lunch hour.

Margaret was optimistic about the Tories' prospects, contrary to the commonly held view, 'Winston Churchill made marvellous speeches and so we thought we had a chance; no one has ever overturned such a colossal majority in one election.'

That campaign was a learning exercise for Margaret. She constantly reiterated the Conservatives' economic message: 'Are you going to let this proud island race, who at one time would never accept charity, drift on from crisis to crisis under a further spell of shaky socialist finance? Or do you believe in sound finance and economical spending of public money such as the Conservatives will adopt?'

That first general election brought home to Denis the often intolerable strain a candidate is under – and how much of it rubs off on those who are close to him or her. For three weeks he shared the all-consuming urgency of a win-or-lose dash for votes. In the end Margaret cut the Labour majority in Dartford by a third, a remarkable achievement. 'You knew in your heart that she wasn't going to win Dartford but she kept on knocking the majority down,' says Denis. 'Christ, I hated elections . . . the physical and mental strain.' Margaret felt it too: 'I was young, I was very active, very energetic, but that first election I fought was the most exhausting I have ever fought. I came out of it thoroughly tired.' But she'd proved herself as a candidate and the Dartford Conservative Association quickly re-adopted her.

Nationally Labour had won such a narrow victory that it was only a matter of time – and a few by-elections – before another general election was called. In the meantime, Margaret moved into a flat in Pimlico and began seeing more of Denis. She also learned to drive and acquired her first car, a humble Ford Prefect that had cost her sister Muriel £129. Cars didn't matter to Margaret so long as they got from points A to B without breaking down.

Denis, however, was not impressed with his girlfriend's runabout. 'It chuntered along, just ... but wasn't something I'd willingly drive to Scotland in.' The previous Christmas he had given Margaret a crystal powder bowl with a silver top and she realized he was becoming more serious. Marriage featured on her horizon more clearly than on Denis's; for her it was part of the bigger political picture, particularly after Alfred, Lord Bossom, her political mentor, told her that to get on in politics she needed a husband and children.

Denis was perhaps more cautious about taking the plunge again, yet he can pinpoint the instant when he made up his mind to propose to Margaret Roberts. 'A friend of mine, an old room mate at Mill Hill, Kent Green, and I went on a touring holiday to France in September 1951 in a sort of "tart-trap" sports car I had in those days. During the tour I suddenly thought to myself, "That's the girl." Well, here she was prepared to go out and canvass in all weathers, despite the odds, etc. I think I was intelligent enough to see that this was a remarkable young woman.'

Neither can remember exactly when and where Denis proposed, but Margaret accepted without being asked a second time. She was a woman ruled by her head, not her heart, and both told her it was the right decision. She later wrote:

> When Denis asked me to be his wife, I thought long and hard about it. I had so much set my heart on politics that I really hadn't figured marriage in my plans. I had pushed it to the back of my mind and assumed it would occur of its own accord at some time in the future. I know that Denis too, because his wartime marriage had ended in divorce, asked me to be his wife only after much reflection.
>
> But the more I considered it, the surer I was. There was only one possible answer.

First, however, Margaret threw herself into electioneering: 'I did work hard and I learned everything I could. In politics you always have a purpose and an objective and we did have a clear purpose on clear principles.'

There was no need to announce their engagement; it was leaked to the press and made public on 24 October 1951, the day before polling day. Margaret was the losing candidate in Dartford again, but had the small consolation of reducing the Labour majority by a further 1,000 votes. When the polling booths closed it was obvious that the general election was going to be a cliffhanger. At the end of a long night Winston Churchill was Prime Minister again; the Conservatives had an overall majority of seventeen.

Shortly afterwards, Denis remembers driving up to Grantham for a formal meeting with his future in-laws. On the way they passed the Gothic monstrosity that is Grantham Town Hall and Denis remarked sarcastically, 'I bet they're awfully proud of that.' Margaret misinterpreted the remark and blushed with pride. 'Daddy thinks it's wonderful.' Denis silently cautioned himself, 'Watch it, Thatcher.'

At the Roberts' family home his reception was only luke-warm. 'Margaret made the introductions and said, "Denis likes a drink," and I swear her father had to blow the dust off the sherry bottle.' The Roberts eyed their future son-in-law warily. After all, he was a divorcee, drove a sports car and lived in fashionable Chelsea – all of which seemed rather racey in small-town Grantham.

After such a long courtship, the couple decided on a short engagement because 'I was getting on a bit,' says Denis, who was then thirty-six. They were married in Wesley's Chapel, City Road, on 13 December 1951. Denis quips that his new father-in-law must have thought the ceremony 'halfway to Rome'. The celebrant was the Revd Skinner, whom Margaret had known almost all her life and regarded as 'the kindest and holiest man'.

She wore a sapphire-blue velvet dress (lacy white was not her style and she 'wasn't going to be cold') – a simple medieval design with a diamond cut-out neckline. The dress was no gamble: while at Oxford she'd had an identical one made out of a length of black velvet she'd been given. As a bride she teamed it with a matching squashy-style beret, trimmed with a fluffy mass of ostrich feathers on the right-hand side.

Denis wore conventional groom's attire, with a carnation in his buttonhole and extra shine on his perfectly polished shoes.

Kent Green was best man and guests at the small wedding included the immediate families, colleagues from Atlas, John and Phee Miller and others from the Dartford Conservative Association.

The reception was held at 5 Carlton Gardens, a magnificent Nash house off Pall Mall owned by Alfred, Lord Bossom, the Conservative MP for Maidstone who'd made a fortune in New York building skyscrapers in the inaugural days of the high rise boom. He was renowned as one of the great political party-givers of his generation. 'The new session of Parliament was launched on a tide of champagne,' the gossip columnists wrote after one of his eve-of-Parliament soirées; and Sir Winston Churchill was heard to end Ministerial dinners at Number Ten by declaring, 'Get off now to Bossom's party.' (Churchill is also credited with the comment, 'Bossom? Bossom? what sort of a name is that? It's neither one thing nor the other.')

For Margaret and Denis it was a glamorous beginning to married life. The celebrations went smoothly, although the bridegroom failed to make a speech – 'I didn't know I was meant to,' says Denis.

The following day the newlyweds flew from London to Estoril, near Cascais in Portugal, where they spent the night and saw a friend of Denis's who was the Atlas agent there. Two days later they continued by flying boat to the island of Madeira, which had become fashionable among Brits after Winston Churchill's visit in 1949 (he painted several famous views of the pretty fishing village of Camara do Lobos).

'There was some doubt whether we would be able to land because of the swell,' recalls Denis, who describes the honeymoon as, 'quite pleasant'.

December in Madeira isn't sunbathing weather and neither he nor Margaret was the sort to lie around the swimming pool. 'We stayed in the capital, Funchal, and did a sort of economic survey: we went and looked at people making lace and other things and toured the Madeira Wine Company.'

After Christmas they took a boat from Madeira because the weather stopped all air connections. 'It was a small boat and a hell of a crossing – terrible,' says Denis. 'It took about three days and it certainly wasn't smooth. I wasn't seasick but Margaret was, awfully.' My mother has hated boats to this day, fearing that anything smaller than the QE2 is liable to sink unless the conditions are duck-pond calm.

In the New Year they moved into Denis's flat at Swan Court in Flood Street, a red-brick block where Agatha Christie penned a number of her novels, and on a summer's day when the windows were open Dame Sybil Thorndike could be heard rehearsing her lines.

Denis had spent quite a bit of money decorating it, buying comfortable cherry-red sofas that matched the Venetian red-and-white glass table-lamps. A set of much-loved Bateman drawings decorated the walls. 'It had a very big open-plan drawing room and dining room, which overlooked Flood Street. There was a large main bedroom and two smaller bedrooms. I didn't do any cooking as a bachelor – or only a bit – and when Margaret first wanted to use the oven she said, "It hasn't got a bottom."

'"I'm not surprised," I said. "I keep the gin in there."'

Margaret was an instantly proficient housewife. If her father had made her a true blue Conservative, it was her mother's training and her innate efficiency that taught her how to organize a household.

If marriage is either a takeover or a merger, then my parents enjoyed the latter. There was a great deal of common ground and a tacit *laissez-faire* agreement that they would get on with their own interests and activities. There was no possessiveness, nor any expectation that one partner's career should take precedence.

Denis's life changed very little. He continued to spend long hours at Atlas, where the employees nicknamed him 'the Major' and could always tell when he was in: Basil Tuck, who ran the industrial cleaning section, recalls, 'There was a buzz in the place and every day Denis would come around talking to the staff. He used to open the door of my office, and in a man-in-a-hurry tone of voice demand, "How's biz, Bas?"'

Man management was one of his strong points and his capacity for energizing people helped him to turn Atlas into an exponent of low-batch, low-cost production. After the difficult early post-war years the old-fashioned family business was transformed into one of the most competitive in its sector of the market place. The company never turned business down, according to Tuck: 'When anyone approached Denis and asked him, "Can you do this or can you tackle that?" the answer was always yes. He had a saying that he quoted almost daily: "When the walls are bulging and the seams are bursting you are making money."'

There was enough arsenic on site at Atlas to poison quite a slice of the population – it was a basic ingredient in many of the products. Drums of a toxic white powder were carefully stored and great emphasis was put on safety. 'All the Atlas products were arsenic-based when the company started in New Zealand. Our first wood preservative was caustic soda and arsenic. Then we had another preservative product, Atlas S, and that did very well in Africa because when the hunters shot lions and tigers they dumped the skins in it and anything smelly disappeared.'

By the mid-fifties the company's range of paints, wood preservatives and other coatings had expanded, along with new chemical cleaning products; domestic and international sales were strong. The Atlas *Newssheet and Information Bulletin* proudly proclaimed:

> 'Atlas Paints – made at Erith, used throughout the world' is no mere cliché ... Atlas Paints have been used on goldmine installations in Africa and Fiji; on tea estate buildings in Ceylon and oil installations in the Middle East ... and even petrol filling stations in Bangkok ...
>
> Whether you have to paint a fire hydrant or the Eiffel Tower, or indeed, any project needing a heavy duty paint for iron and steel, you can be sure of maximum covering and minimum operating costs with Atlas Ruskilla Triplecote.

In one year alone, Atlas paints were used on twenty-six race-courses in Britain, including Kempton Park, Lingfield and Newmarket. The stand at the Chelsea football ground was given a fresh coat and visitors to London Zoo could finger the velvet sheen of Atlas Thixacote eau-de-nil Flat Finish on the walls of the Reptile House and Atlas Super Finish Black on the bars of the lion and tiger enclosure. The *Cutty Sark* in Greenwich – and the decks of many ocean-going liners – were kept dry and sound by Atlas WP Wood Preserver and Deck Cleanser. At Heathrow Airport the runway thresholds and apron markings were painted with Atlas Safety Rubber Line Paint.

One project close to Denis's heart was the painting of the world-famous gasholder that dominates the Oval, home to Surrey Cricket

Club and scene of many heroic battles between the England XI and the old enemy Australia in the final Test of each Ashes series.

Although he loved watching the game, Denis gave up playing cricket after his marriage because he felt guilty being away every Saturday in the summer in addition to refereeing rugby on winter weekends. However, he maintained his contacts with the Old Millhillians' Club and the London Society of Rugby Football Union Referees.

Meanwhile, Margaret had become a young married woman of very comfortable means. Any thoughts of a political career were put on hold, although she still accepted occasional invitations to speak at Conservative Party functions. Instead she decided to read for the Bar. Denis supported her decision: 'Do what you like, love,' he told her, and it became his standard response.

Fortunately, a barrister's life is also highly compatible with motherhood, an event pencilled in to begin on 29 September 1953.

SEVEN

A DISTANT DAD

'He was very good at remembering to wave up at the nursery window as he left for work, whereas Mrs Thatcher, whose mind was already on her job, would forget.'

NANNY BARBARA on Denis Thatcher

I CAME INTO THE WORLD with two extraordinary people as parents, but that didn't necessarily make them extraordinary parents. Margaret went into hospital on 14 August 1953 suffering from labour pains, although 'the baby' wasn't due for another six weeks. The first shock was being told that she was expecting twins; the second was that our arrival was imminent. The doctors scheduled a caesarean operation for the following day and at three o'clock in the afternoon we arrived, weighing about four pounds each.

Unaware of the drama that was unfolding, Denis had disappeared to watch the final Test Match at the Oval. He was celebrating England's Ashes victory and arrived home to find a message from the hospital. At Queen Charlotte's they ushered him towards our incubators so that he could meet his 'instant' family. But of course, premature babies don't look very appetizing: Denis took one look at us and gasped, 'My God, they look like rabbits. Put them back.'

So he took to fatherhood with enthusiasm. Margaret, who had felt unwell during much of her pregnancy, was relieved that we had arrived safely. As she now had one of each sex, that was the end of it as far as she was concerned – she needn't repeat the process.

Both parents had spent years answering to abbreviations of their own names, so they chose Mark and Carol, which couldn't be shortened. And because Denis had reached the age of thirty-eight with only a single Christian name, he decided that one would suffice for his son; Margaret had two, so I was given a middle name – Jane.

There was no wallowing in motherhood during the fortnight Margaret spent in hospital; she filled out an application form for her Bar finals in December, so that she had to keep studying. And within days of our home-coming, an Austrian nurse, Gerda, was hired to help look after us. When we were six weeks old our first nanny, Barbara, arrived; she would stay for the next five years.

With twins and a nanny the Thatcher household desperately needed more room. The problem was solved by renting the flat next door in Swan Court and putting a door between the two.

Nanny recalls that no aspect of motherhood seemed to faze Margaret:

> She coped with the babies when I wasn't around, as well as studying for her law exams. She did everything – she was so ultra-efficient that it was very difficult to fault her. If both of you were crying at night, she would get up and help me with the feeding. Basically, my one aim was to let her sleep because she was always studying so late that she rarely had a full night's rest.
>
> Mr Thatcher used to get cross with her sometimes. He'd go to bed and she'd be studying at one in the morning and even later if there was some assignment that had to be done. Meanwhile, we weren't allowed to make any noise and had to keep the radio down.

When Denis and Nanny teamed up for a spot of DIY (Denis under protest because he saw enough paint at Atlas without decorating at home), they wallpapered our day nursery with some farmyard animal design. They stood back to admire their handi-work, only to realize that they'd accidentally hung one panel upside down. The sight of a bunch of animals standing on their heads reduced Denis and Nanny to hysterical laughter and they didn't hear Margaret approaching. 'She was most unamused,' says Nanny. 'She thought it was inefficient and a waste of time because it all had to be redone.'

Mark and I were christened on 13 December – our parents' second wedding anniversary – in the church where they had been married. Margaret didn't consider the number thirteen unlucky. 'It never bothered me at all. I was born on the thirteenth, married on the thirteenth and my children were christened on the thirteenth . . .'

That same month she qualified and went to the bar, joining Frederick Lawton's Chambers in the Inner Temple. 'Mrs Thatcher was the ambitious one,' recalls Nanny. 'She had her sights set very high. He [Denis] supported her absolutely from the day they married. Mrs Thatcher always got her own way because Mr Thatcher allowed her to. She'd say, "We've got to go to this, this and this." And he said, "Oh well," and accepted it.'

Neither of my parents could be described as being natural or comfortable with young children. Denis – like his father and many others of his own generation – never got involved with child-rearing except vicariously, through daily progress bulletins from Nanny. If we were still up when he came home from work he would come along and say hello. A colleague at Atlas who also had a young family remembers discussing fatherhood with Denis occasionally: they would curse 'children' through gritted teeth before comparing notes on survival strategies.

'Mr Thatcher left parenting to Mrs Thatcher and me,' says Nanny. 'When he left for work each morning he'd say goodbye at the front door and then Carol and Mark would run along the corridor to the window overlooking Flood Street to wave as he crossed the forecourt. He was very good at remembering to wave up at the nursery window as he left for work, whereas Mrs Thatcher, whose mind was already on her job, would forget.'

It was hardly surprising. Somehow she juggled working, studying, organizing the household, shopping, cooking, sewing, ironing and liaising with Nanny. In truth, she was a 'superwoman' long before Shirley Conran ever invented the phenomenon. If that wasn't enough, she even took up knitting. 'She made the twins royal-blue jersey-style jackets,' says Nanny. 'Because I could knit and she was so competitive she couldn't bear the thought that anyone might say, "I can do this, you can't."'

Denis accepted all of this, marvelling at his wife's stamina, but he drew the line when he heard her making impromptu changes to Nanny's schedule. 'He was very strict about my having my day off and wouldn't allow Mrs Thatcher to muck up my hours without at least a week's notice.'

Denis and Margaret entertained occasionally, hosting buffet suppers for their friends, who were mainly from the legal world or involved with rugby football. Margaret would make lobster flans and creamy marquises surrounded by sponge fingers. This was far more sophisticated than their usual fare. Denis had very simple tastes in food: he wouldn't have a clove of garlic in the place, hated the smell of frying onions and insisted on keeping the kitchen door closed so that cooking smells didn't waft through the flat.

When our birthdays came round Margaret proved a dab hand at cake-making, producing incredible sponge edifices in the shape of trains or veteran cars, their bodywork elaborately iced.

My father seemed a rather distant figure: he was rarely at home. I think he found communicating with young children difficult, so any dialogue beyond basic commands was postponed until we reached a more civilized age.

During the summers, when most families go off with their buckets and spades, Denis would be overseas on business; he was often in Africa for the whole of August, making sure that he was back for the start of the rugby season. Family holidays didn't appeal to Denis or Margaret. 'We've never been very good holidaymakers,' he admits. 'Neither of us is good at lounging around. When you were small we went somewhere in northern Italy, to a seaside place where we were going to lie alongside a swimming pool and all that sort of thing. Three days of that and we were bored to death, so we went off to Rome to do some sightseeing and had a lot of fun.'

My first holiday by the sea was with Nanny, who took Mark and me to Westgate on Sea; the following year we went to Bognor for the usual sandpie-making and paddling at low tide.

In December 1954, when we were sixteen months old Margaret unsuccessfully bid for the Conservative candidature in Orpington. It was never going to be easy because female candidates – particularly mothers of young children – were still regarded with suspicion.

After all, they could hardly devote themselves full-time to the task; if they did, they were likely to be accused of neglecting their families.

After this disappointment she immersed herself in the law, specializing in tax. She was about to take on another bout of studying when Denis intervened:

> I got back to Swan Court one night and there on the table was application forms from the Institute of Chartered Accountants.
>
> 'What on earth is all this?' I asked.
>
> 'I want to study accountancy.'
>
> 'In God's name why?'
>
> 'Well, they told me if I want to be a tax lawyer I have to know something about accountancy.'
>
> 'Forget it,' I said, knowing it would mean another three or four years' studying. 'I'll do any accountancy you need and help with any problems.'

Denis, meanwhile, was becoming more and more immersed in rugby refereeing and administration. He was severely shaken when his chronic back problem deteriorated and he had to go into hospital over Christmas 1956 for six weeks of treatment.

> It was wear and tear on my discs, probably arising from some injury I got during the war, although I can't put my finger on exactly when. If I'd been ruthless, I might have pulled up and got a disability pension.
>
> In hospital my doctor, a man called Bob McPherson, and the specialist came along and said: 'You'll be all right, but we have to tell you that you will never referee again.'
>
> I said, 'I'll see you in hell and at Twickenham.'
>
> Bob told me: 'I love my patients telling me that. Face it, Denis.'

The doctors should have saved their breath. Defying medics is something my father relishes with the same zeal that Margaret reserves for attacking the Labour Party.

Both of them have been blessed with good health and any pain (Denis's back and Margaret's teeth and other minor problems) has always been glossed over without complaint. I can rarely recall either of them being so ill that they had to go to bed.

Denis 'refereed two, if not three, years wearing a steel jacket.

I'm the only person living who refereed the county semi-finals in body armour.'

Off the field, at the London Society of Rugby Football Union Referees' annual general meeting in 1955–56 chaired by Admiral Sir Percy Royds, Denis ill-advisedly piped up on the subject of their balance sheet. After the meeting the treasurer came up to Denis and said to him, 'Dear chap, the balance sheet doesn't balance, does it?'

'I'm sorry,' said Denis, 'are you offended?'

'Not offended, do you want the fucking job?'

At the next meeting (by which time Cyril Gadney was president), Denis was asked to be the treasurer.

'It's a very great honour and I will accept the appointment with one proviso,' he said.

'Do you want to be treasurer of the society, or don't you?' an impatient Gadney pressed.

'Just listen. I will run the society's accounts and finances my way. If that is what you want of the treasurer, I'll do it.'

Denis was appointed and set about totally reorganizing the accounts and administration. When he took over the balance was about £150; when he relinquished the post in 1968 the balance was £3,500. It was a labour of love.

Sir Percy Royds and Cyril Gadney were legendary figures in English rugby and Denis and his contemporaries revered them.

Sir Percy was one of the greatest experts on the laws of the game at the time and wrote a history of them. Strong willed, yes, but not formidable. A great rugby man.

Cyril Gadney was a wonderful personality and the father of the modern referee. He was a brilliant referee, although like many referees at the end of their time, he possibly got a bit too dictatorial, but he understood the game. His great theory – and what he taught us all – was that any fool can read up, remember and administer the laws, but to be a great referee you have to get a feel for the game and a feel for the players.

The highlight of Denis's refereeing career was to be appointed as a touch judge for the international in Paris between France and England in April 1956.

In 1995, as he watched another English team leave Waterloo station to take the train through the Channel tunnel to play in Paris, Frank Keating, the *Guardian*'s rugby correspondent, reminisced about the 1956 departure:

Of course, history keeps repeating itself. Well, in different ways. Almost forty years ago, schoolboys of a certain age might remember Leslie Mitchell's golly gosh tones of utter amazement on the Movietone newsreel reporting, wonder of wonders, that the England XV of 1956 were actually flying to the match in Paris.

There they all were on grainy monochrome grinning sheepishly and standing in front of the stepladders alongside a tiny BEA twin-propeller aircraft with the couple of Nissen huts which then comprised Heathrow airport – Eric Evans in his first year as captain, Peter Robbins, Sandy Sanders and all, plus a lanky London Society referee who was to be touch judge the following afternoon in the old Paris stadium at Colombes, one Denis Thatcher!

Denis has his own memories of that special match:

They insisted in those days that the England touch judge was a top referee. When you went on [as a touch judge], you put a jacket over your jersey and a pair of grey flannel trousers. If the referee was injured during the game, all you did was take off your jacket and trousers and you were ready to go on in his place.

Of course everybody prayed that the referee would have a heart attack or something. It did happen occasionally. The great Johnnie Johnson – a policeman, charming chap – was a touch judge in Cardiff when the referee twisted his ankle and Johnnie stripped off and refereed.

England lost in Paris in April 1956 and Denis can still clearly identify the turning point of the match.

The scrum half was an Old Mill Hillian, Johnny Williams, and he gave away a penalty kick straight under the French posts – he literally gave it away. When he came off the field, he was cursing the refcree and I said, 'Johnny, for Christ's sake – you're running for the ball, there's a Frenchman behind you, you turn your head, look over your shoulder and then deliberately obstruct him from getting the ball. For God's sake, a blind man would have given a penalty kick.'

Poor Johnny, he was a great scrum half but famous for not having any brains – he was as thick as hell.

Although rugby was her husband's great passion, Margaret accompanied him when refereeing only once, and that was enough. 'It was soon after we married,' says Denis. 'She came along to a game – I think it was at Southgate – and didn't like the way sections of the crowd criticized the referee – namely me. That was enough for her, although she occasionally came to the international games at Twickenham. She liked those.'

However, she dutifully washed Denis's muddy kit and prepared the picnic basket for the traditional car-boot lunch in the car park at Twickenham. She rarely asked how the match had gone, but Denis would re-referee every one of his games as he drove to work on Monday mornings: 'I had a picture of the game and would think back about whether someone might have been out of position. You always know when you make a really bad mistake. No sensible referee has ever gone off the field and said, "I never made a mistake." It's not possible. All you really prayed for was that you didn't make a mistake that affected the result of the game.'

Denis refereed up until the 1963 season and was mortified not to make the top rung of the refereeing ladder – the international panel. 'Of course you're always disappointed when you don't make the top. I was always ambitious, that's why I worked at it. I nearly made it on the international panel. It would have taken a bit of luck to get me there, that's all. My worst enemy wouldn't say that I wasn't close.'

He did, however, have the satisfaction of ending his career without ever having sent a player off. 'You avoided it if you could in those days. It was a hell of a blot on a player's reputation. But today they're sent off left, right and centre.' He credits his father with impressing on him just what an appalling fate this was: 'I will never forget his look of horror when Cyril Brownlie was sent off at the very first international he took me to at Twickenham in 1925. I'd rarely seen him so upset.'

In addition to the pleasure rugby gave Denis, it served another purpose for a man who had been to a minor public school and hadn't gone to university – it plugged him into a network of contacts he met again and again as his wife entered politics and rose upwards. These included Ewen Fergusson (later Sir Ewen and

British ambassador to France), who played for the London Scottish; Irishman Tony O'Reilly (later the boss of Heinz); and Robin Butler (later Sir Robin and head of the Civil Service.)

In 1956 Margaret's political ambitions surfaced again and she had her name reinstated on the list of candidates seeking a safe Conservative seat which, having served her apprenticeship by standing twice in Dartford, she had clearly earned.

It was a time for change on all fronts and that included a new home. The problem with having growing twins on the sixth floor of a block of flats was that everything had to be planned: we couldn't just pop out into the garden because there wasn't one; expeditions to Ranelagh Gardens twice a day had to be organized. When it rained and these were cancelled we infuriated everyone by trundling our tricycles up and down the corridors connecting our two flats.

The problem was compounded one weekend when we went down to visit John and Phee Miller, who had a lovely house in Kent with a huge garden. According to Phee, no children could have been happier than we were with a patch of dirt and a toy spade and fork. Weeding became our newest craze and we eventually made the nursery carpet in Chelsea quite threadbare.

The crunch came when renting the two flats in Swan Court became exorbitant following the abolition of rent control. Margaret and Denis decided it was time to move out of Central London.

Mark and I complained like mad at the tedium of house-hunting weekends but adored the final result – a white-washed house in a large private avenue in Farnborough, Kent. The Dormers was a magical childhood home in a long avenue of detached houses and generous gardens. Holwood Park Avenue had a dead-end which meant it was absolutely safe for dashing around on bicycles to friends' houses; we could also explore the large wood, lake and fields at the end of the road.

Although exceptionally convenient for Denis – Erith was an easy drive – Dormers was not particularly handy for Margaret, who had to commute up to chambers in Lincoln's Inn. I remember her leaving home each day and coming back in the evening, when she would sit in the living room with a pile of papers on her knee.

At weekends my parents took to gardening with manic zeal. Being in the chemical and weedkiller business, Denis was obsessive about the lawns, scanning them constantly for daisies – public enemy number one. Margaret concentrated on the flower beds: a pond was filled in and planted with a blaze of scarlet, and the crescent-shaped dahlia bed in the front was the envy of the neighbourhood. Unfortunately, the crazy paving terrace overlooking the rose garden didn't pass the spirit-level test thanks to Mark who, in a burst of the mischievousness that he specialized in, hammered in the levelling pegs when the workman had his back turned.

On Monday 14 July 1958 Margaret's search for a safe Conservative seat ended successfully. At a packed Constituency Association meeting for Finchley and Friern Barnet in North London she was elected as the Conservative candidate by 46 votes to 43. Some of the executive couldn't disguise their disapproval at a woman being chosen.

Typically, Denis was overseas on business:

> I was in Africa – coming back from Johannesburg to Lagos. I'd said goodbye to my cousin Tom Pellatt; we were fairly wound up, I'd had a lot to drink and I staggered aboard the plane. I had to change in Kano in Nigeria and on the seat next to mine was the *Evening Standard* of the night before. I hadn't been in England for about three weeks so I picked it up and turned over a couple of pages and there was this tiny little paragraph accouncing that Margaret Thatcher had been adopted as Conservative candidate for Finchley.
>
> That was the first I'd heard about it. I was delighted, but I've always said that it was bloody lucky that I was away because it was a close-run thing and if they'd taken one look at me, they would have said, 'We don't want this pair.'

Finchley had a Conservative majority of nearly 13,000, which more or less guaranteed that Margaret would enter Parliament at the next election, less than a year away. Not only was it a highly desirable seat; it was geographically feasible for a working mother. 'I had a young family and I could never have done what I did unless everything had bounced right for me,' says Margaret. 'I just couldn't have had a constituency a long way away. I was very lucky ... In these days of feminism I am the first to say that had I got a seat in Yorkshire or Lancashire I could not have gone for it.'

In the summer of 1959 we had our first proper family beach holiday at Seaview in the Isle of Wight. The first year we stayed at the Pier Hotel right on the seafront. It was a rambling family hotel with ping-pong tables in the games room and fancy dress parties in the ballroom. Outside, you could go left to a sandy beach or right to the shingle one; offshore were the two squat silhouettes of the forts built to repel Napoleon. The great liners – the old *Queen Elizabeth* with two red funnels and *Queen Mary* with three – used to fill the horizon as they made their way to Southampton. I loved watching them come in, not just for the spectacle but because of the large rollers that they sent crashing onto the beach as they passed.

We went to Seaview several years running and rented a flat just up from the sailing club almost opposite the Seaview Hotel. I went back there recently and, although the Pier Hotel has gone, I was thrilled to find much of my childhood holiday haunt unchanged. I looked along at Ryde pier as I drove off the ferry and remembered how the same scene had always announced to me that the holiday had really begun. Memories of my first sailing lessons (getting soaked and cold) flooded back when I saw the varnished dinghies rocking and bobbing on their moorings.

On holiday I spent my days scampering over the rocks wielding a flimsy net and not catching much; swimming and recoiling when my legs came into contact with the slimy seaweed that low tide left in heaps on the sand. There were also family excursions to see the Admiral's Cup yachts racing past the Needles, and to Carisbrooke Castle or Queen Victoria's old home at Osborne.

When I was ten I used to stop and read the tabloid newspaper in the newsagent's rack to glean the lowdown on the scandal of that summer – the Profumo affair. The juicy details were never printed in the broadsheets that my parents read.

As fate would have it, we were in Seaview when the general election was called and Margaret had to rush back to begin campaigning. Right from the beginning Denis maintained his 'hands-off' stance, smiling for the cameras but taking no active part. 'I didn't do anything by day, I just went to work,' he says. 'I don't think I did any canvassing, I certainly didn't knock on a door.' Being incurably shy, the thought of confronting perfect strangers and asking for their vote wasn't something that Denis relished. He did, however, make sacrifices in his own way: he even gave up refereeing during the campaign; this was, Margaret admitted, 'quite something, considering he wouldn't do it for our wedding anniversary'.

Denis went to the evening meetings and speeches, often sitting on the same platform but avoiding speaking himself. 'We never speak on the same platform. It makes us nervous,' Margaret said.

The campaign was set against a difficult background. The *Daily Mail* on 22 September 1959 summed up the mood.

> Rosy dreams, an easy canter home to victory, were ripped to shreds yesterday by the cold-blast of the national opinion poll carried out by the *Daily Mail*. Reduction in the Tory lead by half from 7% to 3.5% has dangled the rattling spectre of the Labour government before their eyes for the first time ... another women candidate who is as certain to get in is Mrs Margaret Thatcher. She too is 34. Mrs Thatcher, the Conservative Candidate for Finchley where the 1955 majority was 12,825, is expected to be the first woman barrister to become an MP. She is the wife of a company director and has twins, a boy and a girl. She is a graduate of Somerville College, Oxford and was president of the Oxford University Conservative Association ...

A young, attractive woman destined for Parliament was wonderful material for the women's pages. On 5 October, the *Evening News* ran a feature headlined MRS THATCHER IS THE TYPE WHO CAN COPE: 'My husband is thrilled to bits about this campaign and naturally I could never have considered it without his blessing,' said Margaret. 'He is a tremendous help to me and comes to all my meetings. The twins, they are a bit young yet and all they can say is when are we going to have tea at that place on Westminster Bridge, Mummy? It's taking you so long to get there.'

When asked the inevitable question about whether she should be at home looking after her husband and children rather than running for office, Margaret replied: 'I should vegetate if I were left at the kitchen sink all day. The twins are at school and in any

case I have a full time nanny. I have time to cook the family breakfast before I go to town and do the shopping before I set out. I get
the washing and ironing done at odd times and I don't think the
family suffers at all through my political ambitions. An MP has
the advantage of having vacations during the school holidays so
the children will be able to have their usual holiday treats.'

Margaret campaigned for Finchley as if the seat was a marginal,
quickly silencing her critics in the local association through sheer
hard work. The experience of having fought Dartford twice was
invaluable. 'It takes time before you know what to worry about
and what not to. You know you can cope and stamina comes with
experience and then the accumulated experience takes you through
because you've seen it all before and you learn not to get depressed
about something which would knock a less experienced person
rather hard.'

On election day, 8 October, she and Denis left early to tour the
polling stations while Mark and I were shuttled to our respective
schools by friends' mothers. We were only six years old and didn't
understand all the commotion. The house was full of rosettes and
posters; neither of our parents was at home to tuck us into bed.

Denis remembers being relatively confident and from early on
he could see which way the votes were stacking up. Shortly after
midnight at Christ's College, the counting headquarters, the
returning officer called the candidates onto the platform and read
the results. 'Thatcher, Margaret Hilda: 29,697.' She had increased
the Tory majority by 3,500 to an extremely comfortable 16,000.

A few hours later the new MP was back in the kitchen at The
Dormers, seeing us off to school. There was no question of her
sleeping in or nursing a hangover. As I waited to be collected for
the school run, satchel ready and school hat on, she came to the
front porch and urged us, 'Do go and have a look at the car, before
we take everything off.'

I ran across our crunchy gravel drive and struggled with the
heavy shiny black gloss-painted doors. As I prised one open, the
sun flooded in and I gasped wide-eyed. Margaret's humble little
blue Ford was in fancy dress – festooned with Tory-blue streamers,
balloons, and a VOTE THATCHER poster bearing a photograph

of Margaret. That mystified me; what was my mother doing on a sort of WANTED notice straight out of a cowboy film? Then I spied the loud-hailer on the roof. Here was the reasons she'd nearly lost her voice and was popping throat pastilles at a rate I'd never been allowed to guzzle sweets.

'Mummy's very important, she's an MP,' I crowed to my school-friends while my six-year-old brain tried to join up the pieces of a jigsaw – the car that looked like a circus prop, a place called Finchley and another called the House of Commons. Margaret had patiently tried to explain the latter to me but all I could remember was that it had green leather seats.

From chemist to barrister to Member of Parliament – we were all in a new act of the Margaret Thatcher production, with Denis playing his standard, understated part.

EIGHT

STRESS FRACTURES

'My doctor said that I was making myself ill working
at that pace and if I carried on then I was endangering
my health. And then he handed me an ultimatum.
"There's nothing wrong with you physically but if
you don't stop working so hard, you are going to be
very ill indeed."'

DENIS THATCHER

DENIS MISSED THE TRIUMPH of his wife's maiden speech to
Parliament on 5 February 1960, which was hailed as one 'of front
bench quality'. He was away on business. Margaret spoke in
support of her own private member's bill, designed to give the
press greater access to meetings of local councils and their sub-
committees. 'Things always seem to happen when he's away,' she
observed to a journalist without any hint of resentment.

Being the husband of the Rt Hon. Member for Finchley and
Friern Barnet never transformed Denis's life in the way that it often
affects a female spouse: he was not plunged into constituency duties
like organizing coffee mornings or attending school fetes; he was
anything but an all-embracing constituency husband.

In truth, he was entirely unmoved by having an MP in the family;
after all, his wife had always studied or worked and now she had
simply swapped law for politics. Even though conversation around
the breakfast table was now often peppered with jargon like 'three
line whips', 'public sector borrowing' and '*Hansard*', Margaret's
backbench duties rarely impinged on Denis's routine – 'Not on
daily life, although one did come to spend an awful lot of time in
the damned constituency,' he says. 'I always did the annual dinner
and dance of the Conservative Association and was certainly up
there a couple of times a month at dinners Margaret was speaking
at and that sort of thing.'

Atlas was growing steadily. Although building restrictions had been imposed during the immediate post-war years, several major additions were made before 1950, which saw production increase. By 1957 the factory had been expanded to 60,000 square feet, storage to 25,000 square feet, and new road linked up the various sections. The company was developing new products and one, the contract cleaning business, was very successful, particularly the marine chemical cleaning service for ships in the royal and merchant navies.

After Jack Thatcher's death Arthur Colley had become chairman and helped guide Atlas through the difficult years. When he died in 1951, Denis took over and six years later, on the fiftieth anniversary of the company"s incorporation, 200 men and women were on the payroll throughout the UK.

South Africa was an important market for Atlas products, with a number of mining companies using various paints, and it gave Denis ample opportunity to explore the terrain that he loved deeply.

> I used to do a sort of a U-route on my visits. I'd start in West Africa, maybe Sierra Leone and then go to Ghana, Nigeria – once to Cameroon – and then I'd go down to South Africa to Johannesburg where I used to stay with my aunt Doris and cousin Tom. I'd return northwards to Rhodesia, Zambia and then Kenya. I love the scenery, it's absolutely wonderful, almost out of this world.

Denis rarely kept in touch with home while overseas. We'd get a standard postcard with about half a dozen words scrawled on it. Inter-continental calls were an expensive luxury in those days, but this wasn't the reason for his silence – he simply hated the telephone. 'I don't like them. I think it is a method of communication, not of social intercourse. I'm not a chatterer on the telephone and, to be absolutely honest, I'm not very good on one.'

Thirty years later, when Mark had married his Texan wife Diane, she sometimes complained that he never rang her during the long periods he spent away from home. Denis was totally unsympathetic: 'Well, when I was away, I never rang up,' he told her.

Margaret embraced her new career with a workaholic zeal. Drawing second in the ballot to introduce private members' bills

Thomas Thatcher, Denis's grandfather, who put the name Thatcher
on the map in Wanganui,
New Zealand

Madge, Denis's New Zealand
grandmother, the first formidable
woman he ever encountered

Jack Thatcher, Denis's father, whom
he remembers as 'a gentle man and
a gentleman'

Kathleen, Denis's mother, a
flame-haired extrovert

Public schoolboy Denis

LEFT Denis (middle row, centre) captain of Holyrood School rugby XV, 1928

BELOW Wartime Denis (right) in Sicily

ABOVE
The first Mrs Thatcher

LEFT
'Refereeing rugby football is one of the most rewarding things I've ever done'

New Dad – Denis finds
one-year-old twins a handful

The ambitious young Parliamentary
candidate Denis met on a blind date. Margaret
is wearing the hat she later had copied to
match her sapphire-blue wedding dress

Mark and me,
aged one. My
mother still
carries this
photo in her
wallet

Denis admires the posters for his wife's election campaign in 1959, while she discusses a speech with her constituency chairman Bertie Blatch

BELOW LEFT My wife the MP. The Thatcher family outside the House of Commons

BELOW Denis and Mark in Lenzerheide, Switzerland, on the family skiing holiday in 1962

ABOVE Mark, Margaret and Denis celebrating Margaret's 1975 Leadership victory. Denis confessed that he didn't know what he was in for

RIGHT The Leader of the Opposition and her husband walked into some flak from professional decorators after a photocall of them doing a spot of DIY in their holiday flat in Scotney Castle, Kent

ABOVE Denis learning the tricks of the trade ('hands behind back, ignore garland') tries to look at ease on his first official overseas trip, India, 1976

LEFT Finchley Town Hall, election night, 1979: the beginning of eleven and a half years as husband of Britain's first woman Prime Minister

In the line of duty as consort:

RIGHT A rescue 'victim' at the Boat Show

BELOW Total immersion course in teabags

ABOVE
Being presented with a memento of his visit to Bahrain race course

RIGHT
Photocall with Beefeater Gin Boat Race blondes

was a huge bonus. Her youth and good looks made her stand out among the newer members. One commentator wrote in *People* magazine: 'I prophesy a brilliant future for Mrs Thatcher, the new Tory member for Finchley. She possesses "all the qualities", handsome, very well dressed and attractive. She has a very considerable knowledge of politics, the result of long studies, and a friendly tolerance towards opponents that would make her an asset to any party' (25 October 1959).

Somehow she conjured up the energy to race between The Dormers, the House of Commons and Finchley, making it seem remarkably easy. 'There are twenty-four hours in a day and if you fill them with activity, your mind is always active and you're not thinking of yourself,' she says, 'you're just getting on with whatever you have to do next.'

She explained her daily routine to the *Evening News* on 25 February 1960:

> The timetable of being a Member of Parliament fits in quite well with family duties. The parliamentary recesses coincide with the school holidays so I can see a lot of the children at the time when they are home most ... However busy I am, I always manage to phone the twins shortly before 6 p.m. and sometimes go to see them and return to Parliament later in the evening ...
>
> You will be wondering what happens to my husband in the evenings when the House is in session and I am not at home. He is every bit as busy as I am, if not more so. Wives whose husbands are in top jobs see very little of them as they work late, have to travel to different parts of the country and sometimes have to go abroad. My husband was on a tour of the Middle East when I made my Maiden speech. His busy life would go on whether I was a Member of Parliament or not and it is rare for him to be at home for more than one evening during the week.
>
> Family life is centred around the weekends, when we are at home together and devote most of the time to the children ...

This was very true, but then Mark, aged eight, went off to Belmont, the prep school in Mill Hill, and the following year I became a boarder at Mymwood, the prep school in Queenswood, near Hatfield in Hertfordshire. We were together as a family only at half-terms, summer holidays, Easter and at Christmas.

I saw more of Margaret than I did of Denis in those early years. She never missed one of my Saturday leaves from school. I carted her off to see *Those Magnificent Men in Their Flying Machines*, which was something of a novelty for her because she was never a cinema-goer. My next choice was a romantic film, *Mayerling*, starring Catherine Deneuve and Omar Sharif. It had a tragic ending and Margaret shed a few tears – to my great embarrassment. She also made a point of coming to the important school functions, often working on constituency papers in the car until the last minute and then ducking into the marquee for the Speech Day presentation.

She had the most impenetrable tunnel vision. When the mother of a friend of mine was discussing arrangements for getting her daughter and me together during the holidays, Margaret declared that a particular date was unsuitable because she'd be 'in the House'.

'Oh, so shall I,' replied the other mother, thinking it tremendously odd to state the obvious.

Margaret, of course, missed it. No other house registered with her except the House of Commons.

Margaret's childhood had been very strict, highly regimented: her parents had insisted that certain things were done and at certain times. When it came to being a mother herself, she favoured a much more flexible approach and gave us the opportunity to make up our own minds. When Mark and I declared that we didn't like going to church, she and Denis continued to attend irregularly but didn't make us go with them. And when my bedroom needed redecorating, she asked me what sort of wallpaper I wanted. 'Flowers in baskets,' I decided and that was what went up.

I was brought up to see home life as a base or launch pad for everything you did in the outside world. I didn't always understand this as a child. I remember finding my mother in the kitchen one day making Scotch pancakes and I said: 'Why can't you be at home more? All my schoolfriends' mothers are around. Why can't you be more like them?'

She stopped making the pancakes. 'Darling, you have to understand that you have a lot of benefits that other children don't have:

you can come to the Opening of Parliament and have supper at the House of Commons. You can go on overseas holidays.'

She was quite right, of course, although it wasn't until I was older and wiser that I realized it.

She had once made us a ginger cake – other mothers baked and so would she – but when it was sliced, we found a teaspoon in the middle. She'd obviously been mixing the ingredients when the phone rang and had forgotten the spoon.

'Oh look, you got it wrong,' I laughed, surprised that she'd made a mistake; it rarely happened.

Yet as I grew up, I knew rather more about what Margaret did for a living than about Denis. I only knew that Atlas made paint, which gave my mother an excuse for changing the colour of the walls twice as often as anyone else.

Margaret would often take Mark and me to the House of Commons members' canteen for tea or supper and then we'd sit and doodle on House of Commons notepaper while she dictated replies to constituents. Sometimes, more grandly, we'd get tickets to one of the stands on Horse Guards Parade for ceremonials like Beating the Retreat or Trooping the Colour. I couldn't count how many times I stood in Central Lobby to see the Speaker's Procession.

We rarely went to Atlas. In fact I remember only one visit – when the oil tanker *Torrey Canyon* hit the rocks off Cornwall in March 1967 and started to leak oil, threatening one of the first major environmental disasters. Atlas manufactured the foam used to break up the oil slick and, over Easter, we went down to see the barrels being filled. I think Denis thought we were a bit of a nuisance and kept telling us, 'Don't tread on that. Stay out of the way.' It was reminiscent of his arrival home after one family holiday: his first words to our nanny were, 'For God's sake teach the children some manners.'

Just as Jack Thatcher had taught Denis how to play cricket, Denis began to teach Mark. We had a cricket practice net in the back garden and he used to bowl underarm because of his back injury. On summer evenings Mark would face up as Denis threw down deliveries, teling him, 'Keep your eye on the ball ... left elbow up ... straight bat.' But he never took Mark to Twickenham to introduce him to the game he loved. However, when Mark wrote home from prep school to say that he'd made the rugby team, Denis decided to go along and cast a referee's eye over his son's debut.

He was heartened by the team warm-up – 'They were passing the ball like they were at Twickenham' – but his spirits sank when the game got under way. He left at half-time, telling one of the masters, 'God and all the angels couldn't turn my son into a rugby football player.'

Denis gave up refereeing in 1963, when I was ten. I can remember seeing him in action only once and I'm sure it's stuck in my mind because, when he blew the whistle and indicated a penalty, all I could think was, 'I'd get into awful trouble if I went home as muddy as Daddy is getting.'

As Margaret's political career took off, more and more of her weekends were taken up with constituency engagements and a terrifying volume of paperwork. Mark and I were away at school so Denis increasingly found himself alone at weekends. He turned to his old Mill Hill friends for company. The club kept a yacht, *Winnie*, in the Solent and Denis found sailing far more fun than staying at home.

He also dined regularly with his mother and his sister Joy, who lived in a flat in Notting Hill Gate. After Joy's marriage broke up she moved in with my grandmother and they became very close. They both doted on Denis who, since his father's death in 1943, had become the 'man' of the family.

My grandmother's high spirits had not toned down with age. She remained outrageous and full of fun – completely different to my mother, which is why they never really got on. Margaret never even had a meal in her mother-in-law's house, but Mark and I used to see our aunt Joy and grandmother several times a year.

When I look back I have no doubt that my mother's political ambitions – and the singlemindedness with which she pursued them – eclipsed our family and social life. But no woman gets to the top by going on family picnics or cooking roast beef and Yorkshire pudding for Sunday lunch with friends.

It's equally true that work took Denis away a lot. If Margaret hadn't worked, it would have been she who sat at home alone, twiddling her thumbs. It was for this partnership of parallel lives that they married each other and it worked.

Margaret notched up thousands of miles driving her blue Ford Anglia to and from the Houses of Parliament and her constituency office in Finchley. Meanwhile, Denis drove daily to Erith and winged his way around the world on sales drives.

A two-income household in an era when it was the exception rather than the rule (I always seemed to be the only child in my class with a working mother) did mean that we could afford to go abroad for holidays: at Christmas we even went skiing, which became extremely popular with all the family after our first trip in 1960 to Lenzerheide in Switzerland. The idea came about when our planned summer holiday to France – our first overseas trip – had to be cancelled because Mark caught chickenpox. A huge pall of disappointment descended on the house and, by way of consolation, my parents arranged a winter holiday. Lenzerheide was recommended to Denis by a pal of his who sold sports-wear.

While Mark and I enrolled in ski school, Denis and Margaret had private lessons. At forty-six and thirty-five it was certainly plucky of them to take up skiing – especially Margaret, who had done nothing remotely sporty since leaving school. She was a cautious skier, working hard on perfecting her technique but eschewing speed: she had no intention of returning home with a leg in plaster. Denis was also very methodical but immensely frustrated when not every one of his turns lived up to his high expectations.

There were plenty of other British families in the Lenzerhorn Hotel in the early sixties when the exchange rate was ten or twelve Swiss francs to the pound. There were group fondue evenings and we'd watch the ski instructors' torchlight processions down the slopes. The Ski Club of Great Britain held regular races for the children and I remember winning a cup. Margaret, being an MP, was asked to present the prizes, which were given in reverse order. She shook hands with the third place and second place winners and then I came up. I could see she was about to kiss me and, through gritted teeth, I hissed, 'Shake my hand. Shake my hand.'

I blushed and thrust out my hand, desperate to avoid the embarrassment of such an excruciating public display of maternal affection.

The holidays were so successful that we went back for five years,
every Christmas and New Year, staying at the same family-run
hotel at the bottom of the nursery slopes.

Denis was abroad again in October 1961 when Margaret was
appointed to the government as Joint Parliamentary Secretary to
the Ministry of Pensions and National Insurance. His congratulations were delayed and Margaret celebrated alone by simply getting on with her new job. 'I think they were all thinking, We must
have one more woman in, and they picked me and put me into
Social Security, for which I was very grateful. It's highly complicated and if you don't learn to handle it as a junior minister it's
very hard to get on top of it afterwards.'

Her workload increased dramatically. A typical day saw her up
at 7.00 making breakfast and reading through the papers, this was
followed by the school run, domestic organization, the drive to the
House of Commons, dealing with her mail, a visit to the bank,
dashing to catch a train out of town for a political engagement,
back in the House for Prime Minister's Question Time, and then
possibly a late-night sitting.

Arriving home, she would labour into the small hours, psyching
herself up for an appearance at the Despatch Box and scanning
reports for the statistics she needed to ram home a particular point.
She would block out almost any distraction. I can remember watching 'Top of the Pops' with Mark while she sat on the sofa working
through a file of papers. An ear-splitting song came on and I looked
up, sure that she'd tell us to turn down the volume.

'Is the television disturbing you, Mum?' I asked.

She didn't answer so I repeated the question.

She looked up. 'Pardon, dear? The TV? Oh, I didn't realize it
was on.'

Margaret never ever relaxed; she never slept in, she never let up.
The really fraught times were when she was preparing a speech:
the nervous tension would increase until she resembled a tempera-
mental leading lady on opening night. She couldn't disguise her
nerves, and she always chafed for perfection: 'I've always been

worried about making speeches because you always fear that you're not going to get it right. You get pretty scratchy because you've got one thing [the speech] in your mind and you have to down tools for others.'

Meanwhile, Denis was also working incredibly long hours. Basil Tuck at Atlas recalls, 'We spent a lot of time going through business together in the evening and then we'd go up to the Black Prince at Bexley and have a drink before Denis went home. Often he wouldn't leave until half past nine.

'It was said at the time that Margaret was very ambitious but he was also very ambitious for her and said that he stayed at work because she was busy working as well.'

Although Atlas was successful, Denis was responsible for the financial security of his mother, his sister and two aunts and the obligation weighed heavily upon him. 'Atlas was always under-capitalized,' he admits.

Perhaps it was inevitable that the pressure of their parallel careers and nature of their home life would eventually tell on my parents' physical and mental health. It finally showed in about 1964, when Denis was pushed to the verge of a complete nervous breakdown.

My doctor said that I was making myself ill working at that pace and if I carried on then I was endangering my health. And then he handed me an ultimatum, 'There's nothing wrong with you physically but if you don't stop working so hard, you are going to be very ill indeed. You've simply got to take some time off.'

I got myself on a boat – it shook Margaret – and took myself off to South Africa. I went on the *Warwick Castle*; it was a fabulous boat – the best ship in the fleet. On board, I played deck games with the other passengers and after lunch most days I went into the gym. I said to the purser when I got off at Durban, 'I'm pleased to tell you that I'm three pounds lighter than when I got on.' He was most disappointed. Of course, there was non-stop food of the highest possible quality.

This sabbatical was a crunch point in Denis's life, with far more at stake than just his health. According to a friend he confided in at the time, he was also deeply worried about the future direction of his life: 'He was terribly depressed and decided to go to South

Africa to sort himself out. I knew he was unhappy because he discussed it with me. He had his mother and Joy, who doted on him, and a wife who was totally absorbed in her political career.'

Perhaps it was simply a mid-life crisis. He admits that approaching his half century was a landmark that he dwelt on. 'You really think in terms of time marching on when you move out of your forties into fifties. It seems to be more of a psychological hurdle than any other change of decade. You move out of being an up-and-coming young man. If you haven't arrived by then you're not going to.'

In South Africa Denis spent a great deal of time thinking. He went on an extended safari. 'From Durban, I went to Johannesburg and then did a tour of several of the best game reserves in the world. I went to Kruger, Wankie, saw friends in Rhodesia and then went to the Nairobi game park. I suppose I was on the trail for three months.'

He was bitten by the photography bug: he loved all the paraphernalia and came back with hundreds of slides and miles of cinefilm. 'I took a wonderful still picture of a lion in the Nairobi game park. I had my own jeep and a guide and as we inched up, he kept saying, "No closer, master, no closer." The lion was feet away and I had the camera in my hand just when he woke up. I very nearly photographed his back teeth!'

After describing the journey in detail, he finally gave me a glimpse of what was really going on:

I had some thinking time and at the end of it I concluded that I wasn't being fair to my family to go on running Atlas. I came to the conclusion that this wasn't a bad company – making quite a bit of money – and my shareholders were doing very nicely, thank you. But here was a medium-sized [small today] business that was dependent on the life of one man and if I kicked the bucket they could be in real bloody trouble.

There was my aunt Doris and my mother – both stockholders. In the case of Doris, she had the most, and my aunt Ede had a whole chunk, too, and she needed it. I thought, supposing something like this happens again [another breakdown] or if I peg out?

The economic policies of the new Labour government included an enormous capital gains tax which I thought would ruin the Thatcher family because we had all our money in the bloody business.

Denis returned home looking tanned and fit and in the relaxed frame of mind that follows major decision-making. But he found his wife very run-down and in low spirits; she hadn't bounced back after the October 1964 general election.

The campaign had been particularly strenuous because Margaret faced a stronger Liberal challenge in Finchley than in 1959 and had driven herself back and forth across London at all hours of the night. Although her own seat was safe, polling day saw Harold Wilson lead the Labour Party into government with a majority of four.

Defeat was a blow for Margaret, who was already at a low ebb because of Denis's illness.

It was a big disappointment. I remember – and I'll never forget this – when we won in 1959 with a majority of about 100 and there were quite a lot of new Conservative members, we had a dining club and Rab Butler, who was then so very senior, came to this dining club and he said to us, 'We've got a very good majority and if we play our cards carefully and well we should be in office for twenty-five years.' And we weren't, we didn't play our cards well, a lot went wrong and we were out of office in 1964.

Denis immediately set off for Lenzerheide ahead of the rest of the family to continue his convalescence. We joined him for Christmas and the New Year, but the alpine air couldn't restore Margaret's deteriorating health: she came down with pneumonia in January 1965.

For someone who had never known serious illness, it came as a shock. 'I was very surprised. I've enjoyed very good health, [although] I haven't looked after it in particular. Denis hadn't been well and Mark had pneumonia. After having tried to cope with absolutely everything, I came down with it. I remember it so very well because Winston Churchill died in January 1965 and I couldn't go to the lying in state in Westminster Hall. I had to watch the funeral on television.'

Having made his decision about Atlas, Denis contacted George

Williams, the projects and developments director of the Castrol Oil company. Several years earlier Williams had approached him with an offer to buy part of Atlas and the answer had been, 'We ain't for sale!' This time, however, my father was ready to consider an offer – not for part of Atlas but for the whole company.

Williams recalls the lunch: 'I was immensely impressed by the fact that he [Denis] had total command of every aspect of his business, but perhaps even more so by his compassion for the people in the business. Although he had accepted that it was in the family interest to consider selling it I don't think he would eventually have come to a deal unless he felt Castrol was a compatible company from the personnel point of view.'

Denis sold the Atlas Preservative Company to Castrol Oil for £530,000, of which his personal share was £10,000. He didn't discuss it with Margaret because they had an unwritten rule that neither interfered in the other's professional life. He wrote this memo to the staff:

> 26th August 1965.
> The directors have received an offer from CASTROL LIMITED to purchase the whole capital of the company and are proposing to recommend to the shareholders that the offer should be accepted.
> One of the main reasons which will prompt me, as a shareholder, to accept this offer is that I believe that the rate of growth and expansion of Atlas will be faster when we work within a large Group than it would be by remaining independent, thus the opportunities for the staff would be wider and more exciting in the future . . .

All the personal and professional decisions had been made and Denis had a much more settled and confident view of the future. He looked forward to the last decade of his working life and assumed that he'd continue running Atlas for Castrol, avoiding the stress of being top dog. But instead, Castrol offered him a job on their board.

Making such a major career move worried Denis and he wondered whether he was going to be out of his depth. He sought the advice of a close friend, Jim Jackson, who had been with him on the board of Atlas. 'It was one hell of a change and I said to Jim, "They'll take one look at me and I'll be out of work."'

'He said: "Oh, don't underestimate yourself, I think they'll find you're much better than you think you are."'

Denis knew nothing about the oil business and was moving from a relatively small family-owned company to a multi-national where every figure had a string of noughts at the end. 'It took a certain amount of adapting but I found the approach to the work was pretty well the same except I wasn't concerned with sales policy or manufacturing policy; I was merely concerned with trying to get the costing system under some sort of control.'

His new office was in Marylebone Road, which was particularly convenient when we moved from The Dormers to London in 1966 to cut down on Margaret's travelling time. Home became a rented flat on the seventh floor of Westminster Gardens in Marsham Street minutes from the House of Commons.

Margaret's career was also going through a period of rapid change. Now in opposition, she was reshuffled from Pensions to Housing and Land. Edward Heath had replaced Alec Douglas-Home (later Lord Home) as Leader of the Tories and the party was on election footing because the government had such a small parliamentary majority.

In March 1966 Harold Wilson called a general election and increased the Labour majority to 97 seats. Margaret was facing a long period in opposition. She was appointed Spokesman on Treasury and Economic Affairs under Iain Macleod – climbing the first rung on the ladder towards her ultimate ambition: to be the first female Chancellor of the Exchequer.

Denis was also on the move. He'd barely got his feet under his desk at Castrol when the company was taken over by Burmah Oil, the oldest established British oil company. He went home that night fearful of his prospects, given the time-honoured rule of 'last in, first out'. The security of running a small family company was already a distant memory. 'I probably won't have a job, love,' he told Margaret.

His fears were groundless. His employer simply changed from Castrol to Burmah. The new executive appointed him divisional director of the planning and control department and a senior divisional director. He became responsible for setting up a new planning and control unit. Pat Davies, who worked with him, recalls:

> He took to the oil business like a duck to water. He understood it and he had a rapport. He was always very keen to define the objective; he had a vision of things and didn't get bogged down with detail. Business acumen is something he had and not everyone has. Wherever you are, and whatever the size of the company, the principles are the same.
>
> He worked very hard, I suppose it is partly reflected in your mother's expectations. Denis would arrive before ten in the morning and work through until past seven in the evening, which was different to most people. His main quality is his loyalty. He was so straightforward but at the same time very loyal.

The same was true of his marriage. Although only a part-time political husband, he was proud of Margaret's growing reputation: she now shared the mantle of the most prominent female politician of the day with Labour's Barbara (later Lady) Castle.

Politically, Denis agreed with her on almost everything except capital punishment. Margaret was for it; Denis opposed. 'It is an absolutely barbaric way of taking people's lives; it really is absolutely awful. Secondly, of course, there is always the possibility of making a mistake and I think, too, from a conscience point of view juries who are terrified of making a mistake will tend to find someone accused of murder "Not Guilty".'

Although he worked in London, Denis loathed living there. He was a Kent man and he and Margaret rented a small cottage near Horsmonden in the hop-producing county that Denis knew well from his searchlight duty stint more than twenty years before. Then they fell in love with a mock-Tudor house with polished wooden floors on the edge of Lamberhurst, near Tunbridge Wells. 'The Mount' became Denis's favourite of all the houses we occupied.

It had an outdoor swimming pool – which neither parent used – and a redundant grass tennis court. Rotary mowers were quite new and Denis cut a slightly comical figure pushing the machine up and down the banks in his ski boots to protect his toes from the blades.

The Mount offered panoramic views over the village and across the valley, but Denis's eyes were drawn to the neatly raked, kidney-shaped bunkers on the local golf course. Now he took lessons – he hadn't lifted a club since those few boyhood rounds with his father – and golf soon filled the sporting void left by his retirement from refereeing.

When not at boarding school, Mark and I divided our time between the London flat and Lamberhurst. Family holidays had been abandoned because we each wanted to do our own thing.

Although politics never completely dominated the househould, it encroached more and more. I remember sitting on the terrace at The Mount on a glorious summer's day and Margaret holding forth on the invasion of Czechoslovakia. She had drummed into us at an early age the importance of having some direction in life and she, rather than Denis, had overseen our day-to-day lives.

Denis had a unwavering policy of never arguing with members of the family. He'd do anything for a quiet life and if trouble was brewing he would make himself scarce. However, if you started something, he made sure that you finished it; which meant you didn't drop out or flunk exams.

Not surprisingly, both my parents were sticklers for presentation, and I remember them cringing when I took to wearing an old fireman's coat from an army surplus store and a three-mile-long scarf that I knitted – probably the result of having grown up in a house full of hat boxes and blue suits.

After an unexpected victory in the June 1970 general election, the Conservatives were back in government for the first time in six years with a majority of 31. We were on our way to Lamberhurst when the news of the early exit polls came over the car radio.

'If that result is right, we've won,' exclaimed Margaret, obviously surprised. Denis turned the car around and we went to the *Daily Telegraph* party at the Savoy. Late that night, when victory was assured, journalist Andrew Alexander tried to convince me that my mother had a very good chance of becoming the next Chancellor of the Exchequer. Surely not, I thought; not a woman.

As it turned out, Margaret was appointed Secretary of State for

Education and Science and became famous for two policy decisions. In June she revoked Labour's policy forcing secondary schools to become comprehensives, and the October Budget ended free school milk for children over the age of seven. The media dubbed her 'Thatcher the Milksnatcher' and the *Sun* ran the headline: THE MOST UNPOPULAR WOMAN IN BRITAIN.

Although some political commentators have since claimed that Denis was so upset by the ridicule and condemnation that he tried to persuade his wife to chuck in the towel, he says this was never the case. 'It was hurtful but you didn't show it. If you're in public life then you're going to get hammered. I suppose it wasn't bad training. After a bit it just washed over me and I certainly didn't lose any sleep over it.'

George Williams, by then with Burmah, comments, 'The great thing about Denis having to tolerate all those terrible things said about his wife was that he is in love with Margaret and that, to me, is the essence of the whole thing.

'He was so fond of her and so supportive that he never wanted to do anything to let her down. But sometimes he'd hint at the loneliness and used to say, "I just wish we could have a private life. I'm getting old and I'd just like to enjoy life."'

The strain of being unpopular toughened Margaret up for the challenges ahead and taught Denis that he would have to live with the fact that his wife wasn't everyone's cup of tea. Often I didn't recognize the Mrs Thatcher described in newspapers and magazines as my mother; the 'ice maiden' image was so different from the private person I knew.

I noticed it most when I left school and went to University College, London. To my student friends and contemporaries, the Minister of Education was public enemy number one and I was her daughter. There were dozens of anti-Thatcher demonstrations and marches by protesting students: I sometimes tried to explain to them that Margaret wasn't the inhuman dragon they imagined; that she wasn't trying to starve the nation's children of milk but arranging the public spending priorities in her Department. It was a bit like having a split personality – one as daughter of a Minister and the other as a student – and it meant that I never brought student friends home to the townhouse we'd bought in Flood Street, Chelsea.

Meanwhile, Denis turned up when required at constituency functions – even if they were dreary Chamber of Commerce dinner-dances on wintry Saturday nights. Occasionally he had to psych himself up between the car park and the entrance with an audible, 'Thatcher, get your enjoyment shoes on.' He had little time for the pomposity of local government officials, who were inevitably on the cast list at constituency functions. 'Christ, he's even wearing his bloody chains,' he once observed rather too loudly as he spotted the mayor a few places away.

But, as a minister's husband, he did sample the perks of higher political office, including lunch at Chequers for the New Zealand Prime Minister and a concert there given by the pupils at Yehudi Menuhin's school.

Although his policy was never to interfere, occasionally Margaret asked for his advice. When one of her constituents – a shareholder of Rolls-Royce – expressed unhappiness with the state of the company, Denis obtained copies of the previous six annual reports and accounts and cast his eye over the figures. My father could read a balance sheet from a hundred paces and duly reported back to Margaret that Rolls-Royce had been treating research and development costs as capital, rather than charging them to the profit and loss account.

The company was basically bust and Margaret amazed her colleagues with her knowledge of the position when the crisis blew up a few days later and a Cabinet meeting was called. The company was allowed to go into liquidation and the aerospace division was nationalized.

'Don't ever do that to me again,' Denis made her promise. He didn't enjoy the sort of stress involved in giving advice at that level. 'Supposing I'd been wrong?'

Prime Minister Heath had promised a 'quiet revolution' – curbing excessive trade union power, cutting back on public expenditure and trying to encourage a free market economy. Eventually his government became famous for its policy U-turns and was widely considered a failure. Heath's one undisputed success was to take Britain into the EEC. Margaret supported this as best for Britain, although she didn't have any grand vision of being a 'good European'.

The government's failure to curb the power of the trade unions was graphically illustrated in the winter of 1973–74. Successive 'states of emergency' were called to beat the various strikes; power cuts and shorter working weeks became commonplace. Denis recalls:

> The unions were ruining our country – always on strike, which was a failure of nationalized industries – a monopoly they had. The dockers, of course, were a bloody menace. You shipped your goods down to London and the dockers wouldn't touch them. They were capable of holding the country to ransom and did.
>
> The restrictive practices on ships was awful. When Atlas was doing ship repairing and de-greasing heat exchange equipment, unless our chaps were all members of the union they wouldn't even take your kit aboard. Our chaps had to learn to work alongside them and there were certain things they wouldn't let us do at all. You might have to connect your vaporizer up to a flange and you couldn't touch it until one of their chaps turned up and did it. It only took three minutes.
>
> One of them went to lunch and I remember our fellow connected the flange. When the union member came back he said, 'Who connected that?'
>
> 'I did,' said our chap. 'I can't hang around all day waiting for you.'
>
> So the dockers all downed tools and walked off the bloody ship. They wouldn't come back until the flange was disconnected. That's the sort of thing we were up against.

The general election on 28 February 1974 left no single party with an overall majority, although Labour won the largest number of seats. After Ted Heath failed to form a coalition with the Liberals, he resigned as Prime Minister and Harold Wilson formed a minority Labour government.

'You have to pick yourself up and keep on going,' Margaret told one journalist in March but, after four years totally absorbed in a Department, Opposition was a traumatic readjustment. There were no more Cabinet meetings or tell-tale red boxes or invitations to Chequers. She lost her research assistant but retained a miracle secretary in the shape of Alison Ward, who could do twenty-one jobs at once, including organizing Flood Street, chauffeuring her boss to the hairdresser's and looking after constituency matters.

The extra free time meant that Margaret and Denis could take a holiday, but it didn't mean they had to enjoy it. They set off for a fortnight in Corsica; a week later Alison received a call from a phone box at Heathrow. 'We're back,' said Margaret. 'Corsica wasn't a very interesting island – there wasn't much to see and we've done it.'

Not surprisingly, Harold Wilson called another general election in October 1974 to try and win an absolute majority. He succeeded by three seats, leaving the Tories demoralized and Ted Heath facing a leadership challenge. In November, after a great deal of thought, Margaret announced her decision to run and the first ballot was scheduled for 4 February 1975.

Denis had too many of his own work problems to worry about Margaret's gamble: he, along with a few others at the new Burmah headquarters in Swindon, voiced his concerns about the company's spiralling finances.

We spent Christmas in Kent, sitting down to a traditional turkey dinner and opening our presents after the Queen's Message. There was no hint of the drama about to unfold, not just in Westminster but also at Burmah Oil. At 8.30 p.m. on New Year's Eve the company logo flashed onto the television screen and a spokesman reported:

Since the interim announcement in September there has been a sharp downward revision of the anticipated results for 1974, largely due to the tanker operation, which are now expected to show a substantial loss . . . [Therefore] the company expects it will not be able fully to comply with certain provisions of loan agreements with bankers under which foreign currency loans amounting to $650 million have been advanced to the group . . .

. . . the following arrangements have been agreed between the company and the Bank of England to provide interim support to the company pending realization of certain major assets in continuation of a programme already in hand . . .

Burmah was effectively bust and the Bank of England had to bail the company out.

When Denis arrived at Burmah House he had a taste of what it was like to be chased by the press. Photographers were snapping and journalists waylaying any Burmah employee going through the front door. Denis had never been on the main board but was an obvious target because of his wife's high profile. The following morning newspapers pictured him high-jumping a wall to escape.

It was a dramatic start to a year, and this was only the beginning. Six weeks later, on 11 February, Margaret would become the Leader of Her Majesty's Opposition.

NINE

APPRENTICE CONSORT

'I realized I was a shy man who had to un-shy myself
pretty damn quick.'

DENIS THATCHER

DAILY LIFE IN 19 FLOOD STREET was conducted at a flat-out
sprint. No one walked up or down the stairs, they dashed; no one
talked calmly, they barked and gabbled; even the arrival of the
morning newspapers caused eruptions.

The house was a rather boxy terraced townhouse with a bleak
paved front yard cheered up by potted plants and trees in tubs.
Inside, its main disadvantage for the new Leader of the Opposition
was that it wasn't designed for a constant stream of visitors. Guests
waiting for an audience with Margaret in the first-floor sitting room
could only stand, shifting from foot to foot or leaning against the
wall of the coral-papered entrance hall – hardly ideal.

When finally ushered upstairs, they would discover green carpet,
chintz-covered sofas, Denis's treasured red-glass Venetian lamps,
and an oriental-style cocktail cabinet bought with the insurance
proceeds of a brooch Margaret had lost in Richmond Park. (Rather
than buy another piece of jewellery she chose something she
couldn't lose.) Three tall windows looked down on Flood Street.
At the back of the house were two small single bedrooms and a
bathroom; on the second floor were two more bedrooms, including
my parents', and a bathroom. Denis always complained that the
house was too dark. Funnily enough, it was Swan Court which
stole all the light from our side of the street.

After the excitement of victory – and the novelty of having a
female leader – had worn off, sections of the press and the Conservative Party began promulgating the idea that Margaret's grip
on the leadership was both tenuous and temporary. She was a

misfit: a woman in a man's world, a political curiosity and – worse – a feminist experiment. How long could she survive before the Conservative Party regained its senses and dumped her for a man?

Bill Shelton, who became one of her first parliamentary private secretaries, remembers, 'For the rest of that year Ted ran a campaign: "She must be out by Christmas."' Heath referred to her as TBW – That Bloody Woman – and he wasn't the only one. Many in the Establishment and the City were appalled to find Conservative MPs apparently embracing feminist principles. They were confident that she would be ousted at the first opportunity her opponents could find. Funnily enough, many of these same doommongers and critics later became the most fanatical converts to Thatcherism and vehemently denied they had ever harboured any doubts.

Even before her elevation, columnists such as Bernard Levin of *The Times* had warned that the 'Tories must look before they leap into line behind a new leader': 'The male chauvinism of the people of this country, particularly the women, is still dreadful and her sex would be a severe handicap. Besides, there is her too-cool exterior (if only she would burst into tears occasionally); if the Tories would not warm to Mr Heath, they are unlikely to warm to Mrs Thatcher, and there is no point in the party jumping out of the igloo and onto the glacier' (16 October 1974).

After witnessing the mauling his wife had been given by the press as Secretary of State for Education and Science, Denis was suspicious of journalists as a breed, although Bernard Levin was one of the three newspapermen he most admired – the others being Bill (later Lord) Deedes, editor of the *Daily Telegraph* from 1974 until 1986, and Lord Rees-Mogg.

My father wasn't interested in the equality debate; nor did he listen to the sociological waffle about the resentment of the subordinate male. Matthew Arnold's description of someone 'Who saw life steadily, and saw it whole' applied to Denis. The thought of playing second fiddle to his wife didn't even occur to him. After all, he was a businessman, not a political consort – at least for a few more months.

The arrival of security men marked a change in our lifestyle. We had a uniformed policeman on the doorstep (Mark and I were most affected because we were in the habit of opening the door to pick up the milk or the papers wearing only a dressing gown and slippers). Following the assassination of Ross McWhirter, Margaret was given Special Branch protection. It was the first time that a leader of the Opposition had ever been granted such protection on an everyday basis.

No one told Denis, of course, who arrived home to find Mark in the drawing room talking to a man in a dinner jacket.

Mark said to me, 'This is Mr Kingston,' and I assumed he was one of his friends and they were going out somewhere.

'Good evening, sir,' said this very polite chap. 'Please call me Bob.'

We talked for a bit and then I explained that I was going out to dinner and disappeared upstairs to change. I said to Mark, 'If you're going out, you'd also better think about changing.'

When I came back down this chap was still there and when Margaret arrived we started leaving and, bugger me, if this chap didn't follow us out. No one told me who the hell he was.

Denis soon got used to introducing himself to strangers he encountered in the kitchen or the sitting room – mostly secretaries, aides, ad men and speechwriters. As a Cabinet minister, Margaret had kept the Department at the office and rarely invited anyone from her political life home. Leadership was different, and when a major speech was due the wordsmiths practically took up residence in Flood Street, covering the sitting-room floor with paper.

Denis was amazed at the effort that went into a speech and tried in vain to inject some perspective into these write-a-thons. 'Oh, darling, you're much better off the cuff,' he'd reassure her, remembering how often she'd boasted of her ability to arrive at a dinner unprepared, confident that inspiration for the speech would come during the soup. But that was in her backbencher days; this was the big time. Bill Shelton's abiding memory of those first months in the Leader's office is simply, 'We kept on writing speeches for her.'

The speechwriting sessions at Flood Street would continue until my mother could no longer politely ignore the sound of rumbling tummies. A scratch supper was then rustled up downstairs and work was halted until shepherd's pie or the ubiquitous lasagne was consumed. One regular on the team refused to come if he was fed lasagne again.

Afterwards it was back to work again, leaving the kitchen in a mess. One or two of the boys, noticing the lack of any domestic staff, helpfully attempted to clear a plate or two but were summoned back to the draft by my mother, who declared, 'Denis will clear and wash up.'

One of her secretaries, recruited to type the emerging speech, volunteered to help and Denis showed her how to keep a wooden salad bowl in pristine nick: 'No water ... clean it out and then wipe it over with oil before putting it away,' he explained.

The army was one of the lasting influences on Denis's life and he approached washing up with military discipline. Eschewing a dishwasher (which we didn't possess anyway), he would stride around the kitchen with a tea towel tucked into his trouser waistband.

According to Gordon Reece, the Opposition Leader's press secretary, Denis treated Margaret's aides like junior officers in a new regiment. 'It was almost as if he said that if Margaret trusts these new young officers I'm going to trust them as well. I was one of them, and as far as I was concerned Denis trusted me from the beginning. He would always ask my advice about what was happening and what should be done.'

From the moment Margaret became Opposition Leader Denis understood that his life was politically and administratively circumscribed to her career; he didn't want it any other way. But while she was trail-blazing, he would live life the way he always had, however old-fashioned or out of vogue it might seem. The goalposts might have moved and strangers taken over his house, but throughout it all Denis remained unceasingly gallant and courteous.

He needed to be: political staff were buzzing in and out of his home, totally consuming Margaret's life. Occasionally someone paused to inform him that his presence would be required at a particular function – often at very short notice – but he never exploded; typically, he'd sigh and say, 'It's a bloody nuisance but I'll be there.'

At the same time Denis is the first to admit that Margaret's position gave him a remarkable opportunity to meet and mix with those responsible for running the country. True to his nature, he was always pedantic about getting their names, titles and positions absolutely correct.

Denis never bothered the Leader of the Opposition's Private Office. Quite the reverse: Margaret was always grumbling to her staff that no one could find him when they needed to have a word. Bill Shelton remembers one of Denis's rare appearances in the office in the House of Commons. 'We had made the mistake of taking over all of Ted Heath's engagements from his diary. His [Denis's] words were, "Unless you lot do something about her diary, she won't be Leader much longer." I thought, 'My gosh, here is someone who speaks his mind and had seen what we hadn't seen.'"

Denis made no secret of the fact that he preferred our weekend bolthole – a rented flat in Court Lodge, bang in the middle of Lamberhurst golf course – to Flood Street. The lodge was twenty-five yards from the first tee – a refuge where he could indulge his love of golf, good company and a large drink. He'd try to get down early on Fridays to light the fire and turn the lights on before Margaret arrived later. Her weekends were largely taken up with paperwork, with brief intermissions for shopping in nearby Wadhurst and a brief stroll around the golf course.

This was my father's domain. Because he so often went alone to the flat, the freezer and larder were filled with his favourite dishes – soups, tins of tongue and corned beef, and jars of his favourite marmalades and jams.

For the new Leader the first nine months of the job were hell:

It's not easy to be Leader of the Opposition, it really isn't, and opposition is not my natural habit. Opposition is certainly about getting the right policies, which we did. We reshaped all of the policies from the first principles but I like to be a doer rather than a talker.

Then there's the element of frustration – trying to get adopted as policy the things in which I believed. So many people were still thinking of socialism as the flavour of the age and we'd better have a milder version of it, and that wasn't my idea at all. It wasn't Keith Joseph's idea and of course it was failing and they did fail – it's the first cousin of communism.

Denis retired in June, a month after his sixtieth birthday. At a low-key lunch with colleagues at Burmah he was presented with two silver signet spoons, a silver cigarette case and a company silver salver. Phyllis Kilner, his long-time secretary, retired on the same day.

He had no intention of genuinely retiring: he already had several non-executive directorships – Chipman Chemicals, Halfords and Quinton Hazell (an engineering subsidiary of Burmah Oil) – and planned to add to this portfolio. Yet his retirement could never be totally as he'd anticipated because he was about to embark on a very hazardous voluntary job – that of male political consort – and he had one major handicap: despite having been a major in the army, a successful businessman and a high quality referee, he was still painfully and, he assumed, incurably shy: 'If anybody had said to me when I was fifty that I would go round roomfuls of complete strangers, start shaking hands and try and talk to them, I would have said, "You have got to be out of your mind,"' he recalls, laughing. 'That's what happened. I realized I was a shy man who had to un-shy myself pretty damn quick.'

His sister Joy comments, 'When Den was young I could never have imagined that he would become so good with strangers as he has over the years . . .'

The first real taste of the 'press the flesh' circuit came when the Opposition Leader embarked on a series of 'get-to-know-you' tours of Tory constituencies. These were an eye-opener for Denis. 'Christ, what on earth are all these people doing here?' he blurted out as the bus drew up in front of a welcoming crowd outside a local town hall.

'Mr Thatcher, they've come to see your wife,' an aide informed him helpfully.

Denis sighed. 'Well, they don't want to bloody see me.'

One of his first tours was to Derbyshire and it brought home to Denis the enormous reserves of stamina required. 'We had a hell of a day meeting and greeting and lunching,' he recalls. 'It was non-stop and by early evening we arrived somewhere and the chairman of the local association asked me if I'd like a drink. He poured me a tumbler full of whisky ... there wasn't any room for the soda. It barely touched the sides and he poured me another. It was sinking in fast, what I had let myself in for.'

In those first few months Denis, the apprentice consort, approached his public duties with a degree of pragmatism and an eagerness to learn. 'If I was available, I went ... Opposition was a learning process – at least it was for me.'

He was most comfortable when visiting factories – far more so than Margaret – because he had spent his entire working life in them.

> I saw some bloody awful places. We went to one big factory in the southern counties where the chairman took Margaret around and I had the finance director with me. We went into a machine shop and only about half the total kit was working but there was tons of work in progress on the ground waiting to be picked up.
>
> I know from experience that creates a hell of a problem for monthly accounting because how do you value it? So I asked this chap and he just shrugged.
>
> 'You must have an under-recovered overhead factor here because only half of it is working,' I suggested, and he looked at me blankly.
>
> This went on and on and when I got into the car, I said to Margaret, 'What did you think?'
>
> 'I didn't think it was very good; what did you think?'
>
> 'It's bloody ghastly and I'll tell you another thing: I've got fifteen thousand pounds invested in that dump and I won't be able to sell the shares quick enough.'

Later on, Denis became more discriminating in his choice of engagements and would ask himself the question, 'Can I do any good?' If the answer was yes, he tagged along; if the answer was no, he bailed out. Having decided against a visit to Scotland, he welcomed Margaret home and looked forlornly at the stack of tartan-emblazoned tins of shortbread she'd been given. Rather laconically he suggested, 'Next time, why don't you tell them you're also very partial to Scotch whisky?'

There were never any arguments between the Leader and her

consort except on the issue of punctuality. Billed to depart at 19.30, my mother would be pacing the sitting room, speech in hand and ready to go with fifteen minutes to spare. Denis would appear at 19.28, casually open the drinks cabinet and pour himself a gin. 'Plenty of time,' he said, spying Margaret's imploring look. Then he'd remind her of the time they went to catch a train and she had insisted they were on the platform in time for the one before theirs.

Having spent sixteen years reading his wife's press, Denis wasn't tempted to become a media-friendly consort. Instead, he made one of the most important and valuable policy decisions of his new career: he decided never to give an interview. For Gordon Reece, the link man between the Thatchers and the media, this was a perfect example of Denis being his own man: 'He laid down his own rules, nobody else.'

The issue surfaced when Gordon was approached by John Junor, the editor of the *Sunday Express*, who asked if the newspaper could possibly interview Denis.

> I told him I didn't think Denis would agree. John Junor was insistent: 'Well, this is going to be most important: he's a very attractive personality and people would like him. I've been very good to you ... to Mrs Thatcher and the Conservative Party and an interview with the *Sunday Express* would be wholly beneficial ...'
> I was a bit anxious and approached Denis to sound him out. 'Gordon, I'm amazed,' he said. 'You have taught me what I'll never forget and so far I've always done what you told me to do because I thought it was right. But if I see this friend, I've got to see every friend you have; everyone who's been kind to me, to Margaret and the party. I'll have to see them all.'
> I told Denis I was sorry that I raised it.

The decision not to speak to journalists when it was fashionable to court the press was both brave and brilliant. It removed Denis from the firing line because he couldn't unwittingly say the wrong thing and provide ammunition to be shot back at his wife. With hindsight, he calls his decision 'a bit of common sense' and says it wasn't based on any spin doctor's rule book but on a line that he'd heard fifty years earlier. 'My father told me as a boy: "Whales don't get killed until they spout."'

Margaret's political machine was still feeling its way, particularly when dealing with the unexpected. General Franco's death in 1975 was a perfect example. Instead of buzzing with energetic and intellectual discussion on the dictator's contribution to Spanish history, the Spanish Civil War and the literature of Ernest Hemingway, the corridors resounded with Alison Ward's anguished cry: 'Oh shit, I've sent your mother's funeral gear to Sketchley's!'

A turning point for Margaret and her staff was her first address to the Conservative Party Conference in Blackpool on 10 October 1975. The speech went through umpteen drafts as the team paced, argued and scribbled in the Thatcher suite at the Imperial Hotel. At 4.50 a.m. Denis was snoozing in his dinner jacket on the windowsill when he started awake and very loudly declared, 'That's the one!' According to Ronnie Millar, this utterance immediately ended the session. Without Denis's intervention, the exhausted wordsmiths would probably have been honing, paring and reworking the draft until 11.30 the following morning.

Ronnie Millar was making last-minute adjustments to the text when Margaret came out of the bedroom, ready to leave. 'She looked as though she had just come from a health farm,' he said. 'She was wearing a conservative blue dress with a wide skirt which was very becoming. She was three days short of fifty but she looked young and vulnerable, pretty and scared and I felt very protective.'

In the car she and Denis held hands every second of the short ride from the Imperial Hotel to the Winter Gardens. It stopped him shaking, too – he later confided to a friend that it was one of the few occasions he felt truly scared for her. Their nervousness was fuelled by the 5,000 people crammed into the body of the hall and the upper level.

As they arrived on the platform, a woman in the front row handed Margaret a large feather duster. She examined it very closely, as if wondering what it was for, and then proceeded to dust the chairman, Peter Thomas. The crowd roared with laughter. The ice had been broken.

Margaret began: 'During my lifetime all the leaders of the Conservative Party have gone on to serve as Prime Minister. I hope that habit will continue.'

'Hear! Hear!' said Denis, appointing himself chief cheer leader. The laughter and applause subsided.

'Our leaders have been different men with different qualities and different styles but they all had one thing in common – each met the challenge of his time . . .

'What are our chances of success? It depends on what kind of people we are. What kind of people are we? We are the people who have received more Nobel prizes than any other nation except America.'

Denis: 'Hear! Hear!'

Growing in confidence, Margaret continued. 'We are also the people who among other things invented the computer, the refrigerator, the electric motor, the stethoscope, rayon, the steam turbine, stainless steel, television, penicillin, radar, the jet engine, hovercraft, carbon fibres and the best half of the Concorde.'

Denis: 'Hear! Hear!'

When the speech was over Margaret acknowledged the applause, keeping her arms by her side to stop them shaking. Afterwards she returned to the hotel suite, on a high but already coming down. Ronnie Millar dropped in to congratulate her; he had lunched with journalists who described her performance as fabulous.

Margaret: 'Well, if they're right what are we going to do next year? Brighton could be the most dreadful anti-climax.'

This was too much for Denis: 'My God, woman, you've just had a bloody great triumph, and here you are worrying yourself sick about next year.'

Millar wrote later: 'So long as she has this man around she's going to be all right.'

The headlines the next morning heralded the speech as a triumph. The *Daily Mirror* wrote: 'Super-Mag came to Blackpool yesterday and not since Moses came down from the mountain has the message been more effectively spread to the gathering of the faithful at the Winter Gardens . . .' Margaret had been confirmed as Leader and was now secure in the job. She had shown her strength, her determination and vision – silencing a legion of critics and snipers in the process. 'Blackpool 1', as Denis took to numbering the party conferences, had been a success.

Within twenty-four hours the foot-stamping and applause were a distant memory as the Thatcher family exchanged Court Lodge for another weekend flat in Scotney Castle – a romantic spot owned by the National Trust, surrounded by rhododendron and azalea gardens, with a ruined moated castle built in 1378.

But political danger stalked in even the most innocuous pastime. Newspaper photographers recorded Denis and Margaret attempting some DIY: some voters were incensed and Denis received the first critical letters of his new tenure. 'There must have been at least half a dozen accusing me of taking the bread out of the mouths of honest wallpaper hangers or accusing us of indulging in a stupid bit of publicity. For goodness' sake, we were decorating our holiday flat.'

Denis was learning that anyone with even a walk-on part in public life was setting himself up for target practice. He was already developing his own defence – a simple but effective policy: 'I'll keep my head below the parapet.' During the conference the *Evening Standard* had observed: 'Mr Denis Thatcher is still fighting shy of playing the role of full-time consort to Margaret . . .' This article missed the point. Denis was simply performing the role on his own terms – as Gordon Reece saw from the Leader's inner circle. 'He was wonderful with her and she was wonderful with him. People mustn't underestimate that she had loyalty to him; many think that it was his loyalty to her that mattered, but it was her loyalty to him that was even more important because she knew that he was the commonsense point of view. That's what Denis has always been.'

Denis trod very warily during his first year of retirement. It would have been easy and very tempting to enlarge his portfolio of non-executive directorships with the help of the great and the good, but this was never his way. He had a stable of established companies and they were enough. He had regular board meetings and irregular golf games, lowering his handicap into the mid-teens and constantly searching for the perfect swing.

Meanwhile, Margaret's second full year as Leader began well. On 19 January 1976 she made her first major foreign policy statement in a speech entitled 'Britain Awake', delivered at Kensington Town Hall. Vigorously anti-Communist and anti-Soviet, it caused a stir at a time when East–West relations were supposedly in a phase of détente:

> Look at what the Russians are doing. Russia is ruled by a dictatorship of patient, far-sighted men who are rapidly making their country the foremost naval and military power in the world. They are not doing this solely for the sake of self-defence ... No. The Russians are bent on world dominance and they are rapidly acquiring the means to become the most powerful imperial nation the world has seen ... They put guns before butter, while we put just about everything before guns.

Margaret and Richard Ryder, her political secretary, and a handful of others from her office came back to Flood Street after the speech and sat listening to a rather antiquated transistor radio to see if it had been picked up by the media on the One O'clock News. It got a mention – relief enough – but none of us could have foreseen the impact it had on the corridors of power in the Kremlin. Three days later the Soviet Defence Ministry newspaper, *Red Star*, branded her the 'Iron Lady' and accused her of trying to revive the Cold War.

Moscow's sobriquet was meant as an insult but it became a powerful and popular 'badge'. The *Daily Mail* commented, 'Who could have dreamed that her first year as leader of the Conservative Party would be climaxed with her emergence as a world figure by courtesy of a tirade from Moscow . . .' Hilarious posters and cartoons showed Margaret 'handbagging' a Soviet tank with Brezhnev's intimidating visage, or sitting Boadicea-like on horseback ready to fight off the Communist hordes.

Denis recalls: 'It was a brilliant speech and the Iron Lady tag turned out to be a gift.'

Margaret always appeared brimming with confidence and conviction, but 'You're never free of self-doubt because you always want to do better than you've done last time; whether you've done comparatively well or not, you always want to do better. You're forever striving.'

I saw a flash of this self-doubt in April 1977 during an unofficial trip to China, Japan and Hong Kong. I was on my way to Australia and Margaret had suggested that I accompany her before going on to Sydney. After qualifying as a solicitor and doing shipping law for a City of London firm, I had decided that I wanted to travel.

We flew first to Beijing, where an official banquet was arranged in the Great Hall of the People. A limousine picked us up from the Embassy and, as it edged through the dimly lit streets, we talked about the years to come in the UK. Having planned to be away for at least a year or two, I wanted to talk to Margaret. 'Good luck. I hope it all goes well and you win the election when it comes,' I said.

Looking out of the window, she whispered, 'My great fear is that when the test comes I might fail.'

Denis had no such doubts and was in awe of 'the sheer sort of feeling of leadership and determination that she brought to the job. After about a year, or perhaps eighteen months, I never seriously thought we would lose. I think I can say that I never honestly, thought we were going to lose.'

According to Tim (later Sir Tim) Bell, who handled the Tory Party advertising when Saatchi and Saatchi won the account in 1978, Denis was delightfully naive about Margaret's importance. Her advisers were discussing how to raise her profile in a Labour seat in Cardiff, when Denis weighed in. Cardiff to him meant one thing: his beloved rugby football. 'Look, I think it might be a very good idea if she appeared at Cardiff Arms Park. I can't be sure to get her a seat in the stands but I do know one or two people who might be able to. I'm sure you chaps can make sure that the camera is pointing into the crowd where she's standing.' It never occurred to Denis that the Leader of the Opposition could get all the seats she wanted at any sporting or cultural event in the nation.

'Clearly he didn't think being a political leader was anywhere near as important as being a member of the Rugby Football Refereeing community,' jokes Tim Bell, who also commented on Denis's survival mechanism, which was simple but very effective: 'He paid absolutely no attention to anything that was not the way he wanted it to be. If it was the political scene, he took the view that you can't run them all, can't make them all behave, so if they do something wrong he would just ignore it. In that way he didn't have to get excited and worked up about it.'

His rather cynical and ironic view of politicians was an asset: if he didn't like people, he had a wonderful habit of mispronouncing their names to show his aversion. For example, someone called Parkin would become Parker; Price would become Bryce.

He was also quite capable of telling Margaret's advisers exactly what he thought. 'He didn't hesitate to completely debunk some proposal we were putting up to Margaret,' says Bell. 'We'd be sitting there and anguishing about doing this or that or not and he would never stir, argue or debate but come to his verdict and declare concisely and decisively, "Not a vote in the box."'

Nothing in Denis's diary for March 1979 gave a clue to the momentous end to the month. It looked quiet enough: England versus France at Twickenham the first Saturday; Chipman board meetings in Horsham; off to Jersey on Quinton Hazell business – all familiar territory. He could never have predicted the events leading to his one and only visit to the Chamber of the House of Commons.

Jim (later Lord) Callaghan's Labour government had clung to power through a variety of alliances with minor parties and the Opposition had been on full alert for a general election for more than a year: the call was expected in the autumn of 1978. Instead, Callaghan had decided to go on – a disastrous decision: within months the nation was chilled by the 'Winter of Discontent'.

Nightly images appeared on TV of garbage piling up in the streets and violent confrontations on the picket lines as a wave of public sector strikes crippled industry, outraged many voters and played into Margaret's hands, for Labour could control the union militants no better than the Tories.

On 28 March the Conservatives forced a vote of No Confidence in the government. It was a real cliffhanger; the most dramatic vote ever seen in the post-war House of Commons, with the result in doubt right until the end.

Denis was sitting next to Maggie Atkins, wife of the Chief Whip, in a box on the floor of the House. He wasn't going to miss this;

after four years in opposition this might be the night the balloon went up.

Margaret made a speech that electrified the house and the atmosphere was supercharged as MPs began to file into the division lobbies to vote. At about 10.30 p.m. the result was announced – Ayes 311; Noes division 310. Denis threw his arms in the air and yelled, 'Done it!' as if celebrating a try at Twickenham. Unfortunately, this was not deemed appropriate conduct in the gallery of the House of Commons. 'A nearby waiter [as the attendants are known] tapped me firmly on the shoulder and said, "You are not a Member of this House, sir."'

Afterwards, he joined Margaret, her staff and supporters in the Leader of the Opposition's office.

'Everyone was mesmerised that we'd won the vote,' recalls Crawfie (Mrs Cynthia Crawford, personal assistant to David Wolfson – later Lord Wolfson). 'Denis was very ebullient and genuinely thrilled.'

I was waiting nervously by the phone 12,000 miles away on a sunny morning in Sydney. It only rang once before I grabbed it and heard Alison Ward squawking ecstatically: 'Your mother wants to tell you herself, but we won.'

'By how many?'

'One.'

'Yes, but by how many?' I thought she was repeating the fact that they'd *won*.

Then Margaret was on the line, explaining that the government had fallen by a single vote.

'That's not many,' I gasped.

'We didn't need many,' she said pointedly, thinking my brain had been barbecued on Bondi Beach.

'So when is the election?'

'We don't know. Probably in early May.' She sounded absolutely effervescent; on the same sort of high that I remembered from four years earlier when she became Opposition Leader.

Parliament was dissolved on 7 April and the election set for twenty-six days later. This was the big one: if she lost, she was out – no questions asked.

'It was a pulverizing campaign, but for most of the time it was looking good,' recalls Denis, who worked 'the other side of the street' – his least favourite duty as consort. 'I hated every minute of campaigns. The days of gin and tonics and sandwiches; the tension, the strain of reading the papers and studying the opinion polls the next day.'

It was also overshadowed by tragedy when, two days after the election was called, Airey Neave was killed in a terrorist bombing in the garage of the House of Commons. Margaret only heard that Airey was the critically injured victim when she arrived at the BBC studios for a party election broadcast. She couldn't bring herself to broadcast and returned home to Flood Street to hear that he had died.

Denis could only console her. He had also had the greatest admiration for the man who had been so prominent in helping Margaret become Opposition Leader.

I flew back from Australia for the last ten days of the campaign, taking time off from my job at the *Sydney Morning Herald*. Margaret and Denis weren't thrilled about my choice of career. Denis regarded 'reptiles' as the enemy, but he accepted that it was my decision. My mother certainly couldn't criticize me for changing horses. She had set the precedent by being a chemist, a barrister and then a politician.

The ferocious pace of the campaign staggered me. Throughout one plane trip Caroline Stephens, my mother's diary secretary, was furiously typing out a new passage for a speech to be delivered on landing. As we piled onto the 'Battle Bus', the various copies were separated, stapled and stacked while someone yelled into a mobile phone, others discussed security and Margaret read a last-minute briefing and checked her hair. There were constant photo opportunities – Margaret cuddling a calf, Margaret at a fish factory, Margaret going walkabout in Huddersfield. I had the unnerving feeling that everyone was waiting for her to make a mistake or show signs of cracking under the pressure.

At times Denis's patience was stretched to breaking point. After a particularly pushy cameraman had jostled him once too often, he calmly muttered in the offender's ear that if it happened again he'd 'fill him in'. At the end of one eleven-minute factory tour amid a sea of 'reptiles', he thanked the managing director and said he would come back at a quieter time to see what was actually made there.

Home late at night, Margaret would continue speechwriting with her team, while Denis was upstairs glued to the TV, listening to reports of the campaign. When some particularly hostile barb annoyed him he would yell, 'Rubbish' or worse.

The last flight of the campaign had an end-of-term atmosphere, with the travelling press busily consuming champagne and contemplating their expenses. We landed at Gatwick after a rally and the pilot announced that Denis had been at the controls for part of the flight.

'Why are we at Luton, then?' yelled a wit from the press corps.

After three-weeks spent travelling 3,000 miles to more than thirty cities and towns, Margaret and Denis were up early on election day listening to the radio: the morning polls gave the Tories a lead of between 2 and 8 per cent. At nine o'clock they went out to vote before touring the constituency. The hours ticked away very slowly.

They returned to Flood Street for the most fraught hours – late afternoon and early evening. There was nothing anyone could do now – votes were being cast and the contents of the ballot boxes had to be counted. These are the hours when every candidate feels like a student awaiting an exam result.

Margaret couldn't sit still for more than a few seconds and eventually took to clearing out drawers and piles of papers in her office, tearing redundant notes into confetti-sized pieces. It wasn't in anticipation of winning. Prime Ministers-in-waiting all have their ways of dealing with nerves, and being a personal shredder is as good as any.

Shortly before midnight we went to the count at Barnet Town Hall, where we were ushered into a private room to watch the results on television. The ITN exit poll predicted an overall Conservative majority of 63.

No one had a broader smile than Denis when victory was

confirmed. During those four years of opposition Denis had spent very little time speculating about life at Number Ten. It had been a case of waiting and seeing.

Now the waiting was over, and at 5.15 a.m. he returned to Flood Street, buoyed up by victory and the cheers and the applause at Central Office. The Conservative Party had won a respectable working majority, although Denis admits he anticipated an even more sweeping result. 'I thought the majority would be higher than 44. I just didn't think that after the Winter of Discontent the great British people would vote for the Labour Party again.'

TEN

A TIED COTTAGE IN
DOWNING STREET

'When we landed in Northern Ireland the first time
to visit the troops, the divisional commander, a major-
general with all the scrambled eggs and red braid on
his uniform, was there at the bottom of the aircraft
steps. Margaret went down first and then I go down.
He salutes me and says, "Good Morning, sir." 'I
thought, By God, I've arrived.'

DENIS THATCHER

SHORTLY BEFORE 3 P.M. ON the spring afternoon of May 5th
the Leader of the Opposition's car was proceeding so slowly down
the Mall it was virtually kerb crawling.

As soon as the call came through to Conservative Central Office
from the Palace that the Queen wished to see Margaret Thatcher
to ask her to form the next government, my mother simply couldn't
wait to be off.

I remember her saying,

'Come on, let's go now.'

'Christ, there aren't any traffic lights – you'll be early,' declared
Denis. It was the story of their life – loitering in lay-bys or parked
in side streets (to the chagrin of her detectives) because Margaret
insisted on leaving a buffer zone to ensure she was never late. As
they drove off in the Leader of the Opposition's car (the car swap
takes place at the Palace) I had a farcical vision of them continually
circling the Victoria monument trying to kill time.

As the car 'trod water' Denis had time to admire the architecture
on one side of The Mall and the leafiness of St James's Park on the
other. Although it didn't show, his mind was racing. 'I suddenly
started to worry about what I was going to be doing while Margaret

was seeing the Queen,' he recalls, with visions of being 'totally spare' and having to kick his heels on the red carpet, twiddling his thumbs or staring up at the chandeliers.

In fact, it was far less intimidating. 'I was carted off into a small drawing room where there were one or two of the Queen's staff.' Lady Susan Hussey (a lady-in-waiting to the Queen and wife of Marmaduke Hussey) – 'a wonderful lady' – was among them. 'Colonel Blair-Wilson was another and there were two or three others. I think possibly a cup of tea was on the go. They were so incredibly kind and nice and I thought, Golly, if these are the people in the Palace then we've got no problems.'

When the formalities were over, the new Prime Minister swapped cars and a motorcycle escort swept them to Downing Street. Mark and I had already gone ahead in a taxi and had been let into the hall of Number Ten. The mustard-yellow carpet was barely visible as the staff lined up along it to receive Britain's forty-eighth Prime Minister.

The cheers of the crowd (Downing Street was then still open to the public) signalled her arrival. Ann Morrow of the *Daily Telegraph* wrote: 'By 4 o'clock she was at Downing Street looking very much as if she belonged there . . . Mrs Thatcher's son, who is 25, waited with his father in the doorway like a couple of well trained guards' – an accurate description of the latter.

I stood behind them, totally over-awed, and kept telling myself, 'Don't do anything wrong, don't embarrass anyone.'

Margaret recited the prayer of St Francis of Assisi.

> Where there is discord, may we bring harmony.
> Where there is error, may we bring truth.
> Where there is doubt, may we bring faith.
> Where there is despair, may we bring hope.

Then she turned and walked through the door into Number Ten to be greeted by an admiring burst of applause from those inside. Made famous by the tabloids for her 'guts, grit and determination', Margaret nevertheless looked rather emotional: she paused inside the front door and confessed that she'd been overcome by the mêlée outside.

Having been introduced to her staff, Margaret was scooped up by her political team and I saw blonde hair and a blue suit disappearing at a fast walk.

Denis, Mark and I were suddenly surplus to requirements and no one quite knew what to do with us. The Callaghans had not yet moved out of the Prime Minister's private flat above Number Ten, and my parents wouldn't move in for another month. 'A car will take you back to Flood Street,' a messenger told us. As we left, Crawfie and the other girls from the House of Commons arrived. They all wore T-shirts emblazoned with the campaign slogan: I THOUGHT 'ON THE ROCKS' WAS A DRINK 'TIL I DISCOVERED LABOUR GOVERNMENT.

Denis escaped from the hubbub, heading down to the flat at Scotney for the bank holiday weekend. He was perhaps the only man in my mother's life who wasn't sitting by the telephone wondering whether he was being pencilled in to her new Cabinet.

That evening, as the Prime Minister and her new staff sat down to a working Chinese takeaway in the State Dining Room, Denis opened the freezer, perused the selection of ready meals, and opted instead for an old favourite – baked beans on toast.

If he was struggling to comprehend what had happened in the previous twenty-four hours, he didn't let it show. Only later would he admit, 'When Margaret became an MP, I thought the highest she'd get – and the highest she wanted to be – was Chancellor of the Exchequer. It never occurred to me she could possibly be elected as Leader of the party, let alone become Prime Minister.'

Every headline and news bulletin was dominated by Margaret's elevation, but some columnists found time to consider Denis. Laura Tennyson of the *Glasgow Herald* wrote: 'Husband Denis: more of her shadow than the former Opposition Cabinet Members, constantly attentive, steadfastly loyal; like Prufrock he is "politic, cautious, and meticulous" but not Prime Minister, nor meant to be.' She also warned him, 'At this very moment cartoonists are certainly sharpening their pencils ready on one false move to draw pictures of the archetypal hen-pecked husband.'

Where did Denis look for guidance? His new position had very few parallels anywhere in history. Margaret was only the fourth female this century to have achieved the leadership of a nation – the others being Eva Perón, who succeeded her husband in Argentina, Golda Meir in Israel, Indira Gandhi in India, and Sirimavo Bandaranaike in Ceylon. All were widows, so there was no one to provide clues about being a male consort.

Margaret Truman, daughter of President Harry Truman, wrote a book about the role of America's First Lady, commenting, 'The job remains undefined, frequently misunderstood and subject to political attacks far worse in some ways than those any President has ever faced.' The experiences of prime ministers' wives in the recent past were no more encouraging. Audrey Callaghan hadn't liked life in Number Ten; Ted Heath was unmarried, and Mary Wilson disliked the place so much that she wouldn't live there.

In theory, because he was a novelty, the media interest in Denis should have been huge, but the reality was very different. Margaret took the spotlight: she was the seventies version of John and Jackie Kennedy rolled into one.

The Cabinet was announced on Saturday evening and there were few surprises: Geoffrey (later Lord) Howe was Chancellor, Lord Carrington the Foreign Secretary, and Keith Joseph the Industry Secretary. Among the junior ministers, named on Sunday, were several politicians whose careers would be closely linked with Thatcherism over the next decade, including Cecil (later Lord) Parkinson and Norman Tebbit, who would become chairmen of the party and friends of Denis.

A week later, on my father's sixty-fourth birthday, the Prime Minister hosted her first official dinner for a visiting foreign leader, Chancellor Helmut Schmidt of West Germany. She kindly insisted on inviting Mark and me, which gave me the opportunity to look around Number Ten before I went back to Australia. A number of the Cabinet were invited, including Geoffrey Howe and Peter Carrington. Other guests included Bill Deedes, Sir (later Lord) Marcus Sieff, head of Marks and Spencer, and Trevor Nunn of the Royal Shakespeare Company.

We gathered in the Blue Room for drinks beforehand, beneath portraits of Nelson and the Duke of Wellington. The house manager, Peter Taylor, rapped three times on the floor and announced,

'Ladies and gentlemen, honoured guests, dinner is now served,' and we all filed into the oak-panelled State Dining Room, which was dominated by a chandelier suspended above the horseshoe-shaped table.

Denis found himself with Helmut Schmidt on his left. Much to his relief, the Chancellor spoke beautiful English, although he was slightly perturbed when Herr Schmidt lit up a cigarette between courses of fillet of sole in champagne sauce and roast sirloin of Scotch beef. Denis, a heavy smoker himself, had always considered it rude to light up before the loyal toast.

My father says he wasn't nervous that evening, but it was another milestone in the 'learning curve'. Although he had never been particularly fond of Germans or Germany as a nation, he was quite capable of hiding such thoughts behind a genuine air of bonhomie and diplomacy. He would never visit his prejudices on individuals, as he demonstrated time and again in his dealings with dignitaries, the media and politicians.

The dinner wasn't starchy or formal and I remember being surprised at the animated hubbub. Afterwards, Margaret sat down to review the evening with a circle of advisers in the Pillared Room; the general opinion was that even though Schmidt might have been a bit closer to Callaghan politically, the dinner had gone off very well. But Denis was worried by something quite different: on the way back to Flood Street he added his domestic observation to the general post mortem. 'Look, love, the so-called silver was so awful it wasn't true. It nearly had the broad arrow on it. In the name of God what goes on here? It was appalling. It looked as if it had come out of the Sergeant's Mess.'

The new PM didn't fuss; she just arranged for new silver to be loaned to Number Ten. She also began collecting Crown Derby candlesticks and Denis later complained that we had 'more than any human being needs'.

My father's personal diary for Monday 4 June is clear except for four words: 'Move to Number Ten.' The vans arrived at Flood Street early, loading up with tea-chests and suitcases for the short journey to Downing Street. Number Ten appears deceptively small from the outside, yet inside the shiny black door, dubbed by

Churchill 'the most democratic in the country', there are more than sixty rooms, three staircases, and offices for 140 people.

In the old days, when governing the country was a rather more laid-back occupation, Number Ten was described by an official as 'a gentleman's home in which a little government takes place from time to time'. Nowadays, it is basically a set of offices over which the Prime Minister has a self-contained flat, converted out of the attic rooms by Mrs Neville Chamberlain.

Denis spent most of the day unpacking and sorting through clothes, golf clubs and books. They brought very few large items from Flood Street because the flat was already plainly furnished with regulation government issue. This had a practical bonus because defeated prime ministers, in common with detected Russian spies, had to move out in a hurry.

The ground plan of the flat resembles an extended railway carriage. The hallway is usually cluttered with red boxes. On the left is the main bedroom, with two single beds pushed together and an en suite bathroom which doubled as a hairdressing room in the mornings.

Further along the hallway is the drawing room, which overlooks Horse Guards Parade. With its television, comfortable sofas and bookcases, this became the main social area for the family, and Margaret would work here late at night. Next door is another bedroom which was used as a dressing-room and occasional guest room. Further along, on the right, is a laundry with washing machine, freezer and fridge, Mark took over the bedroom opposite and Denis snaffled another for his study. Up three steps is a guest room which I used when I came over.

At the end of the corridor Joy Robilliard set up her office. As Margaret's constituency secretary, she took on the extra role of organizing the flat, shopping for food and fielding phone calls. She was a mad keen golfer and helped us all, especially Denis, whom she kept up to date with my mother's schedule.

At the very back of the flat, down several steps, is a small galley kitchen and an unimposing dining room for a squashed eight.

There are several ways of reaching the flat, but most people take the lift or climb the main staircase past the first-floor State

Reception Rooms and the Prime Minister's study. I always joked that Margaret had one of the world's shortest commutes – it was only seconds from the end of her bed to her desk.

The popular image of grand living in Number Ten, with hot and cold running footmen and maids, is sadly a myth. The Prime Minister pays a service charge for living over the shop and makes his or her own domestic arrangements. Margaret took Mossie, our daily from Flood Street, with her, and then hired Edwina.

Separate staff cleaned downstairs – normally very early in the morning, which meant that Margaret and Denis were occasionally woken by the sound of strong-armed dailies energetically plumping up the cushions in the State Room like boxers hammering training bags.

The catering arrangements were typically haphazard. People would arrive for a drink and be mildly astonished to find the new Prime Minister alone in the flat, dashing around trying to coordinate glasses, lemon, tonic and gin. She often had to send someone to the ice machine downstairs because nobody had filled the ice-trays in the freezer. It was probably Denis's fault: he didn't like ice in his drinks, claiming it diluted the alcohol!

Food was also a problem. My mother didn't give dinner parties, but colleagues or speechwriters would qualify for supper if they were working late in the flat. Usually Joy or Crawfie would try to be around, but occasionally Margaret had to manage on her own. One MP was so horrified to find his train of thought constantly interrupted by the Prime Minister bobbing up and down to check on the simmering frozen peas, that he read the riot act to her. Eventually she solved the problem by getting the girl who did her office lunches downstairs to make loads of 'shove-in-the-oven-and-heat-up' dishes for the freezer. The net result? More bloody lasagne or shepherd's pie.

Despite the fact that he had no secretary of his own, Denis carved out a fairly relaxed daily routine. Because the en suite doubled as the Prime Minister's hairdressing salon, he was regularly evicted at 6.30 a.m. so that the beds could be made, the shampoo and rollers located and the hairdrier wheeled in.

Ousted from the master bedroom, he occasionally found one of my mother's female staff asleep in the bedroom which doubled as his dressing room, yet also housed much of the PM's burgeoning wardrobe.

If his luck was really out, he would even find in the kitchen one of the ladies who looked after Margaret's clothes monopolizing the kettle in order to steam brush a pair of her suede power heels.

Normally, Denis at least had the privilege of a lone, peaceful breakfast in the small dining room. One end of the table was laid for him and he would eat toast and marmalade while browsing through the morning papers. 'I used to read quite a range of newspapers every day. Over breakfast, I would get through the *Express*, the *Mail* and the *Sun*, then move on to the *Daily Telegraph* and *The Times* and see what their leaders had to say, and end with the *FT*. The object of the exercise was to keep as well informed as one could.'

Afterwards he would wander along to his study, sit at his desk and start preparing for a board meeting or answering his mail. Within weeks, eager correspondents had realized that writing to Denis could be the back-door route to the Prime Minister. His daily mailbag was soon bulging but he refused to shunt the letters along to the correspondence department. Instead, he answered them personally, averaging at least fifty replies a week.

> I decided it was better to do it that way rather than just sending out a printed reply. I thought it was more useful from the party's point of view – i.e. Margaret's point of view.
>
> The very difficult ones I sent down to the political office, but after a time you got a feel as to whether they [the writers] were on your side or whether they were digging up information to possibly use against the Prime Minister. You had to use a bit of common sense and read between the lines.

When it came to writing implements he was a dedicated ink-and-fountain-pen man; biros, felt tips and other disposable pens were simply sloppy. His favourite fountain pens never left his desk.

By contrast, Margaret would delve into her handbag (dubbed 'the mobile filing cabinet' and surface with a fistful of lurid plastic pens – gold felt tips for autographing champagne bottles for auction, highlighters for marking up research documents and *Hansards*, and black and navy blue for signing and initialling.

Although my father's office was only seventeen stairs up from the Prime Minister's, it was a world away from the corridors of power – and as close as he ever wanted to be. He had no desire for power or influence and, by his own admission, understood little of the workings of government. 'I had no contact with the action going on below – don't forget that the private office was two floors down. From my point of view it was absolutely ideal because I wasn't in the act.'

The reason few spouses like Number Ten is that you are living over the shop and, if you haven't got a job in the shop, cabin fever – or more accurately flat fever – can set in. Denis hated it because 'the only time the sun comes in – if at all – is at seven o'clock in the evening'.

Downing Street was built by a spy, George Downing, and that sense of being under surveillance – or at least having your privacy compromised – continues. Everyone knows whether you're in or out and there are no private telephone lines – you always have to go through the switchboard.

However, both my parents adored Chequers, the Prime Minister's country residence outside Great Missenden, near Aylesbury. For Denis it was love at first sight and he promptly decided it was the best perk of the job. He enjoyed playing tour guide, showing weekend guests through the historic house and telling them how much he loathed a Henry Moore sculpture which was marooned in concrete in the middle of the back lawn. Denis would have liked to hide it behind a dense thicket of trees, and guests who expressed a partiality would be quizzed as to exactly what they thought it was.

Before I returned to Australia, Mark and I drove down one Saturday afternoon and got hopelessly lost. I did the navigating and Mark drove like a maniac (as always) and we just made it for dinner.

Gun barrel-straight Victory Drive, lined with beech trees planted by Winston Churchill, swept up to the house's familiar Tudor façade and we skidded to a halt in front of the magnificent red-brick and grey-stone building.

Margaret met us in the Great Hall, once an open courtyard until it was roofed over in about 1870. Along one side was an ornate carved gallery and a glistening chandelier hung from the ceiling. We went straight into the large wood-panelled dining room. The four of us sat next to the deep bay window at the smaller of two dining tables, normally used for breakfast. My mother, a chocoholic, was delighted when gooey chocolate profiteroles arrived for dessert.

Afterwards, she gave us a guided tour. The 1,000-acre estate and house were given to the nation by Lord Lee of Fareham in 1917 for the use of the Prime Minister as a weekend retreat. At the top of the staircase in an anteroom to the Great Parlour two stained-glass windows explain the gift:

This house of Peace and Ancient Memories
was given to England as a thank-offering
for her deliverance in the Great War, 1914–1918,
and as a place of rest and recreation for her Prime Ministers forever.

Lloyd George, the first tenant, didn't care for the place, saying it was 'full of ghosts of dull people'. I found it grandly comfortable, rather than sombre. There were wonderful paintings on the walls, roaring fires and comfortable squashy sofas. The estate itself had a number of tenanted farmers and you could look out of the dining-room window and see cows grazing along Victory Drive.

This was my parents' chance to live in a stately home; and it gave them an excuse to entertain the great and the good without lifting a finger.

'Chequers is why you get the job,' Denis declares. 'We depompozised it. I used to say to people coming to lunch on Sunday that if they were early they shouldn't sit in that lay-by in the lane but come in because my woman didn't like me to start drinking before the guests arrived.'

Harold Macmillan was a guest at Chequers one weekend and, while Margaret submerged herself in a stack of red boxes, Denis cracked open a bottle of champagne and entertained the former Prime Minister in the Long Library. He was intrigued by Mac's best yarns and by his moustache, which rose and fell in time with the tempo of the tales. 'He stayed the night. It was an experience, of course, one can never forget. He wasn't all that old really. He must have been over eighty but had an enormous intellectual capacity, was extremely well-educated and quite fascinating. You would throw out a question or make a statement and before you could say "knife" he was back with Churchill and telling stories.'

I asked Denis if he had welcomed the election of the first woman Prime Minister.

'Not really, I don't think he was in tune with modern Conservatives. He was a bit on the left.'

After years of self-service from the fridge, Chequers offered catering par excellence. A marvellous caretaker, Vera Thomas, saw to it that my parents had whatever they desired. She told the staff: 'If the Prime Minister or Mr Thatcher want moose on toast at midnight, then they get it.'

Margaret also loved wandering outside among the daffodils, working in the hidden garden behind the indoor swimming pool, or sitting on the terrace overlooking a magnificent walled rose garden. In comparison, the private flat in Number Ten felt claustrophobic, particularly at weekends.

Until Margaret reached the top of the political tree, family life had been disrupted by an underlying conflict of interests and the perpetual need to be in at least two different places at once; now the family was more unified. Previously she'd gone out to work; now a considerable amount of her time was spent in Number Ten and Chequers – Denis's homes, too.

Not that she let up at Chequers – it was just a more beautiful, countrified environment in which to do red boxes. She had a book-lined study with one of the best views out over the rose garden and all the way down Victory Drive. She would emerge from this bunker at meal times and disappear again afterwards. Poor Denis did his best on Saturday nights – when they rarely entertained in the cause of a good night's sleep – to persuade her to abandon work in favour of a TV supper in the White Parlour watching a video of 'Yes Minister'. He liked this den-like sitting room decorated in fresh white and yellow tones. In winter a crackling fire made it welcoming and in summer the sun poured in.

My father soon realized that being this Prime Minister's husband meant organizing his own entertainment; Margaret was devoured by her job. He enjoyed walks through the surrounding farmland, favouring those which ended at a licensed premises. Otherwise he'd grab a couple of golf clubs, plant his brightly coloured umbrella upside down in the lawn, then, having paced out the requisite number of yards, start raining balls down on it.

Charles Powell (private secretary to the Prime Minister 1984–1991, later Sir Charles) says that many a time he'd be sitting inside with Margaret while she roughed up a foreign head of government who was reluctant to toe the line, 'and my eyes would wander out of the window and see Denis practising his putting on the lawn. I knew there was a real world out there somewhere. It was a great reassurance.'

On Sunday mornings Margaret continued working on her red boxes, jumping up five minutes before guests were due for lunch to comb her hair and get into her hostess-mode. After drinks in the Hawtrey Room and a four-course meal, she would say goodbye and go straight back to her study.

Denis was determined not to let what he called his 'vicarious public life' intrude upon his private pursuits. An early casualty, however, was his beloved silver-grey Rolls-Royce. He's no car buff, but he insists that once a man has driven a Rolls he can never be truly happy without one. After the ghastly M4 commute he decided that motoring was going to be fun: he'd have the car of his dreams.

Unfortunately, the Downing Street security personnel decreed it had to go.

They thought it was too dangerous. I mean, it was fairly conspicuous. Initially, I asked them if I got rid of the personalized number plate [DT3] whether that would be enough, but they said no. So I sold the plates for £1,800.

I told them, 'Fine, I'll buy a Ford.'

'Don't be silly,' said Margaret [obviously thinking this was a massive over-reaction]. I bought a blue Ford Cortina station wagon and drove it into the ground over the next eleven years. It was a great car – never once opened the bonnet.

Despite the increased security at Number Ten, Denis was much less affected by it than many imagined. Once out of the front door, he would stride along Downing Street into Whitehall and his escape was complete. The lack of 'protection' surprised many people he came into contact with, including one City chairman who had invited him to lunch. A welcoming committee was downstairs looking out for a motorcade, when Denis strode around the corner, having walked from the nearest tube station. When his host expressed surprise, Denis replied, 'No problem. No one's going to waste the price of a bullet on me.'

He always kept a low profile. Mick Giles, chief executive of Quinton Hazell, recalls Denis arriving in Leamington Spa for board meetings, 'in the clapped-out Cortina and wearing a baseball cap . . . you had grave difficulty knowing who he was. The car has broken down when he's been here and we've had to fix him up to get him home.'

One of my favourite images of Denis is as someone far more flamboyant and theatrical than the man in a grey suit two paces behind the Prime Minister. He liked wearing capes, particularly a black Nelson-style evening cloak with a scarlet lining. It made him look like a cross between Batman and Dracula as he marched quickly across the wide expanse of Horse Guards Parade on his way to dine at a club in St James's.

When he came home, normally quite late, he always insisted on walking. Peter Yarranton (later Sir Peter, a former England rugby international) offered to get Denis a cab after a rugby dinner at the Savoy, but was told firmly, 'Peter, my boy, if I can't walk through the streets of London half an hour after midnight on my own it will be a very sad day indeed.' Denis then disappeared into the mist shrouding the Embankment. The policemen on front-door duty at Number Ten claimed they could sometimes hear my father's parade-ground walk before he even got to Trafalgar Square. If anyone recognized him, Denis was always courteous in the extreme. Late one night a demonstrator outside South Africa House tried to needle him: 'You're married to that bitch Thatcher, aren't you?' he yelled.

Without missing a stride, Denis replied, 'You've got the wrong person, old chap,' and carried on.

Even now, more than fifteen years later, he is still surprised when people recognize him. On a recent weekend he went for a stroll along the Thames because I'd mentioned I was considering buying a flat over Blackfriars Bridge near the new Globe Theatre. I was also having another look and we bumped into each other on Blackfriars Bridge.

'Hello, Dad, how are you?' I said.

'Fine. You know it's very pleasant on a bank holiday Saturday. I was recognized by a couple of people. You'd have thought they'd met Jesus Christ.'

Denis has never had a problem with keeping himself company. Although his diary was quite full when he arrived at Number Ten, there were times when he found himself alone – although 'never lonely', he says.

Even so, he cut a solitary figure sitting in the stands overlooking Horse Guards Parade, watching the bands practise for Trooping the Colour. The music appealed to the military in him, which was lucky because the rehearsals began as early as 6 a.m. and made further sleep impossible. Instead, Denis would have breakfast, wander out of the back door, past Number Eleven and down the steps behind the scaffolding stands. One morning he had a visitor. 'There I was – only me in the stands – and one of the non-commissioned officers came up and saluted, "A shower, sir, aren't they, a shower. But we'll get it right."'

It was Denis who was on parade at 7.30 p.m. on 12 June 1979 for a state banquet at Buckingham Palace in honour of President Moi of Kenya. He had been once before and occupied a lowlier position on the seating plan:

Margaret was way up the top of the table and I was so far below the salt it wasn't true . . . Buck House state banquets are the grandest things I've ever been to in my life. I mean, it's always a breathtaking table; it's wall-to-wall gold; the plates are gold. Margaret turned over a side plate to see what it was. I saw her do it and the next time we attended there was a little printed card alongside the place settings explaining what the porcelain was. On that occasion it was George the Third.

Of course, he still had a constant battle to overcome his shyness. He had, however, picked up a few tricks of the trade. As co-host at Number Ten receptions, he would often break the ice and steady the nerves of guests anxiously waiting to be received. Similarly, he tried to make sure no one was left out by steering them into a conversation.

Henry Blofeld, the cricket commentator, has developed the useful trick of addressing people whose name he had forgotten as 'My dear old thing...'; Denis adopted a similar tactic. When he couldn't remember a wife's name, he would call her 'Dear lady' and do it with enormous charm. Similarly, a man would become 'My dear boy...' with just the right mixture of bonhomie and gentlemanly warmth.

He had another huge advantage, as he explains: 'If you have got some slight position – e.g. you're married to the Prime Minister or Leader of the Opposition – then the other chap is bound to be even more shy, particularly if he's never been to Number Ten...' My father can pinpoint the moment when this realization suddenly hit him. It was on Margaret's first trip to Northern Ireland after she became Prime Minister.

This is the best example I can give you of the total change: when I was a soldier, if you were a major-general you were second only to Jesus Christ himself. When we landed in Northern Ireland the first time to visit the troops, the divisional commander, a major-general with all the scrambled eggs and red braid on his uniform, was there at the bottom of the aircraft steps. Margaret went down first and then I go down. He salutes me and says, 'Good Morning, sir.' I thought, By God, I've arrived.

Reams have been written on the privileges that go with the premiership. At Chequers it wasn't the centuries of history that impressed Denis but, as he confided to a former neighbour of ours

in Lamberhurst who asked him what it was really like, the fact that
'They even turn the pages of the bloody TV guide onto the correct
day for you.'

ELEVEN

DEAR BILL

'You get fuzzy wuzzies going on the rampage down in Brixton, you people sort it out in no time at all, but have you noticed one thing: when peace is restored there are no television cameras in sight. I'll tell you why – because the media are closet pinkoes.'

DENIS THATCHER to a member of the cast of
Anyone for Denis at No 10.

ALTHOUGH DENIS THATCHER was married to a famous wife, he wasn't yet a famous husband. 'Invisible' was the adjective most often used in scant mentions in the national press. Normally the feature-writers are put on the scent and told to prepare profiles on the nation's new consort, dissecting everything – fashion sense, hairstyle, public utterances and influence on the Prime Minister's choice of tie or government policy.

Traditionally, these articles appear on the women's pages because, after all, the subject is invariably a woman. So where did this leave Denis?

Quite relieved, I suspect. There wasn't much point in analysing his dress sense – even less his hairstyle. He had barely uttered a word in public since Margaret became Opposition Leader and was notable only by his absence from most political occasions. When pressed into duty, he would blend into the background.

Bernard (later Sir Bernard) Ingham, who became the PM's press secretary in the autumn of 1979, believes that Denis benefited from having public attention focused almost exclusively on Margaret: 'I don't think that journalists had a very clear impression of Denis other than that he liked sport and a drink; and I think he was fortunate that she was the first woman PM because, for a time, they were less interested in him.'

Bill Deedes agrees: 'The fact is that the first male consort in our history was never thought about – or given full frontal treatment – because Margaret was an exciting enough figure and they dwelt on her.'

One publication with an influence way beyond its circulation changed all that. It was *Private Eye*. John Wells, actor, writer and co-founder of the *Eye*, had taken more than a passing interest in the Conservative Party leadership ballot in 1975. During the Harold Wilson premiership Wells had written a column called 'Mrs Wilson's Diary', a satirical creation which allowed him to use the 'innocent lens' by fictionalizing the views of the Prime Minister's wife.

When Ted Heath entered Number Ten, and there was no 'Mrs Heath', the column was shelved, but with Margaret and Denis Thatcher it gained a whole new dimension.

In 1975, when Margaret emerged from nowhere to win the Tory leadership, Wells was watching TV as cameras caught the celebrations.

I can remember it very vividly: there was a hand-held camera and I thought it was like one of those Jacques Cousteau submarine cameras because there at the back was Denis grinning very widely – obviously he'd had a few – and the television lights reflected off his glasses.

He immediately seemed to me to be a very attractive comic character; a really charming saloon bar figure; like the person who you see in a pub saying, 'I'm in the chair. Have another drink.' There was something very theatrical about his appearance; as though he should wear spats and hold a cigarette lighter. Straight away, I thought he was a well-drawn, possibly Wodehouseian figure.

After the general election John Wells, Richard Ingrams, the editor of *Private Eye*, and the late Peter Cook, another founding member, sat down and began discussing how to exploit Denis's comic potential.

Ingrams suggested they do 'letters' rather than a 'diary', written to a fictitious golfing pal called 'Bill'. Wells thought that the pomp and ceremony of the State Opening of Parliament would provide an ideal launchpad. 'We knew if we set him at the State Opening it would be funny because he was actually a full-blown comic character. If you think in terms of glove puppets, he did actually talk for himself; he just wrote himself and that was very enjoyable.'

The inaugural 'Dear Bill' appeared on 15 May 1979.

10 Downing Street
London S.W.1

Dear Bill,

So sorry I couldn't make it on Tuesday ... M. [Margaret] insisted I turn up for some kind of State Opening of Parliament or other. I had assumed now the election was over I would be excused this kind of thing, but oh no. I had just carried my spare clubs out to the jalopy when heigh ho! – up goes a window and M. is giving me my marching orders. It's off to Moss Bros. for the full kit, and at that moment, I don't mind telling you, I couldn't help thinking pretty enviously of you, Monty and the Major enjoying a few pre-match snifters at the 19th without a care in the world.

It took me ages to get kitted out. The staff at Moss Bros. all seem to be gyppos these days, and there was a bit of a communications problem. But eventually I managed to get a cab back to the House of Commons, only to find that I'd left my invite back at Downing Street. I told the chap on the door that I was Mr Thatcher, and he said, 'That's what they all say.' After about 20 minutes they agreed to go and get M. out to vouch for my bona fides and, as you can imagine, I wasn't top of the popularity stakes at that particular juncture!!

M. then had to go off to do her stuff, so I just mooched around for a while, looking for a watering hole. What a place, Bill! If you ask me, it's just an antiquated rabbit warren – miles and miles of corridors, with chaps in evening dress wandering about like a lot of super-annuated penguins. Luckily I bumped into a familiar face in the shape of George Brown. He seemed to know his way about, and we ended up in a nice little bar overlooking the river, with an awfully jolly crowd of chaps who were watching the show on the TV.

It all seemed to go quite smoothly, but I was a bit miffed to see M. fussing over that fellow Stevas [Norman St John Stevas, leader of the House of Commons], and taking the fluff off his collar. To tell you the truth, I don't like the cut of that chap's jib. If you ask me, he's not absolutely 100 per cent and when I said as much a lot of the fellows at the bar agreed.

Must close, as M. has got some Hun coming to dinner and I've got to do my stuff again. I sometimes wonder who won the bloody war!

Yours aye!

DENIS

What Wells and Ingrams couldn't possibly have known – something that made it all the funnier to Denis and those of us who did – was that Denis's last encounter with Lord George-Brown, the former Labour Deputy Leader, was at a meeting with Margaret at Scotney Castle in Opposition days; on that occasion it was Denis who played navigator. 'After they'd finished I asked him if he knew the way back to his route and he wasn't sure. I drove to the Kent–Sussex border with him following and the last I saw was him hooting thanks as I waved him on before turning around and coming home.'

Wells and Ingrams swiftly twigged that gin and golf were to Denis as shoes were to Imelda Marcos. As more letters were published, his 'character' developed: he was a boozing, smoking, sports-loving male chauvinist who was married to a domineering wife and deserved the sympathy of every man.

'Dear Bill' was universally acknowledged as a hit and quickly became one of the most widely read features of the magazine. John Wells generously credits the real Denis with the success (after all, he provided the raw material) – rather than the creative flair of the 'Dear Bill' team. 'There are very few people who are absolute archetypes and I think he is a living archetype of a great many Englishmen and that is why he became so popular. I thought he was an endangered species. Like anybody who smokes, I could see him attributing his longevity to smoking tipped cigarettes and drinking a lot of gin . . .

'He is very politically incorrect and the fact that anyone like that could float to the very very top was very unusual.'

Of course, the letters had a sharp satirical edge, normally directed at Margaret. This meant that Denis had to be a sympathetic figure; through him, the Prime Minister could be portrayed as a

'She Who Must Be Obeyed' who made cabinet ministers tremble and union leaders splutter into their pints.

Even Denis became a keen reader of his fictitious epistles – largely because so many people he met kept on referring to them, some under the impression that he was ghosting them himself. On one of the 'Thatcher Tours' (as the Prime Minister's overseas trips were dubbed) a member of Margaret's Private Office went into the hotel suite one day and found him bent over a side table, reading. The 'document' captivating his attention was not the day's programme but the latest 'Dear Bill'.

One of the most astonishing things about the letters was how often they got it right. On a whole range of subjects, the creators managed to give, in somewhat exaggerated prose, a sample of Denis's views.

'Dear Bill' on the 'filthy reptiles of Fleet Street': 'Oh God! I expect you saw that I made page two of the *Telegraph*. Not exactly calculated to ease my lot with the Boss over Yule. Talk about shits of hell: Fleet Street takes the biscuit. God knows I'm let off the leash seldom enough as it is, sitting in Downing Street all day long being told to lift my feet up every time little Cosgrove comes by with the hoover, and now this comes up . . .'

– on Commonwealth Heads of Government Meetings: 'Personally, I thought the whole business had been wound up years ago, but not a bit of it. All the Coons, the Gandhi woman, little fellows who've obviously never had a suit on in their lives from places you only hear about if you collect stamps: there's nothing they like more, it seems, than having a week-long get-together to talk about the old days . . .'

– on the BBC: 'I kept telling the Boss, if ever there was a state-owned industry ripe for privatization, it is that nest of Pinkoes and Traitors at Shepherd's Bush. Fifty quid a year they charge now, just so we can watch highlights from the Argentine evening bulletin. And that's an awful lot of snorts in anybody's language . . .'

– on poor sportsmanship: 'I don't know if you've been watching the tennis. I find it all a bit depressing. You settle down with a snort in your hand on a sunny afternoon, expecting to hear nothing but the thwock of ball on gut, the occasional cry of the umpire and the rustle of applause as you drift away into a deep sleep, and all you get is one or other of these superbrats effing and blinding at the authorities like Question Time in the House of Commons . . .'

Perhaps the ultimate compliment paid to Wells and Ingrams was the accusation that they must have had a mole within Number Ten feeding them information. Wells denies this totally, although he admits they had occasional flukes. In one 'Dear Bill' Denis refused to walk around a golf course because the detective assigned to protect him was wearing short socks, the wrong kind of trousers and the wrong raincoat. 'Someone rang us up and said: "How did you know that?" And we said: "We had no idea, we made it up." Apparently, almost the same day that we wrote it, Denis really was playing golf and refusing to have a detective because he said he was improperly accoutred.'

Similarly, the tennis anecdote was remarkably close to the mark. Denis hates the game and always declined to accompany Margaret when she was a guest in the Royal Box on finals day.

I was once the guest of ICI and we had a very good lunch in their tent. I went up into the stand on No. 1 court after lunch and there were junior players on court.

There was an American girl playing and she got a very very bad call. There was no doubt about it, I saw it. She was about nineteen and she said to the linesman, 'You must be fucking blind.' A hell of a lot of people heard her and I was appalled. I got out of my seat, went back to the tent and said, 'I will never come here again.'

According to John Wells, the language for 'Dear Bill' came from two sources. One was Jeremy Deedes, Bill Deedes's son, who used to ring in with particular phrases like 'bib and tucker'. The other was discovered during a holiday in Alderney.

I was in a pub and it was a reunion of The Few, and The Few had just been burying so there was one less. They came back from the memorial service and one said: 'I suppose it will be me next.' And the other replied: 'No, no, I shall be very sorry to see you crippled under.' I used that.

Once you start writing people actually come up and give you lines like: 'He's so stupid he has to look up his arse to see if he's got his hat on.' That came from Mary Ingrams, who discovered it in a pub.

Many of the expressions that appeared in 'Dear Bill' uncannily resembled Denis's own turn of phrase. According to Denis, expensive hotels 'charged like the Light Brigade' and he and his cronies often 'drank enough to sink a battleship'.

Aside from the Denis persona, several other memorable characters – just as alive to their creators and the *Eye* readers as Denis and Margaret – were created. The 'Major' was a popular favourite, an ageing throwback to the Raj and the days when Britannia really did rule the waves. Peter Cook had the idea for 'Boris', the Russian spy and gardener at Number Ten; and Wells's favourite was 'Maurice Picarda', a golfing pal who was based on a contemporary of Wells's at Oxford, Noel Picarda, 'who was always engaging in fly-by-night schemes and always having very ambitious ideas'.

Later, when someone sent a photograph of Denis quaffing champagne in the Twickenham car park, from the boot of a Rolls Royce, the 'Dear Bill' team felt like cheering because he was surrounded by a group who looked exactly like the people they had invented.

'Dear Bill' was also innovative and deliciously entertaining in dreaming up ever more outrageous names for the many 'tinctures', 'large ones', and 'copious snorts' of alcohol that Denis encountered in his capacity as consort – or, occasionally, failed to encounter. Typical examples included, 'the magnum of some unspeakably vile Cuban whisky' (produced by 'Boris', the Russian spy and gardener at Number Ten); 'Number One Tiger Breath Whisky' (a Christmas pressie from Mark acquired at some duty free boutique in Macau); 'some ghastly sticky made out of rotting edelweiss' (Denis feared it was all he was likely to find on the PM's alpine holidays); and an 'emergency transfusion of damson vodka' (again courtesy of Boris).

From my father's point of view, the letters were amusing – at least to begin with – but he became annoyed when they were published in paperback and fans began sending books to Number Ten for his autograph; they even expected *him* to fork out for the return postage.

One episode irritated Denis enormously: a television station commissioned a poster to advertise a series about Number Ten. It depicted Denis washing up in a floral pinny and was displayed all over the London Underground. When Denis, a keen user of the Tube, marched onto the platform at Westminster station one morning, he found himself face to face with this awful poster of himself. As he waited for the train, people began staring at him, then averting their gaze to check the poster again, before giving him a final 'it is, isn't it' look. He hated the attention and, when one of the secretaries suggested that the quickest route to his next appointment was on the Underground, he rolled his eyes and grumbled, 'I can't. That bloody poster.'

'I take a "lot of stick" from the left-wing press, *Private Eye* et al in, I hope, philosophical good humour,' he said, 'but the use of the hoardings of the public transport system to "take the mickey" out of me and, by implication, the Prime Minister presents the standards of advertising at a pretty low level in the eyes of decent people.'

Yet on the rare occasions that he did complain about 'Dear Bill', others were swift to remind him that the satirical ruse had turned into his personal fortnightly press release. Robert Morley, the wonderful character actor whose portly girth and gargantuan personality endeared him to everyone, was once on hand when my father protested about 'those buggers at *Private Eye*'. Morley's reply was bang on target: 'You should be very grateful, my darling; they have given you a personality.'

The 'Dear Bill' letters cumulatively did more than anything else to cement the image of Denis Thatcher in popular mythology and transformed him into an affectionately regarded and genuinely respected institution. They also had a less obvious but immensely valuable political advantage in that their protective smokescreen ensured that my father was never accused by the media of being an *éminence grise*. Bill Deedes, who could see things with crystal clarity from both sides of the fence, is convinced of this:

> But for the Dear Bill letters – now Margaret accepts this but I don't think Denis does – I can think of many occasions when he would have been credited with unpopular steps taken by Margaret.

Private Eye made him look a man who would not have an idea in the back of his head except gin and golf. His friends knew how astute he was; reading a balance sheet upside down/sideways, etc. and with a considerable knowledge of human kind and a very good judge of character. But *Private Eye* established him as a completely different figure, which meant that it would look ridiculous if a tabloid came out with a story saying: 'There's no doubt that Mrs Thatcher's new measure against the BBC, or whatever, owes much to the thinking of Mr Thatcher because they are very close and he is known to be outspoken . . .' As far as I know, from start to finish, Denis was never accused of inspiring any piece of legislation or any idea. That is very important.

It never happened because of the value of 'Dear Bill' . . . once that image was indelibly imprinted on the voting public, how could you pretend that he was a serious figure. It was therefore very difficult to paint Denis as an *éminence grise*.

For John Wells, the fortnightly letters were to develop into a full-time career. Not long after 'Dear Bill' was born he was asked to appear on a new chat show hosted by the then up-and-coming Terry Wogan. The plan was simply to read one of the letters; Wells had never done an impersonation. 'When I was sitting in make-up putting the wig on for the first time, I noticed that when I grinned I had the same bone structure. He has got prominent teeth and a big lip. I painted in the gap and put on a pair of Denis's glasses that we had got copied and it was amazing, I did look quite like him.'

Expecting a one-off performance, Wells was astonished when Robert Fox, the theatre impresario, suggested a stage play and Richard Ingrams came up with the title *Anyone for Denis*. Most of the 'Dear Bill' creative team were involved and Dick Clements was brought in to direct. The project went without a hitch until it came to filling the leading role. Eventually John Wells suggested himself and showed them a videotape of his Wogan performance.

Anyone for Denis opened at the Whitehall Theatre on 7 May 1981 and, not surprisingly, was highly offensive to Denis, particularly one scene where he was portrayed as a man unable to tell a urine sample from a glass of whisky.

The play is set at Chequers: Denis has invited a bunch of his hard-drinking golfing pals round while his wife is overseas at a Euro-beetroot convention. The fun starts when she unexpectedly turns up with two eurocrats and the US envoy and the drunken golfers and delegates come to blows.

I reviewed the show for the *News of the World* and wrote: 'John Wells, who plays Denis, doesn't look like Dad, he doesn't sound like Dad and he doesn't behave like him, either.

'The ['Dear Bill'] letters are funny and affectionate towards the foibles and mannerisms of my father and mother. The play is still very funny – but it removes all the affection for Dad and replaces it with ridicule.'

A few weeks later a special charity performance was arranged and two extremely unlikely guests were among the audience. Somehow Robert Fox and Tim Bell of Saatchi and Saatchi had come up with the idea that the Prime Minister could boost her popularity by showing that she was 'a good sport'. A fortnight before the performance, word arrived from Number Ten that my mother would indeed be attending but that Denis was unavailable. John Wells had a bet with the cast that Denis would have his 'forearm twisted into a reef knot' and be forced to turn up. He won.

No theatre seating plan was ever more carefully arranged: Robert Fox was nervous that if 'Joe Public' found themselves next to their esteemed leader they might be cowed into embarrassed silence, so he wanted the seats surrounding the Thatcher party packed with the Old Etonian backers of the play; because they had money in the show, they would laugh uproariously whatever happened on stage.

However, the Prime Minister's party had a different buffer zone in mind. Initially the detectives were to sit alongside my parents, with Bernard Ingham immediately behind them. But, according to Ingham, 'a dirty trick' was played. The detectives foresaw the embarrassment of being caught laughing at an inopportune moment and told Ingham that, 'as a security matter', he would have to sit next to Margaret. 'It was one of the most embarrassing, teeth-gritting things I ever had to do,' he recalls, still grimacing at the memory.

The curtain went up and John Wells immediately spotted Denis because the theatre lights were bouncing off his glasses and bald forehead. He ad-libbed a joke about his left-handedness, which was quite gentle compared to the ridicule that followed. Denis came across as a prototype 'little Englander', full of ghastly, off-hand class and race prejudice, but really asking for nothing more from life than a few simple pleasures.

My mother was acutely offended, and as she left the theatre she couldn't hide her annoyance. When asked for her opinion, she gritted her teeth and told a journalist, 'Marvellous farce' – which is exactly what she thought it wasn't. Yet she maintained the façade long enough to guarantee favourable coverage in the morning papers, which were full of 'Maggie able to laugh at herself' reviews.

At a reception for the cast at Number Ten the atmosphere was equally strained. Denis looked like a fish out of water among so many paid-up members of Equity but bravely greeted his 'alter ego' John Wells. Shaking hands, he said, 'If I had any kind of *esprit de l'escalier*, I would say "Snap!"'

Then it was upstairs to meet the Prime Minister. My mother, who likes to be in control, quickly polished her receiving line technique: guests inclined to chat instead of shaking hands and getting out of the way find her handshake actually moving them along a conveyor belt. That night she was on autopilot: 'Do come in, I am sure you will see lots of your showbiz friends,' she said to John Wells and his wife.

However, the classic confrontation was between my father and Nick Farrell, who played a plainclothes policeman on stage but had come to Number Ten as a plainclothes actor. John Wells witnessed the meeting.

Clearly Denis latched onto the idea that he [Farrell] was indeed a policeman and I overheard him saying, 'I can't tell you how much I admire you people.'

Nick was totally confused. What did he mean? Were heterosexual actors over the age of twenty-five what he meant by 'you people'?

Then Denis said: 'You get fuzzy wuzzies going on the rampage down in Brixton, you people sort it out in no time at all, but have you noticed one thing: when peace is restored there are no television cameras in sight. I'll tell you why – because the media are closet pinkoes.'

Nick Farrell was amazed but I was delighted because it confirmed everything. I realized that we hadn't gone far enough . . . the fuzzy wuzzies in Brixton was an extraordinary line.

It was vintage Denis. He would often regale the family with his thoughts on the long line of crooked and despotic leaders that Africa had spawned in the years since independence.

Several other stories emerged from the Number Ten party – not all of them so easy to confirm. One was that Margaret waited until the last of the guests had left before giving instructions for heads to roll. The following morning, when the headlines suddenly bestowed upon her a sense of humour, she changed her mind. True or not, Tim Bell describes the night as one of the greatest mistakes of his life.

The influence of the 'Dear Bill' letters on my father's public profile turned out to be a gift. Just as the 'Iron Lady' sobriquet had done wonders for Margaret, 'Dear Bill' brought Denis into the public consciousness. Although consistently over the top, the letters became increasingly affectionate towards him – if not to his wife and members of her Cabinet.

Although unwilling to admit it, once he became more confident in his role as prime ministerial consort, Denis ceased to be irritated by 'Dear Bill' and began to play up to the eccentric image he had been given. At a charity luncheon a fellow guest asked him: 'Mr Thatcher, how do you spend your time?'

Rather than banging on nobly about good works, Denis declared, 'Well, when I'm not completely pissed I like to play a lot of golf.'

At another function in the shires, where he was fêted by the blue-rinsed pillars of the Tory Party, one lady took him aside and discreetly sympathized: 'Mr Thatcher, I understand you have a drink problem.'

Denis waved his glass and said: 'Yes, Madam, I have. There is never enough of it.'

TWELVE

TWO PACES BEHIND

'You know me, I never go on one-night stands.'

DENIS THATCHER

DENIS CLUNG TO THE SIDES of an armoured Mercedes; it was careering – apparently out of control – through the streets of Lusaka. Sitting in the back seat, Denis may have been safe from terrorist attack, but was he about to become another Zambian road death statistic?

The host government had ordered up a fleet of Mercs to ferry various heads of state around the capital during the Common-wealth Heads' of Government Meeting (CHOGM) in 1979. Unfortunately, no one had thought to teach the resident chauffeurs how to handle the new vehicles.

Less than two months after entering Number Ten Denis found himself at the first of seven CHOGMs he would eventually attend with the Prime Minister. It was also his first official overseas trip – he had skipped the G7 Summit in Tokyo and also Margaret's visit to Canberra in June.

The Lusaka conference was a difficult one, full of underlying tensions and security problems. Denis wisely didn't voice his private views on the Commonwealth, which he considered to be long past its sell-by date: 'I wasn't keen on it – then or now. I don't think it stands for anything. What does it do?'

The 1979 CHOGM was dominated by the 'Rhodesia question'. Notwithstanding the April elections – held under a new consti-tution which saw a black majority government elected – bloody fighting continued because the guerrilla-backed Patriotic Front had not taken part. Moreover, many black African states viewed Bishop Muzorewa's government as nothing more than a front for continued white minority rule.

The Commonwealth heads were to examine how to end the hostilities and steer Rhodesia towards peace and stability. Margaret saw this as the responsibility of the Commonwealth as a whole and believed that Britain, as the former colonial power, should be ready to resume authority in Rhodesia until a new constitution could be drafted with all sides involved, paving the way for fresh elections.

The trip began inauspiciously: as she emerged from her aircraft at Lusaka airport the Prime Minister was more or less frogmarched off to a hostile press conference convened in an aircraft hangar. The rather amateur motorcade then ferried the British contingent to the Mulungoshi Village, where the accommodation consisted of rather pokey prefabs hastily erected to host some previous summit of African leaders. The Queen's chalet offered a few de-luxe trappings, but its neighbours hadn't fared well in the tropical climate. Margaret and Denis returned one evening to be told by Caroline Stephens, 'The ceiling has fallen down and there's no hot water.'

Denis kept his complains to himself, and during the course of the week-long conference he often stepped in to wind up the all-night working sessions so beloved of the Prime Minister. 'I can't remember the subject matter but everyone was going on and on and, it seemed to me, going round in circles and getting nowhere. I walked across the room and said to Margaret, "Look, you've got an exhausted staff; it's time for them to go to bed," and Peter Carrington, the Foreign Secretary, was there and he said, "Thank Christ!" Obviously, I was the only person who could say it.'

Unwittingly, Denis probably made a rod for his own back because, after Lusaka, the consensus in the Private Office was that the Prime Minister's tours went better when he was aboard: he was able to break up the never-ending late-night political benders; he would want a drink, which meant the gathering immediately became more of a social occasion, and eventually he would tactfully glance at the following day's programme and say, 'We're on the road at half past six. Bed.'

Denis soon formulated a policy on overseas tours: although he never ducked his responsibilities, he refused to be a 'passenger'. When people asked him if he was accompanying the PM on a particular trip, he would amuse them by saying, 'You know me, I never go on one-night stands.' True to his word, he never attended G7 (Group of Seven) summits or the regular European powwows that dotted Margaret's calendar. Similarly, he saw no point in going on 'shorties' like an overnighter to New York for an address to the United Nations.

He did, however, do many of the major tours, which tested human stamina to its limits and set records for the number of long-haul destinations feasible in a day. They were 'flag-waving' exercises from his perspective. On one packed three-day visit to Saudi Arabia he visited the Chemical Insecticides and Disinfectants Company (a joint venture with a British company), accompanied the Prime Minister to the King Faisal Specialist Hospital, and then went solo to the Riyadh Electricity Company. There was also a visit to the British Council offices, a reception for the British community, an aerial tour of various oil installations, and lunches and dinners with members of the Saudi royal family. As a young man Denis had travelled the world selling paint for the family business; now he was 'selling Britain'.

If Margaret took little time out for sleep from her frenetic schedule, when overseas she went into overdrive: nights became merely an interlude best used for travelling because she didn't want to waste valuable working time. This was fine for her because she had a bed on the plane and an astonishing capacity for managing with precious little sleep.

Denis strenuously avoided going on any organized trip for 'spouses', whatever the jolly might be. Fashion shows, recitals and visits to kindergartens were designed for the female consorts rather than someone like Denis, and he was quietly relieved when Benazir Bhutto's husband, Asif Zardari, turned up, doubling the husband quota at a CHOGM. 'I never went on a spouse visit. I didn't like them. I had my own programme. I had to sing for my supper a bit. UK Ltd, I reckon, is what I did and I made a lot of friends, incidentally.'

Also mindful of his hedonistic 'Dear Bill' image, he made sure he could never be charged with treating official overseas tours as junkets. 'In Lusaka I declined an invitation to play golf with

Kenneth Kaunda on his own private course because I didn't want to be accused of having a round at the taxpayers' expense,' he explains.

This was probably just as well, given Margaret's strictly businesslike attitude. She frowned when, at one CHOGM in the posh resort of Lyford Cay in the Bahamas, several delegates took themselves off to a local casino. Similarly, at a G7 Summit in Japan, the participants were all given fashionable new tracksuits and trainers just in case they felt inspired to shake down the endless banquets with a couple of laps of the jogging track. The Prime Minister was appalled at the idea of this distraction from duty and popped them into her suitcase, bringing them home for me.

There was inevitably a lot of hanging around as sessions ran over time. One evening Denis found himself queuing to get into a CHOGM reception when an Australian journalist approached him, thinking he looked a helpful sort. 'What's going on?' he asked.

Denis had to admit he shared his ignorance.

Exasperated, the journalist informed him, 'I don't know why Malcolm Fraser [the Australian Prime Minister] is here anyway. Back home no one could give a monkey's tit about all this.'

Denis grinned and dined out on the story for weeks afterwards. He also roared with laughter when it reached his ears that at the Melbourne meeting in 1981, irreverent Antipodean hacks had come up with an alternative translation of CHOGM: 'Coons Holidaying On Government Money.' He couldn't abide 'sitting next to the leader of some Caribbean island at lunch who, in between wolfing platefuls of smoked salmon, would say, "I really want to come and see your wife, I want some more aid."'

While 'Dear Bill' had invented phrases like 'Big Chief Coon' and 'Ahmed ben Wog', my father had his own composite African leader: 'A proper little shit, a poor little nation, and of course all of them socialist dictators. The first thing they do is set up a Swiss bank account; the second one is they build themselves a damn great palace.'

Yet despite such outbursts, Denis never embarrassed the Prime Minister by uttering such thoughts in public, and he was perfectly charming when he met African leaders, commenting afterwards, 'Not nearly as black as he's painted', or some such nonsense.

Unlike a more modern political consort, Hillary Clinton, America's First Lady, Denis never saw himself an 'equal partner'. Margaret, not he, had been elected. As Gordon Reece observed:

> He always said what he thought because he had confidence in what he thought. But look at the things he didn't do: the capacity for interference was limitless; he could have tried to be a policy-maker, he never tried to do that. He just gave his point of view. He didn't do anything more.
>
> He never wanted to sit on a Cabinet committee, never wanted to be appointed to anything. One of the great triumphs of Denis is what he did not do, not just what he did. That is the basis of why he was so valuable to Margaret. He would do everything to advance her interests but wasn't up to being her Svengali.

No one ever got in to see the Prime Minister via Denis, but he was brilliant at spotting the limpets and hangers-on; at receptions he often intervened when he felt someone was undeservedly monopolising her.

Another of Denis's great attributes was his common sense. When Margaret was having a brainstorm – insisting on wallpapering the Prime Minister's study herself to save taxpayers' money, or electing to take only a cabinet minister's salary and not the higher prime ministerial one – his was the voice of reason:

'Doesn't do you any good out there, Love,' he'd tell her.

With his dry sense of humour and slow smile, he had the knack of defusing a panic. 'Come off it, Love,' he'd say when she was in the middle of a tantrum, 'let's get relaxed,' and offer her a drink. Sometimes when a crisis was brewing, someone from the Private Office would give Denis prior warning so that he could batten down the hatches before the storm arrived.

Despite his inexperience with the media, he possessed a very shrewd sense of when an idea was quite ludicrous or likely to backfire on her. Margaret may have been a self-contained political phenomenon but Denis did his bit to ensure that her feet never left terra firma.

I could smooth her down a bit when she was crisis ridden. To some extent I could bring her back to reality – they [her close political aides] can get divorced from what the hell's going on, you know.

I was talking to different people all the time so I was in a different ball game. So many politicians are under the misapprehension that the rest of us think all the time about politics; the truth of the matter is the great British people don't give a damn. The only people who keep it going is the press.

However, Denis distanced himself from any problem which was strictly the domain of the Prime Minister. Cabinet reshuffles, public service appointments and diplomatic squabbles were, he said, 'nothing to do with me'.

He would offer his opinions to her in the privacy of the flat, over breakfast or late at night. In *The Downing Street Years* she wrote: 'I could never have been Prime Minister for more than eleven years without Denis at my side. Always a powerful personality, he had very definite ideas about what should and should not be done. He was a fund of shrewd advice and penetrating comment. And he very sensibly saved these for me rather than the outside world . . .'

Bill Deedes remembers Denis reporting his input in his modest, measured fashion with the wonderful preface: 'I said to my woman . . .' He would then go on to make some comment about sticking to her guns and not letting the bastards (Labour Party, trade unions, the media, Cabinet critics) grind her down.

Denis was the soul of cooperation in Number Ten. 'I'm easy, I'll do whatever you want,' he told Margaret, and never made any demands on her time or complained about her absences. In Opposition he had honed his antennae to detect when he was 'spare'; 'If you don't need me, I'm off,' he'd say and disappear to his own tasks. This became one of his catch phrases and was mouthed by the Number Ten staff when they saw Denis looking through the Prime Minister's diary for the tell-tale annotations in the margins: '+ DT' or 'No DT'. Occasionally someone's sympathy was articulated out loud: 'Denis, poor bugger, he never knows if he's going to get hot dinner, cold dinner or none at all.'

Although my father's retirement was sabotaged by Margaret's political promotion, the timing was not inconvenient. Had they been contemporaries, with Denis still pursuing his career, there might have been a conflict of interests. He would certainly never have been able to support her with the same energy, nor develop his own role at such a measured pace.

In many ways men are far more promising raw material for consorts than women. From the very first day Denis arrived at his prep school in short trousers, he was taught never to let the team down, whether it be the cricket XI, rugby XV or his beloved house; the army had also instilled in him a sense of duty and loyalty. Moreover, a man's life is less likely to revolve around his wife's career. If your life is entirely bound up in your spouse's, there is a far greater temptation to interfere. This was never a problem for Denis: he always had his own agenda and outside interests, such as golf and rugby.

My father developed a sixth sense for gauging the temperature of the political crisis of the moment. Denis recalls the tell-tale signs. 'I think you get some sort of feel for it. The first thing is, late at night, all the damned lights [of Number Ten] are on all over the place, indicating that people are coming in and out. Like any other establishment, it's either shut down or half shut down or going like a bomb.' At such moments he would slip into his study and put on some music. Whenever Crawfie and Joy heard a symphony blaring out they'd wonder, 'What's up now?'

Everything in 1979 was a 'first' and as the autumn rolled on it was the Prime Minister's annual weekend to Balmoral.

The form was fairly standard: we used to get up at lunchtime and have lunch with the Queen's secretary and then arrive at the castle at around teatime to be met by a lady-in-waiting. After tea and drinks, the Queen would come in and Margaret would go off for her weekly meeting with Her Majesty.

There was a houseparty and some of the people who'd been shooting didn't come in until later and then there were more drinks – because they're very generous with drink – and then we went in for dinner. In their language it's probably very informal but nevertheless you're on tiptoe. There's the usual sort of after-dinner conversation over coffee and then the Queen withdraws fairly early . . .

After Sunday lunch we drove over the estate – the Queen in her Land Rover – and we finished up at afternoon tea with the Queen Mother.

Denis was a big fan of the Queen Mum, particularly when, sitting next to her at a royal banquet, he used the wrong fork to eat his salmon entrée. When the next course arrived, he looked down and said: 'Oh, Ma'am, I seem to be a little bit short here.'

'Oh well, Mr Thatcher, I'm sure we can find you another one,' she graciously reassured him.

Denis refers to the first few years at Number Ten as his 'running-in' time. He exercised supreme caution: you don't relax your guard when you're walking on eggshells. There was little enjoyment to be had at official functions where his main aim was not to stand in the wrong place, say the wrong thing or embarrass the Prime Minister. At official dinners he would sometimes think, 'Christ, what on earth am I going to say to the lady on my left or right?' He was once reduced to 'Likey soupy?' with one shy wife who spoke little English. He even contemplated writing down emergency subjects on a postcard to hide under the napkin on his lap. But eventually, he deserved a diploma in small talk. There were certain fall-back subjects: 'You always ask where they've come from and where they're going to; ask what's on their itinerary and that sort of thing.'

Of course, it helped if the guests spoke English.

If not, there was always an interpreter but that takes a bit of getting used to. You have to concentrate and – I think I read this in a book somewhere – you must forget the interpreter and look straight towards the guest when talking. Don't go on with a 'tell her this' and 'ask her that' routine, which is a temptation at first because it seems the obvious thing to do.

Fix your eyes on his or her eyes, talk and then pause so that the interpreter can catch the conversation. Once you've got it right, you're OK and you can relax.

With the media, Denis's trump card remained his blanket refusal to give any interviews. Nor was he tempted into accepting any number of offers: he could have played a round of golf on any of the hallowed courses of his choice, or test-driven luxury cars or sampled the finest malt whiskies, but he chose to refuse them all. No interviews meant no interviews, on or off the golf course.

He was unfailingly polite when he turned down offers, hand-writing a reply, his gentle humour cushioning any sense of rejection.

Dear Sir,
Thank you for your most charming and indeed persuasive letter.
Knowing, as I do, of your high reputation and standing, be assured that I have no doubt that anything you wrote following an interview with me would be both sympathetic and accurate.

There are several editors and others in Fleet Street whom I number among my friends and close acquaintances. Were I once, even once, to give an interview to so distinguished a journalist as yourself, or to one far less so, they would very properly approach me and I would not in honour be able to refuse.

I have spent some 15 years or more 'keeping my head below the parapet'; that this is misunderstood from time to time is understandable but on balance the policy has paid off.

I hope you will not regard me as ungracious in declining your kind and indeed sincere invitation and will appreciate my reasons for so doing. One day when I have left my vicarious 'public life' I may be persuaded to give an intensive interview if only to provide a single accurate paragraph in the many biographies which will be written of Margaret.

Thank you for writing to me and with warm good wishes . . .

This made life very easy for Bernard Ingham: 'I knew where I stood [with Denis]. I could say that he had never given an interview in his life and he's not going to start now.'

Exactly why he got such an easy ride from the press remains a mystery to Bernard: 'I didn't go around saying, "If you misbehave you'll get clobbered," or anything like that. I do think that what they all felt was that here was somebody who was a pretty decent man, knew how to behave and it wasn't in their interests to slag him off and let him down because they knew that certain consequences might follow. This is where he [Denis] might have been a beneficiary of it being a strong government which wasn't going to stand any nonsense.'

On overseas trips Ingham told the accompanying journalists Denis's programme. 'I never actually said that he was off-limits but I think they understood this . . . All media relations is a balance of advantage in a sense – like a reign of terror – but they knew that if they really did badly misbehave we had a sanction. Now the credibility of a sanction is whether you will actually carry it out and fortunately it was never put to the test because I think the media behaved with uncommonly good sense.'

Bill Deedes was also impressed by the way in which Denis handled his own PR.

> He was always immensely polite to the press; he called them vipers but the word 'viper' was a very affectionate one and they knew they weren't vipers anyway so it didn't upset them.
>
> There were press receptions at Number Ten and one of the great features of them was that with Denis and Margaret as hosts nobody was ever left to wallflower. Denis would be circling round the room, saying, 'You must come and meet the PM,' or 'You must come over and speak to X, Y or Z.' He took enormous pains to get that right.

Denis certainly was lucky, but he earned his luck because, however nice you are, you can always have an accident. He knew that those in public life attracted obloquy, and because his wife had tunnel vision, he could help her most by patrolling the fringes, making sure no one was left out or unthanked.

Although Denis declined to give any interviews, he did occasionally accept a speaking engagement – an astonishingly brave decision for someone so shy. One of the first – and almost his last – was given to his old friends from the London Society of Rugby Football Union Referees at their annual dinner in 1979.

It came in the middle of a growing storm over the proposed tour of South Africa by the British Lions. Denis tackled the issue in his characteristic straightforward manner, speaking as a rugby lover, not as the husband of the Prime Minister. 'We are a free people, playing an amateur game and we have got the right to play where we like. If the soccer players can go and play in Russia and our table tennis team can go to China, as sure as hell we can play our game in South Africa.'

He sat down to rapturous applause. Peter Yarranton recalls, 'Rumour had it on our table that we probably wouldn't see Denis for three or four weeks because the lady wouldn't like it, but that really endeared him to everyone because he was saying what we were all feeling. We were being dictated to by the politicians.'

With hindsight, Denis regards the speech as a huge mistake. He had thought long and hard about the embarrassment it might cause Margaret but eventually stuck his neck out.

Of course, after all the London Society of Rugby Football Union Referees is a club, damn it, and what I didn't realize was that amongst our guests we usually have a few journalists who are rugby football correspondents.

My comments brought the house down but I regretted what I'd said, especially when I picked up the papers the following morning and saw the front pages. It was cheap applause at someone else's expense [Margaret's] – the person I wouldn't disadvantage until I go to my grave.

There was a question in the House of Commons, too, but it was typical of how Margaret and I got on together; she never said a word to me about it. She never said, 'For God's sake, I've got enough problems without you getting in the act and adding to them.'

It made me a damn sight more careful from there on.

This involved finding a safe format for his speeches to ensure that nothing could be misinterpreted by hovering journalists.

When I went to ladies' luncheon parties, I only spoke for three, four or five minutes at the most. I started with an in-joke about Number Ten – half a minute – such as, 'When I was having my weekly meeting with the Prime Minister – that's the only time I see her, you understand – I told her that I was coming to see you today and she sends her very best wishes.'

Then I'd prophesy the brilliant ministerial future awaiting the local Member of Parliament, because although he may not have been in the audience, sure as hell his wife was. 'I'm sure you all know what a wonderful member is Mr So and So; his speeches in the House of Commons are much appreciated and the PM sees a great future . . .'

I'd finish with a call for party loyalty and an appropriate quotation: the one I used more often than not was Henry V's speech at Agincourt. They got a couple of lines from that, including 'Cry God for Henry, England and St George,' although I used to say, 'Cry God for Margaret, England and St George.'

If there were no interruptions, the whole thing was over in three minutes – long enough.

He knew he was on fairly safe ground handing out prizes and awards. At the Boat Show in January 1980 he presented the first Golden Award to a duty winchman on one of the helicopters involved in the previous summer's dramatic rescue of sailors in the Fastnet Race.

Denis became more confident as he went on, writing out his speeches and religiously sticking to the script. 'I got better, but then if you listen to one of the greatest speakers in the world continually – Margaret – you are pretty bloody dim if you don't pick up a thing or two, aren't you?'

There were still occasional blunders, mostly caused by inexperience. In 1980 a minor scandal erupted and ran its course through headlines, editorials and questions in the House of Commons when Denis wrote a letter on Number Ten paper to the Welsh Secretary, Nicholas Edwards, protesting about planning delays on a housing scheme in Snowdonia. He wrote in his capacity as part-time consultant to the IDC group, which was involved in the project. There were allegations that he was using his position unfairly, Denis took the line that he could use Number Ten stationery because, after all, he lived there. 'In future, Mr Thatcher needs to be a little more diligent in his letter-writing habits,' chided the *Sunday Times*, but the incident passed over quickly with no permanent damage to Denis's reputation.

On the whole he'd learned enough by then not to make his personal opinions public. When Russia invaded Afghanistan in 1979 and the international condemnation triggered the boycott of the Moscow Olympics, Denis kept his mouth shut. 'It was messy and controversial but I'd learnt my lesson after my speech to the London Society in 1979. I got pretty tactful and deliberately didn't make any comment even though I thought it was barmy, to be absolutely honest. I was for it [the boycott] on the basis that we'd chucked the South Africans out and I thought, Bugger that for a laugh. These buggers [the Soviets] ought to be out, too.'

Denis was soon earning high praise for the astute way he had handled his first innings in the spotlight. Stephen Pile wrote in the *Sunday Telegraph*: 'The fact remains that Denis Thatcher has conducted his first year in office with total brilliance. Fate, heredity and the General Election have dealt him an unplayable hand and with simple genius he has declined to play it.'

THIRTEEN

CONSORT SURVIVAL:
GOLF AND GIN

'Sometimes he would open up his mind, but never his
heart.'

BILL DEEDES

NO ONE WHO HASN'T experienced it can imagine the sense of
isolation and loneliness involved in being married to someone who
is wedded to a job. For days on end Denis would glimpse only the
back of his wife's power heels as she charged off to fulfil the next
prime ministerial duty.

When they were together – perhaps in the car on the way to a
dinner where Margaret was due to speak – she would have her
head down making last-minute changes to the text. On the way to
and from Chequers, if they went together, one or other of them
normally slept.

It's not easy being an outsider in your own wife's life after thirty
years of marriage. Your shared experiences boil down to the official
gatherings you attend together. Another PM might have had an
interest she shared with her husband, or a desire to spend time
with him relaxing or on holiday, but Margaret desired nothing
beyond being Prime Minister. Their lives ran at different speeds –
hers breakneck and frantic from the moment she woke up. This
was a mirror image of the first years of their married life, when he
was constantly overseas on business, working late at Atlas and
refereeing at weekends.

Occasionally, there were reminders of the past. I dropped in
once when Crawfie and Margaret were having a drink in the flat.
My mother had put on some supper, expecting Denis to arrive
home at any moment. The phone rang and Crawfie answered it.

Denis had left a message: he'd decided to stay on where he was to have a drink and would be delayed. My mother sighed and said, 'That's the story of my life.'

The non-executive directorships that Denis accepted after retiring meant he was reasonably busy and he probably kept himself better briefed than most who take up such positions. He prides himself on never having missed a board meeting; he took his directorships very seriously.

As always, he was scrupulous in running his business affairs. When he joined the American railroad corporation CSX it was as a consultant because he pointed out to them: 'I won't go on your board because in a very short time I shall be above the normal age of American directors. You have to be re-elected every year and that could be very embarrassing for you at your AGM.'

Nor surprisingly, corporations in the City saw some mileage in being 'in' with the Prime Minister's husband and he was snowed under with invitations to enjoy their lavish lunchtime hospitality. He accepted some but never forgot his sensitive position. 'I don't think they wanted to see my beautiful face; I think they were either trying to get information out of me or give me guarded messages – most of which I ignored. I learned never to criticize anybody unless I knew the facts. I never got involved in discussions if I could help it because I knew damn well that somebody would quote me.'

He also became practised at deflecting questions the moment he realized he was being pumped for information on aspects of government policy. 'I think I've got sufficient brains and knowledge of companies to play that one pretty carefully. I have always been terribly terribly careful about insider trading in business and this was the political version of it.'

Denis successfully juggled his private engagements with official duties – no easy task. Take, for example, one week in November 1980, which included the State Opening of Parliament, a formal dinner every evening, including one at Buckingham Palace and another at Claridge's for the King of Nepal; and then a board meeting and dinner in Stratford on the Saturday. He would return from a business trip to America, go straight to his study in the flat in Number Ten, and race through his in-tray dealing with anything urgent. A lightning change into a dinner jacket, a glance at the guest list and briefing, a drink in the sitting room and he was away again, turning on the charm at an official reception a floor below.

At a rare breakfast together, he and Margaret began discussing what they had planned for the day. It turned out that they were booked to open rival antique fairs, one at Chelsea Town Hall and the other at Grosvenor House. Denis made a speech saying how glad he was that his wife had such a busy job because when they'd lived in Chelsea in Opposition days she had enjoyed shopping in the local antique haunts – a costly exercise.

As he grew in confidence, Denis even occasionally performed solo at party political functions. 'Well, I couldn't keep writing back saying no, could I?' he explains. But on each occasion, he made sure he was well briefed, knew what to say and had a stock of safe questions. Kim Coombe, a fellow Old Mill Hillian, says, 'I think he learned very quickly – this is half the intelligence of the man. Whilst he was shy, I don't think he was nervous. I've never seen Denis remotely nervous.'

Rugby internationals at Twickenham were sacrosanct dates in Denis's calendar. The day before, his diary carried a reminder, 'Prepare for Twick'. 'I'd been preparing for Twick for years – still do, of course,' he says. 'I would go up to Harrods and pick up lunch. It was pretty standard – invented by Margaret in the days when she came to one or two international games – a flask of hot tomato soup, smoked salmon and game pie. Then I've got a basket which holds twelve bottles: a bottle of whisky and a bottle of gin, a bottle of claret – at least. Sodas and tonics . . .'

The car park at Twickenham was familiar territory. When he drove himself to an international he always got the same parking spot, under a large oak tree.

> To begin with I had to pay about five bob – slipping it to the gateman so that he would get me my preferred parking spot.
>
> Later the fee went up to a pound, which I was happy to pay, although he always said to me 'Mr Thatcher, just remember to be here early.'
>
> I said: 'I'm always early. I hate arriving any time after ten o'clock.

The fee went up to five pounds, which seemed like an awful lot but I was happy to pay. Then the gateman retired and at his last game, I drove in and slipped him a tenner. Christ knows what this new chap will be like. I hope he'll keep the arrangement going.

Peter Yarranton identified Twickenham's importance for Denis:

He had his political world, he had his own business interests, but all he needed to do was to walk into Twickenham and he had 70,000 people on his side. They just said, 'Hello, Denis,' 'Good Afternoon, Denis.' And he'd reply, 'My dear boy,' and 'Dear lady . . .'

He was very earthy. We all knew he might be meeting a president or prime minister the next day but you would still hear him in the car park, asking around, 'Is there any chance of giving me a lift in the direction of Number Ten?'

It might seem strange that Denis, pillar of male chauvinism at Twickenham, could happily walk two paces behind his wife for the rest of the year. He managed it and probably won over a whole political constituency who wouldn't normally have voted in a woman as Prime Minister. They admired Denis and this made it acceptable to vote for Margaret.

Denis needed no reminder of Boswell's words, 'A man, Sir, should keep his friendship in constant repair.' More than ever before, he came to rely on personal friendships as a retreat from the political relationships where 'friendship' is assessed on a scale of usefulness.

When I started researching this book, Denis gave me a list of his friends: their names were familiar but I had met only a few of them. It was a whole slice of my father's life I knew nothing about. These friendships had been cemented not in any of Denis's homes, but in the boardroom, the car park at Twickenham or his friends' houses, where he was a lone house guest. Denis was known not as a husband, a father, or a consort, but as a man wholly relaxed and happy in his own skin.

Cornishman Vic Roberts, a former rugby international, and his wife, Suzanne, were among these friends. Denis would stay at their home near Falmouth; at a dinner party one evening a glib comment on being the spare man at the dinner – 'You men don't know how lucky you are' – betrayed the depth of his feeling.

Vic and Suzanne welcomed me to their glorious house over-looking the river Fal, just as they had welcomed Denis on numerous visits. I had a smoother journey because I didn't have to slip surreptitiously out of Number Ten with golf clubs and bag, across the garden by the Cabinet Office and through the gate onto Horse Guards, anxious not to be seen skiving off for a weekend of golf. On one occasion, having escaped successfully, Denis was dismayed when, bolting along the motorway towards Cornwall, he suddenly realized that his cash, cheque book and credit cards were still in his wallet back in the flat.

It's all right, he thought, Vic and Suzanne would lend him some money. Then he looked at his fuel gauge and saw the needle hovering perilously close to empty. He made it as far as Honiton, parked the car and strolled into a branch of his bank. Suddenly, he became an impromptu game show contestant.

'May I see the manager?'

'The manager is on leave.'

'May I see the assistant manager?'

'Can I ask why?'

Growing impatient and not averse to pulling rank now and then, he said, 'My name is Denis Thatcher. I am the Prime Minister's husband. I have left my wallet in my jacket in Ten Downing Street and I want to withdraw some money.'

'Have you got any identification?'

This seemed like an extremely stupid question to Denis. 'No, it's in my jacket in Number Ten.'

'Well, you don't look like your photograph.'

'Well, I am Denis Thatcher and would you please ring my bank in Erith to confirm.'

Finally the call was made but the bank employee returned still unconvinced. 'Could you list your standing orders?' he asked.

Denis tried his best, citing a couple of clubs, but to no avail. By now he was fuming and argued that no normal mortal could reel off his standing orders as if they were the first lines of Macbeth.

'No, that is not satisfactory,' said the bank clerk.

'Listen, I'm the husband of the Prime Minister, I'm almost out of petrol and my wallet and credit cards are in London. What do you expect me to do, hitchhike?' Then he had a brainwave. 'The Harlequin Football Club. I have a standing order.'

Rugby football again proved to be his lifeline – if only a temporary one. He was eventually handed £50, not the £100 he asked for.

At the end of the weekend Suzanne Roberts enquired, 'Are you all right for cash, Denis?'

'Yes, I have £32 left.'

'My goodness, Denis, that was a very reasonable weekend, wasn't it?'

It wasn't the first or the last time that Denis had found it an uphill struggle convincing people of his identity. Checking into a hotel in the Midlands before attending a board meeting, he told the registrar his name and, without looking twice, she said, 'That's what they all say ... sign your proper name ... we get a lot of people trying that on.' His telephone calls were often not returned because the message-taker wouldn't believe it was the real Denis Thatcher calling from Downing Street.

He once had fun chatting to someone who clearly hadn't got his name during the introduction and proceeded to ask him what his wife did for a living.

'She's got a temporary job,' Denis replied.

Another story which he delighted in recounting concerned a public engagement in Bristol. It was a highly organized and well-managed cock-up because no car was booked to take him to Paddington station and when he arrived he had no seat on the train.

So, having stood in the queue to get a ticket, I get on the train and there isn't a seat. I wandered up and down and found an empty carriage of the old-fashioned type with seats opposite each other and like a flash I was in.

I noticed on the door a sign saying, 'Reserved for Rosewood Psychiatric Hospital'. In the fullness of time the train stopped at Reading and all these chaps piled into the carriage, shepherded by a very young and very nervous male nurse. He got them settled down and started to count them, 'One, two, three, four ...' and then he got to me and said, 'Who are you?'

'I'm the Prime Minister's husband,' I said.

'Six, seven, eight, nine ...'

Another couple Denis stayed with were George and Diana Williams. He and George went all the way back to the 1960s, when George negotiated the purchase of Atlas for Castrol. Later, Denis and George worked at Burmah together. The Williams lived first in Dartmouth and then in Frome, Somerset, where Denis would accompany them to the local pub and eat Irish stew around their kitchen table. It was a rare taste of normality and relaxation.

My father was also able to be himself on his annual golfing jaunts to the Algarve, La Manga in Spain and various French resorts. His regular foursome included Len Whitting, a quantity surveyor by qualification and a housing company executive involved with the Kent building firm William Ellis; and Bill Deedes: 'He is one of the great men I have met,' says Denis. 'He's an educated man, a gentleman with standards, a first-class companion and a wonderful raconteur. We had a lot of fun in the twenty years that we went overseas playing golf and, of course, played golf closer to home. I love him like a brother.'

The late Ron Monk, a builder who was also involved with William Ellis, made up the foursome, and Denis was fond of joking that he would have made a good sergeant but he didn't really see him as an officer.

The inaugural golfing holiday took place before Margaret became Prime Minister. Len Whitting explains, 'We'd started to work together – with Denis attending our Ellis board meetings. I'd already been going on golfing holidays so I invited Denis with Ron Monk and Bill Deedes to go down to Portugal.' What he didn't reckon on was the Thatcher freneticism.

Before we left, Denis insisted that we put our golf kit – shoes, slacks, socks, and so forth – into our golf bags. I wasn't sure why. We flew down to the Algarve, hired a car and drove to the hotel, and before I could get out, Denis said, 'Sit still.'

He and Bill jumped out, told the porters to take our bags and they both got back into the car and we drove off. The golf course was half a mile away. When we got there Denis said, 'Right, out you come, ties off, get your bags down into the changing-room.' We were straight out for eighteen holes.

I was a bit pale and by the time we finished we all looked rather pink. Back in the dining room that evening people couldn't believe that we'd stepped off the plane, gone straight to the course and teed off. We hadn't even checked in.

That set the pattern for ten or twelve years of eighteen holes in the morning followed by another eighteen in the afternoon.

Len confesses, 'Bill was dancing along like a ballerina at the end of these thirty-six holes and I, the youngest, looked the most beat.' It wasn't until Bill and then Denis – the seniors in the quad – reached seventy (years) that the daily total was reduced from the manic marathon to an enthusiast's round of nine after lunch.

Of the four, Bill Deedes was the best golfer in the early days: he had been doing it all his life and was playing off a handicap of about ten. Denis could play to a handicap of about fourteen for most of a round and then suddenly go to pot. He had an unortho-dox technique, particularly when teeing up because, according to Len, his bottom would stick out. 'I'm not quite sure what that ever did but if you have him as a partner there's always a good chance that – providing you slot in and don't both do badly on the same holes – you can do very well. He takes the game very seriously.'

The four pooled their duty free purchases, designated one of the rooms as 'the bar', and spent balmy evenings on a balcony overlooking the golf course. 'Sometimes he would open up his mind, but never his heart,' says Bill Deedes. 'It was totally relaxing; there was no question of Denis having to leap into a dinner jacket and canter off to some function or stand on parade.' According to Len Whitting:

To be honest, one of the things we all tried to do was not to talk about politics. We didn't want it to appear that we wanted him as a friend to hear all the bits of gossip and inside view of what was going on. It wasn't our job to start prying and asking, 'What do you think is going to happen here?' or 'Is the bank rate going to go up?' or, 'What does Margaret think about this?' because the atmosphere would have been totally different.

It was more often that Denis would be talking away about Bill or Joe and it turned out he was referring to a president or prime minister and we didn't realize.

From the moment they arrived at their destination Denis would visibly relax. There was no red carpet, he was no longer consort, and the goldfish bowl of Downing Street was an aeroplane ride away: he became demob happy. On one trip they arrived at their hotel in La Manga, in southern Spain, to find an exuberant party game in progress on the dance floor. The objective was to pop a balloon attached to your partner's behind without using your hands. Denis was paired up and entered straight into the spirit of things, looking suitably undignified and roaring with laughter.

The golf-and-gin formula was not open to variation: one year Len had the temerity to suggest that they might take half a day off for a spot of sightseeing beyond the fairways. This, of course, was tantamount to treason as far as the others were concerned. Chaps are sent to the Tower for far less.

Undeterred, Len broached the subject again over breakfast as he watched the rain cascading down outside. 'Well, I think we could do it today,' he ventured, knowing it was hardly the weather for golf. Denis and Bill agreed to consider the sightseeing proposal, but not until they had gone up to the golf course to see if the weather there was any different.

'But it's only eight hundred yards away,' argued Len. 'Why is it going to be any different?'

Denis and Bill were adamant and the four dashed through the downpour to the car, scrambled in and drove the 800 yards. There were no officials or caddies around and Len was confident that he had won the argument. Denis and Bill had other plans. 'Without further ado or discussion, out came the golfing shoes and off we went. We were absolutely sodden before we'd even completed the first hole. Then, of course, the sun came out and steam was rising, followed by more rain and the sun again. We played eighteen holes and got soaked and dry, soaked and dry.'

Staggering into the clubhouse, Len assumed the ordeal was over. 'Then they said, "Let's have a light lunch and perhaps it'll be better this afternoon." We went straight out again and I surrendered. "That's it," I said. "I'll never ask for time off again."'

Seve Ballesteros was the club professional at La Manga and

offered to give Denis a game. Denis would have loved to say yes, but knew that 'as soon as I turn up on the tee with Ballesteros, there will be a camera'. Moreover, his back trouble had flared up again. However, the others weren't going to miss the opportunity to play a round with one of the greatest golfers ever to swing a club. Seve never quite believed in Denis's bad back and, accordingly, it developed into a running gag between Bill and Ballesteros, with the Spaniard inquiring about Denis's back every time they met. After the game the foursome invited Seve to dinner at a restaurant of his choice. Unfortunately the offer was made rather too publicly: when they turned up, an enormous table had been prepared and Bill commented, 'Someone's having a big party.' As guests kept arriving, the peseta dropped – it was their party and they were paying.

When the bill arrived, the four hosts reached for their plastic and were sternly informed that no credit cards were accepted. They then emptied their wallets and trouser pockets and, having counted every last peseta in their possession, just managed to meet the total. This, of course, left them without a bean for the return journey to La Manga, several miles away. Piling into a taxi, they decided to keep quiet about their lack of resources until they were within walking distance of 'home'. A furious Pedro cursed their forebears but was finally persuaded to return the following morning when the hotel cashier was open for business.

Golf has given Denis enormous pleasure over the years and made him many friends. He's a staunch fan of the greats like Arnold Palmer, Tom Watson and, in particular, Jack Nicklaus – the man who's won more major championships than any golfer in history.

I met him once, just to say hello. Charming man. I have an enormous respect for him, he's one of the greatest sportsmen in the world. There's a wonderful story: it was at the Ryder Cup and Nicklaus was playing with Jacklin on the eighteenth green in the singles. They were both on the green and Jacklin putted first, leaving himself short of the hole. Nicklaus said: 'I'll give you that,' and tossed him the ball. Then Jack putted from about eight feet and missed, so the hole was halved.

Somebody said to him afterwards: 'What did you do that for, Jack? That was more than generous.'

Jack replied: 'Supposing he'd missed it at this stage of the match.'

For Denis this was true sportsmanship – a player who respected his opponent and didn't want to win at all costs. On the golf course, and elsewhere, he was faultlessly polite – well . . . almost, according to Len: 'If you're on a golf course with him and there are ladies nearby he will quite frequently doff his hat. This happened on one occasion but the ladies didn't walk on far – which Denis didn't know. He played his shot and didn't do it as well as he would have liked and fumed, "Oh, f***!"' I'm not quite sure what the ladies made of the combination.'

Slow play, the bane of a golfer's life, was an issue which Denis felt strongly about.

The editor of a golfing magazine had a dinner to launch a campaign against slow golf. Peter Alliss, who's a great friend of mine – absolutely wonderful man and a great golfer – asked me to go to this lunch and I made a short speech.

The thing about slow golf is that it annoys everybody. Alliss mentioned it again the other day. He was commentating on a tournament and the penultimate pair were on the eighteenth tee, while the game behind had barely started putting on the sixteenth green. It ruins the game for spectators.

Now, the difference between golf and all the other games – and there's a hell of a lot of money at stake – is that thanks to the man whom I regard as the greatest sportsman in the world, Jack Nicklaus, the officials are absolutely rigid about bad behaviour or the slightest suggestion of cheating.

Nicklaus said: 'Our job is to remember that amongst other things we're public entertainers and golf is a game of etiquette – gentlemanly etiquette – and we don't want anybody who can't behave like a sportsman.'

Among Denis's other irregular golfing partners were Cecil Parkinson, MP for Hertfordshire South, Cabinet minister and Tory Party Chairman, Neil (now Sir Neil) Macfarlane, sometime Minister for Sports and, several times a year, the Hong Kong shipping magnate Y. K. Pao, one of the wealthiest men in the world.

Cecil recalls one memorable round:

We always seemed to finish up at Sunningdale because Y. K. wanted us to be his guests. Denis and I put our heads together and said we couldn't have this and we would take him to one of our courses. On the next occasion we played at Huntercombe, which was Neil's home-course near Henley-on-Thames.

Denis and I were playing Y. K. and Neil. We used to have the same stakes every time: £1 on the front nine, £1 on the back nine and a £1 on the match – so the total liability was £3.

We played well that particular day and Denis and I won. Y. K. owed us £3, which he paid up, and then he disappeared into a corner of the locker room and sat staring at the card and scribbling. Finally he came back to us. 'I don't owe you three pounds, I only owe you two. I had a stroke on the sixteenth which I didn't claim; that gave us a win so we won the back nine.'

Denis handed over the £1, adding playfully, 'Now I understand why you're so rich, Y. K.' Continuing to wind him up, he suggested that having lost £2, Y. K. should consider having a rights issue.

Margaret was facing one of the toughest periods of her Premiership during the early years of the 1980s. Having embarked on a radical series of reforms which included slashing public spending and confronting trade union abuses, she was hampered by a world-wide recession. Unemployment reached the two million mark and kept on rising steeply while inflation remained stubbornly high.

Within her own Cabinet the majority of ministers became increasingly antagonistic towards the monetarist policies she had embarked upon. Ian (later Lord) Gilmour was sacked in September 1981 and immediately announced to the press that the government was leading the country 'full speed ahead for the rocks'.

Throughout the summer violent riots had flared up in places like Brixton in London, the St Paul's district of Bristol, Moss Side in Manchester and Toxteth in Liverpool. Unemployment and heavy-handed policing were usually blamed but it gave further ammunition to Margaret's critics.

The government were further shaken by some disastrous by-election results and the success of the Social Democratic Party, formed by former Labour Cabinet members Dr David (later Lord) Owen, Shirley (later Lady) Williams, Bill (later Lord) Rodgers and Roy (later Lord) Jenkins, who had broken with the Labour Party because they felt that it had become too left wing under the leadership of Michael Foot and the influence of Tony Benn.

By the summer the SDP was neck and neck with the Tories in the opinion polls, but worse was to come in November, when Shirley Williams overturned a 19,000 Conservative majority to win the seat of Crosby in Lancashire. Some Tories went into meltdown.

Denis, with his healthy irreverence towards the roller-coaster of Margaret's life, viewed each new scandal or disaster calmly as 'just another bloody thing that happens when you're in politics'. When Roy Jenkins won Hillhead, Glasgow, Denis's reaction was characteristic. Standing by the drinks chiffonier near the door of the drawing room, he opened a brand-new bottle of gin and poured a generous slug. Turning to the despondent-looking Prime Minister, he said, 'Don't worry, Love, you'll get 'em back at the general election.' These few words did more to restore Margaret's buoyancy than any number of flunkeys from Smith Square prancing about with swing-o-meters.

However, notwithstanding all the problems at home, the overseas tours went on. During a visit to an Indian village in April 1981, Denis had the mickey taken by Fleet Street's photographers. Against his better judgment, he was persuaded to put on a bubblegum-pink turban, which looked like something from a provincial pantomime.

Margaret had been photographed in every known bit of kit but I did rather draw the line because I didn't think it was frightfully dignified. I mean, Margaret looked absolutely wonderful – beautiful girl and that sort of thing – but I thought I always looked a bit of a twerp. The pink headdress was a sort of a turban thing and by the time the chaps [photographers] had finished the thing had unwound itself halfway round my neck. I did look a fool. The picture made the front page of *Private Eye*, which is exactly where you'd expect it to be.

FOURTEEN

FRIENDS IN HIGH PLACES

'He's got such a wonderful voice, hasn't he? He's a super chap and an excellent host. He has a natural affinity for putting people at their ease. You're not short of a sentence while you're talking to him.'

DENIS THATCHER on President Reagan

MEETING THE 'GREAT AND THE GOOD', as Denis referred to world leaders and household names, was a very necessary part of his role as consort. But having conquered his stage fright, he soon discovered that the famous aren't necessarily all sparkling conversationalists. Overseas heads of state on standard three-day visits were virtually house guests. When the President of Nigeria arrived in March 1981, Denis accompanied the PM to a state banquet in his honour at Buckingham Palace on Tuesday evening; to a lunch the following day in Number Ten; and on Thursday evening it was Nigeria's return bunfight at Claridge's. By then Denis could be excused for waning (after all, a man can eat only so many canapés), but on Friday evening he was billed to pitch up at a Young Conservatives' wine and cheese evening. Thankfully, there was the prospect of light relief on Saturday – a round of golf and England versus France at Twickenham.

Yet despite occasional fatigue, the role of consort afforded Denis the remarkable opportunity to sit on the sidelines of the biggest game of all – world affairs – and to listen, observe and decide for himself whether great men make history or history makes great men. He admits, 'A vicarious political life is absolutely fascinating because you're not carrying the bloody can.'

Bill Deedes believes that the popular perception of Denis as an unlucky sod who gave up his retirement and spent years being 'handbagged' by the Iron Lady is very wide of the mark. In fact he was a beneficiary.

> I think he may have said to himself, 'Look, here I am, Denis Thatcher, I've got various qualities and I won a military MBE and all the rest of it. Here I am married to a woman who is Prime Minister and I'm going to live as I've never lived before. OK, to some extent I am seen as the husband, but it's not downhill all the way. I'm going to enjoy a life which very few men in Britain do enjoy.' It takes a certain amount of character to say all this . . .
>
> He was married to a famous woman, he travelled round the world, had presidents and prime ministers and monarchs to dinner. Lucky fellow – many people working their hearts out or earning millions of pounds a year for Britain didn't have the same experience.
>
> It can be argued that Denis, who otherwise would have been a rather shy director of companies, mostly retired, would have had a pretty dull life without the amazing coincidence of being married to the first woman Prime Minister of Britain.

Of the many world leaders that Denis met, he always enjoyed seeing former military men, like King Hussein of Jordan and President Zia Ul-Haq of Pakistan.

Hussein is charming, outgoing and amusing – more like a soldier than a monarch. 'He's a terribly terribly nice chap,' says Denis. 'We've seen him regularly over the years. He's a lovely man and I always get on well with those who come from a military background because I loved the army so much myself. He's been here and we've been to the Palace in Amman and his summer villa in Aqaba.' But he balks at calling him a friend; that would be an impertinence.

Denis met President Zia in Pakistan on the way back from the CHOGM in Melbourne. The war in Afghanistan was at its height and Pakistan had been inundated by refugees. He and Margaret visited one of the refugee camps. Later, Denis and the President were in contact again.

'When Margaret was in hospital having her eye operation [in 1982], he rang me up all the way from Pakistan. He asked, "How is she?" and so on. I thought that was very considerate of him.'

Denis met very few of the major European leaders during the eighties: there were not many visits to Britain because the Prime Minister was seeing most of them so regularly at various summits. He avoided the euro-junkets because they fell into the 'one-night stand' category.

Occasionally his eye for detail and growing diplomatic sense proved useful. When François Mitterrand of France and his wife came to lunch at Number Ten in August 1981, Denis suggested that the French President might prefer not to have portraits of Nelson and Wellington staring down at him as he ate.

These were the years when 'Thatcher Tours' were crisscrossing the world's time zones as if trying to defy jetlag. Number Ten had dubbed them 'tours' to give them 'street cred' and commercial clout: vacant seats were flogged off to accompanying journalists.

There was a 'Thatcher Tours' joke that Denis wasn't 'two paces behind' the Prime Minister, he was 'two *places* behind'. You could almost guarantee that when the goodbyes had been said and the limousines were purring, a cry would go up, 'Where's Denis?' A search party would be dispatched and he would be found deep in conversation with some under-manager of the factory or tobacco plant.

The British delegation was always minute compared to the huge casts which arrived from some Third World countries. When Margaret rather grandly introduced one of her party as the 'chief of my diplomatic staff' the fellow had to stop himself looking incredulously over his shoulder: he was the 'chief' and the 'staff'.

On overseas duty Denis was marvellous at spreading the feel-good factor and would discreetly thank each and every member of the aircraft crew, or make sure that the embassy or high commission staff knew how much the Prime Minister appreciated their hard graft.

The Prime Ministerial VC-10 normally left from Heathrow or one of the RAF bases like Brize Norton. The front cabin is basically an airborne office, with working tables which doubled for dining; a pair of bunks meant one could grab some sleep on long flights. The rest of the jet had regular rows of seats for staff and press. The Prime Minister usually worked through the flight, while Denis retreated with a packet of cigarettes and a good book. Although only feet away, you would barely know he was there.

'He was a very relaxed traveller,' says Charles Powell. 'He would settle down with a book – some sort of military history or biography – and the Prime Minister throwing tantrums or hysterics about the briefing or the speech or whatever, just sort of passed him by ... climatically he was far better than the Prime Minister. I think after many years of plodding through Africa and other places doing his business he seemed to thrive on the heat.'

The entourage is the political equivalent of a touring pop group, theatrical company or cricket team. It is all rather rarefied: meeters and greeters and minders know exactly who you are and, if you don't know where you're going, they do and you'll be swept onwards. The tedium of waiting at the baggage reclaim, filling out customs or immigration forms, finding the green channel and fumbling at the bureau de change is replaced by a red carpet welcome, a band striking up the national anthems and, more often than not, a guard of honour for the PM to inspect.

You're then ushered into a fleet of gleaming chauffeur-driven cars lined up on the tarmac. As soon as the lead car moves off the motorcade follows in formation and speeds through streets which are likely to be totally deserted because they've been closed off in your honour.

It was all too easy to get used to this uninterrupted progress. A detective looking after Ronald Reagan during a London visit after he'd left the White House told me that, every time his car was held up at traffic lights or because of congestion, the former President would try to get out for the simple reason that, for years, no car he'd travelled in had come to a stop until it reached its destination.

The American visits were always Denis's favourites. He first visited the United States on business for Atlas in the 1950s and enjoyed going back, particularly in such style. After landing at Andrews Airforce Base, he and Margaret might be helicoptered to the Washington Monument and then transferred to limousines for the short ride to Blair House opposite the White House. There were plenty of Secret Service men – straight out of central casting – wearing shades and dark suits and constantly whispering instructions into their shirt cuffs.

My first view of the White House was in December 1979, when the enormous banks of poinsettias were in bloom and the Christmas lights were blazing, making it look like Fairyland. It was far grander than Number Ten, in the same category as Buckingham Palace. 'It's better than Downing Street. It had an atmosphere,' says Denis. 'But it's only a bit better than our embassy in Washington, which is magnificent.'

On that occasion Jimmy Carter, the peanut farmer from Georgia, was in residence, with wife Rosalynn and daughter Amy. Margaret had met the President at the G7 Summit in Tokyo six months earlier and was impressed by his intellect and sincerity, if not his grasp of economic policy and foreign affairs.

Mrs Carter had organised carol singing in the East Room as the after dinner entertainment. It was impeccably done and dinner guests were all given beautifully hand-scripted carol sheets done up as scrolls and fastened with the Presidential seal.

I found myself standing next to the First Lady, who was wearing a bright red floral-patterned chiffon dress. In a fluster she said, 'I've left my glasses up in the apartment – you'll have to tell me what's coming next.'

I spent the next hour discreetly hissing, 'Away in a Manger' or 'The Twelve Days of Christmas' and prompting her with the first line of each new verse.

The next incumbent of the White House, President Ronald Reagan, was to become a good friend of my mother's. They admired each other immensely and shared very similar views on economics, foreign policy and welfare. Both my parents had met Reagan before he became President. They had been impressed by a speech he gave as Governor of California, at the Institute of Directors' annual conference in 1969 at the Royal Albert Hall in London.

The Governor had thanked his hosts for asking him to address their prestigious forum and continued in this vein of self-deprecating humour: 'You do me a great honour. That honour is not lessened by my faint suspicion that your invitation was prompted, at least in part, by curiosity. After all, it is not everyday that someone who has been riding off into the sunset for twenty-five years with "The End" superimposed on his back, turns up on the State House steps with something he calls a "Creative Society".'

Margaret was the first major foreign leader to visit the new President. Almost every second of an official visit to Washington is precisely choreographed – from the car allocations to the speeches, dinners, ceremonies and goodbyes. The programme for the Washington visit was fifty-six pages long; here is an example of a single hour:

WHITE HOUSE ARRIVAL CEREMONY

THURSDAY
FEBRUARY 26, 1981

9:30 a.m. Members of the Welcoming Committee arrive at the White House (South West Gate) and are escorted to their places on the South Lawn.

9:40 a.m. Members of the Official British Party [including Yours Truly] leave Blair House for the White House (South West Gate).

9:55 a.m. Prime Minister and Mr Thatcher leave Blair House for the White House (South West Gate).

9:58 a.m. President and Mrs Reagan leave the White House Diplomatic Reception Room and proceed to platform area.
Ruffles and Flourishes
Announcement
Hail to the Chief

9:59 a.m. President and Mrs Reagan arrive at the platform area in front of the Diplomatic Entrance and position themselves at the beginning of the red carpet.
Motorcade enters the White House grounds and proceeds to the Diplomatic Entrance from the President's left.

10:00 a.m. President and Mrs Reagan are introduced to the Prime Minister and Mr Thatcher by Mrs Leanore Annenberg, Chief of Protocol.
(*Photo Opportunity*)
President Reagan then introduces the Prime Minister and Mr Thatcher to:
Vice President Bush
Mrs Bush
Secretary Haig
Mrs Haig
General Jones
Mrs Jones

President and Mrs Reagan escort the Prime Minister and Mr
Thatcher onto the platform.
Present Arms
Ruffles and Flourishes
National Anthem of the United Kingdom
National Anthem of the United States
19-Gun Salute
Order Arms

President Reagan escorts the Prime Minister to the Commander of the Troops, who takes his place at the Prime
Minister's right. The Inspection Party turns in front of the
band, and President Reagan takes up position to the right of
the Commander.
Inspection begins at the right front of the band and proceeds
along the front rank of troops. Members of the Inspection
Party salute when passing in front of the colours.
At the left flank of the formation, the Inspection Party turns
and proceeds toward the platform.
President Reagan and the Prime Minister return to the
platform.
Troops in Review

The Marine Drum and Bugle Corps passes in front of the
platform.
Present Arms
Order Arms
The Commander of the Troops concludes the honours at this
time.

President Reagan and Prime Minister move to the microphone
and face the press area.
Remarks by President Reagan
Remarks by the Prime Minister
President Reagan and the Prime Minister face the troops and
the Commander of the Troops indicates that the ceremony
has concluded.
President and Mrs Reagan escort the Prime Minister and Mr
Thatcher to the South Portico Balcony.
Trumpet fanfare
(*Photo Opportunity*)

10:30 a.m.   The Party enters the Blue Room and a receiving line is
formed.

Nothing was spontaneous – every single step of the running order
was stipulated in advance. Even so, the sheer pace was exhilarating.

When Margaret went for talks with the President, Denis was off and running on his own programme of events, organized by the British Embassy and the Foreign Office: he flew to Wilmington Delaware to view a trade exhibition. Meanwhile, I went to the Smithsonian Institution and then attended a large luncheon party at the State Department hosted by Mrs Haig.

The official black-tie dinner at the White House that evening was quite spectacular. The 100-odd guests were mainly politicians, although there was the inevitable sprinkling of film stars like Charlton Heston and Bob Hope. The reciprocal dinner at the British Embassy the following night included Katharine Graham, owner of the *Washington Post*, Gloria Vanderbilt, the fashion designer, and Barbara Walters from ABC television, whom Margaret got on well with.

These were two of the most talked-about dinners of the year and there was obviously a degree of one-upmanship: Lady Henderson, the wife of the British Ambassador, was a renowned hostess. She was justifiably proud of her dessert coup – a luscious vanilla ice-cream dome hollowed out so when you cut a slice an avalanche of chocolate flakes spilled forth.

President Reagan hugely impressed Denis, 'He's got such a wonderful voice, hasn't he? He's a super chap and excellent host. He has a natural affinity for putting people at their ease. You're not short of a sentence while you're talking to him.'

The following day, Denis visited Manassas to meet businessmen, thereby extricating himself from morning tea with the British embassy wives. In the afternoon he was with the Prime Minister when she received an honorary degree from Georgetown University and then continued his own programme while she went to the Pentagon.

By Saturday morning, the circus moved to New York. As we waited for the Presidential helicopters at the Washington Monument, the wind was howling and Alexander Haig said to me, 'I wouldn't go up in weather like this.'

How reassuring, I thought.

Denis met Nancy Reagan again five months later on 25 July, at a lunch at Chequers after the royal wedding. The President was unable to attend because he was still recovering from an assassination attempt.

By the time I returned to Britain at the end of 1981, Denis had had three years to get used to calling Number Ten and Chequers home. I took over our old house in Flood Street which my parents no longer used, until I bought my own home in Fulham.

I was not nearly as newsworthy as Mark, whose motor-racing and business exploits had earned him a number of mentions in the tabloids. Mark's choice of recreation didn't win the unstinting approval of either parent, but Denis had his hands full as consort and, having rarely interfered in our upbringing, he was hardly going to start laying down the law when his children were in their late twenties.

The incident which has continued to haunt Mark was getting lost while competing in the French-run Paris–Dakar Rally in January 1982. He'd undertaken the famous contest in a Peugeot with co-driver Charlotte Verney and mechanic Jean Garnier.

On Sunday 10 January we received a message from the *Daily Express*: a report from the desert claimed that Mark had gone missing. No one panicked because we thought we would have heard if it was anything serious and the rally organizers told us that Mark and Charlotte were being rescued.

Communications were slow and confused, but on Tuesday evening Derek Howe, a member of Margaret's political staff, came up to the flat and explained to Denis and me that Mark was still missing and that it was another competitor who had been rescued. Denis went pale and said, 'Christ, Margaret will go spare. We'd better go down to the study.'

Soon after, Denis was sitting in the bath early one morning, contemplating the day ahead, when Margaret banged on the door. 'Hector [Laing, later Lord Laing, Chairman of United Biscuits] says you can have his plane to go down to Tamanrasset [deep in the Algerian Sahara] to look for Mark,' she said.

All plans were abruptly cancelled and within hours my father found himself flying off into the sandy yonder. He telephoned to say that an extensive ground and air search was under way. Within twenty-four hours Mark and his team were picked up.

Mark, still unshaven and decidedly peeved about all the fuss, greeted Denis rather too casually: 'Hello, Dad, what are you doing here?'

Denis's face was like thunder but he held his tongue. When Mark mentioned that he'd like to go on and finish the rally, he responded, 'Not bloody likely.'

Bernard Ingham was on the sidelines when the prodigal son returned to Heathrow:

> We were standing on this freezing tarmac [it had been snowing], waiting for the plane to come in and we went up the steps. Mark rushed past your father and then me, saying, 'Where's my detective?'
>
> I could see that Denis was rapidly losing his temper in a big way. So I said to Mark, 'Follow us and do not deviate. We're going into an office to talk.' We got into an office and everyone [the media] was trying to break in. Eventually we found somewhere secure and Mark sat down and put his feet on the table. Denis was standing and so was I. Mark was incredibly fierce at this interference. He gave the impression that there was a great deal of fuss about nothing, which even further grated upon your father.
>
> Mark wasn't inclined to listen to anything that I had to say and in the end – through clenched teeth – Denis hissed at him, 'Will you for the first time in your life listen to somebody who might do you some good.' Mark shut up and I said what I had to say.

Not surprisingly, the 'Dear Bill' letter on the débâcle was a mini-classic.

29 January, 1982

Dear Bill,

Thank you for your condolences on the safe return of the son and h. from his Sahara car rally. Honestly, what a prize twerp! I washed my hands of the little blighter years ago, and when the Boss told me he was intending to drive across the desert with some fancy French bint he'd picked up in the pits, my response was that he could go to hell in a handcart for all I cared. Next thing I know, M. is hammering on my door at some unearthly hour to say she has just heard on 'The Jimmy Young Show' that the little bugger has been missing for four days and what was I going to do about it? Answer, turn over and go back to sleep. Cue for maternal hysteria, call myself a man, etc., why yours truly always so pathetic in a crisis?

Eventually I found my glasses and endeavoured to pour a bit of oil on the troubled H_2O, arguing that a) a bad penny usually turns up in the end and b) that being inexperienced in these matters he had probably driven off on one of the B-roads in search of a quiet layby to try a bit of hanky-panky with la belle frog. Need I tell you that this last analysis went down like a cup of cold sick, waterworks turned on, hanky out, male sex maligned, wailing and gnashing of teeth, all culminating in yours truly agreeing to jump on the first Laker standby to Timbuctoo in search of Prodigal Son . . .

. . . I was sitting comfortably enough ensconced in the Lounge enjoying the patronage of the *Daily Telegraph* Motoring Correspondent when one of these pilot johnnies breezed in for a quick one and said would I like to go aloft in his kite for a shuftie at the terrain? Moments later we were bucketing about in the inky blackness, friend wog shouting back incomprehensible references to flickering lights beneath, and it crossed my mind that given a fair wind the Boss might soon have to send out another search party to bring in yours truly.

When we eventually returned, empty-handed, to the Bar, bugger me if young Mark isn't sitting there with a carefully nurtured growth of beard, drawling away to the reptiles, affecting great unconcern about the whole episode, and clearly seeing himself as the hero of the hour.

At the first possible juncture I took the blighter to one side and gave him a pretty largish piece of my mind. Did he realise that the air forces of the entire Free World had been out trying to find him and his bit of French fluff for the last seventy-two hours? That his mother was on the very brink of a breakdown? That I myself had had to come out to this Godforsaken oasis and would no doubt shortly be expected to partake of sheep's-eyes with the wog powers that be, and all this because he refused to take a job like any other man of his wealth and background?

Absolutely no response. Sulky look, not his fault if parental brigade overreacts, he and Mamselle Fifi perfectly happy sitting in the desert waiting for the local A A man to turn up.

The rest, I imagine, is history. Flash-bulbs popping all the way back to Chequers. Unquestionably the worst moment of the whole episode, when Saatchis had invited every reptile in the business down for a photocall on the lawn, and it was suggested I should put my arm round the little sniveller as a sign of delirious happiness at the reunion. I drew the line at this despite a withering look from M., and broke away at the earliest moment to recover my equilibrium in the Waggonload of Monkeys . . .

The observation about my father's obvious reluctance to hug Mark was spot on. John Wells had picked up the signals from watching the TV footage – the body language said it all: Denis was furious. In truth, he had been reluctant to go to the Sahara in the first place, knowing it would turn into a media circus, but he went for Margaret's sake. Throughout the ordeal, she'd been unable to function and one night I had found her surrounded by red boxes and close to tears as she read a note from the editor of one daily newspaper: 'How we hope we will be able to lead our paper tomorrow with the news that your son has been found.'

The day the news came through that Mark had been found safe and well, she went up to the flat to watch the lunchtime news which would confirm it. We watched and Margaret announced that she'd like a drink. 'I'll pour it,' volunteered Crawfie, at which point the telephone rang. Crawfie answered.

'Could I speak to the Prime Minister?'

'Yes, may I say who's calling.'

'Ron.'

'Ron who?'

'Ron Reagan.'

'Yes, Mr President.'

He was calling to express his relief at Mark's rescue and the Prime Minister took the receiver while handing Crawfie the drink with a you-need-this-look.

Jack (later Sir John) Page, who did a long stint as MP for Harrow West, had entertained us at Chequers the previous Christmas by writing and delivering a poem. On Mark's safe return, he put pen to paper again and the composition was delivered to Downing Street with a bottle of Moët:

Just after lunch on Boxing Day
I think you may have heard me say
That 'dashing verve and courage stark
are all embodied here – in MARK'
I never thought these words would be
so quickly proved for all to see.

And now the agonies are through
(and worries only loved ones knew)
Dear Mark has rightly challenged us
with – 'Why ever was there so much fuss?'
So once again now calm and cool
Let's all apply the tried Page Rule
which after crises always is
just 'Say your prayers and pop the fizz.'

Margaret wrote back: 'Marvellous – absolutely marvellous. How do you do it? The best lines of all were, "And worries only loved ones knew," and "Just say your prayers and pop the fizz." We did all that. We feel so lucky. Somehow other worries have been put into perspective.'

The entire episode stamped Mark with a 'lost in the Sahara' image and for a while every other stand-up comic had an opening gag which recycled the incident. There was, however, one benefit: the rest of us could relax a little because Mark had hung an 'occupied' sign on the family's 'embarrassing relative' slot.

FIFTEEN

THE FALKLANDS

'The Falklands marked her soul and mine.'
DENIS THATCHER

ON THE EVENING OF Friday 2 April 1982 Denis was downing a gin and mixed in the drawing room of the flat at Number Ten when a message was delivered by a member of the Prime Minister's staff. Argentina had invaded the Falkland Islands.

Now, Denis prides himself on his geography but this caught him out. 'I remember looking at *The Times Atlas of the World* to find out where the bloody hell they were – and I wasn't the only one.'

The following morning the nation woke to the news that an enemy flag flew over a British dominion. Newspaper headlines trumpeted the humiliation: SHAMED! declared the *Daily Mail* front page. FALKLANDS FIASCO LEAVES GOVERNMENT FACING CRISIS COMMONS TODAY. The *Daily Express* proclaimed: OUR LOYAL SUBJECTS, WE *MUST* DEFEND THEM.

Maps appeared showing the location of the Falklands in the South Atlantic 500 miles from Cape Horn. The European colonial powers – Britain, France and Spain – had all established settlements on the islands during the seventeenth and eighteenth centuries. The first British landing was in 1690 and the current treasurer of the navy, Viscount Falkland, gave the islands their name. The British had claimed sovereignty over the islands since 1833 and the local population 150 years later was composed almost entirely of British stock. But Argentina had always regarded the Malvinas (as the Falklands were known) and the dependencies of South Georgia and the South Sandwich Islands as part of its sovereign territory.

During the 1970s and early 1980s successive military governments had stepped up their claims to the islands. Since 1979 the Argentinian government and British Foreign Office had been trying to reach a compromise over the rival claims. The result was a 'leaseback' agreement, under which sovereignty would eventually revert to Argentina, but the islanders' way of life would be guaranteed by a continuing British presence. This plan foundered because the 1,800 islanders wished to remain 'British' and gained the support of a number of MPs in the House of Commons.

It became obvious that the Argentinian junta had lost patience and opted for a military solution. Perhaps it was gambling that Britain would not bother to defend the islands – not an entirely unjustified belief, given that most people thought the Falklands were probably somewhere near the Orkneys off Scotland.

Denis was already in fighting mood. 'As an ex-soldier I thought, "How the hell are we going to get a force 8,000 miles away?" I looked at the time and the distances – it was a logistical nightmare – but I had no doubt that we had to do something.'

An emergency session of the House of Commons was called – the first time the House had sat on a Saturday since the Suez Crisis.

The Saturday morning newspapers hammered home the government's discomfiture. The finger of blame was pointed at the Foreign Office, with the Foreign Secretary Peter Carrington squarely in the frame; the Prime Minister's own survival was also in doubt.

I had never seen my mother on her feet in the House of Commons as Prime Minister and it occurred to me that if things were as bad as they appeared this might be my last opportunity. I slung on some clothes, caught the Underground to Westminster and joined the queue for the public gallery.

In the Chamber the Labour Party was gleefully heaping scorn on the government. Margaret later described the mood of the House as 'the most difficult I ever had to face'. She rose to face the music and began: 'The House meets this Saturday to respond to a situation of great gravity. We are here because, for the first time for many years, British sovereign territory has been invaded by a foreign power ... I am sure that this House will join me in condemning totally this unprovoked aggression by the government of Argentina against British territory.'

'Here! Here!' came the cries, and I felt things were going better.

Her voice took on a harder edge: 'I must tell the house that the

Falkland Islands and their dependencies remain British territory. No aggression and no invasion can alter that simple fact. It is the government's objective to see that the islands are freed from occupation and are returned to British administration at the earliest possible moment.'

There were several interjections, including one by Edward Rowlands (Labour MP for Merthyr Tydfil and Rhymney) who blanched at the Prime Minister's reference to Southern Thule, occupied in 1976 when the Labour government was in power. Rowlands pointed out that this particular part of the world consists of 'a piece of rock in the most southerly part of the dependencies which is completely uninhabited and which smells of large accumulations of penguin and other bird droppings'.

The debate then moved on to arguments over whether the government should have predicted and therefore prevented the invasion. Referring to South Georgia, the Prime Minister said: 'There is only a British Antarctic scientific survey there and there was a commercial contract [given to an Argentinian company] to remove a whaling station. I suggest to the Honourable Gentleman that had I come to the House at that time and said that we had a problem on South Georgia with ten people who had landed with a contract to remove a whaling station and had I gone on to say that we should send HMS *Invincible*, I should have been accused of war-mongering and sabre-rattling.'

As I left the public gallery, my mind was filled with farcical images of bird shit and scrap metal dealers. It made the cries of shame seem rather over the top. But during the short walk through Parliament Square and along Whitehall, my spirits sank again when I realized how shaky the whole situation was.

At Number Ten I walked straight into the gloom of building work around the entrance to the lift. Peter Taylor tried to lighten the siege atmosphere by nodding in the direction of the renovations and muttering: 'Preparations for sandbagging!' Indeed, I half expected to see blackout curtains going up.

Joy Robilliard told me that Margaret was in the sitting room.

I gently opened the door, not quite sure what to expect. I genuinely feared they might be moving out of Number Ten within days.

A few months earlier my mother had gone round the flat with little sticky dots, marking anything which was ours as opposed to HM Government's. The idea was that if we had to move in a hurry the removal men would find their job easier. It wasn't that she expected to lose the next election or be ousted as leader; she simply had a very ordered and practical mind and she knew that prime ministers don't last for ever.

'Hello,' I said cautiously. She was sitting on a gold-coloured velvet sofa. There was no sign of doubt: this was Britain's first female Prime Minister auditioning for the part of war leader. 'Are you OK?'

'Fine,' she said, stuffing her hands into the pockets of her dress. 'We're down now but not for long. I've just been downstairs and told Peter [Carrington] and John [Nott] that we're going to fight back.'

If her resolution and aggressive intent could have been transmitted to the Argentine dictator Galtieri at that precise moment, he would have been in no doubt that his occupation of the Falklands was purely temporary.

That afternoon my parents drove down to Chequers. By the following morning Margaret's resolution had hardened; it was vintage Iron Lady. She returned from church and marched purposefully across the Great Hall. 'I'm going back to London,' she said. 'I know we can win. I know we can get them back if only I had six strong men and true . . . and I don't know if I've got them.'

She was worried that some in her Cabinet didn't have the stomach for a fight. Her colleagues were talking of compromise; she took the stance: 'If they won't go, we'll throw them off.'

A more immediate problem was to stop the government from self-destructing. Peter Carrington was under enormous pressure to resign from MPs and the press. Margaret was eager to keep him knowing that, now more than ever, the Cabinet needed continuity. She spoke to him several times on that day, urging him to stay.

However, an editorial in The Times on Monday morning made up his mind. Two senior Foreign Office ministers also resigned and the sharks in the press gallery tasted blood. Now they began circling John (later Sir John) Nott, the Secretary of State for Defence, blamed for the crisis by many backbenchers because of the defence review and budget cuts. His poor performance during the emergency debate on Saturday didn't help his cause. He offered to resign but my mother insisted that he couldn't go until the crisis was over.

The Task Force sailed from Portsmouth on 5 April, led by the carriers HMS *Invincible* and HMS *Hermes*. It included eleven destroyers and frigates and the amphibious assault ship HMS *Fearless*. The cruise ships *Canberra* and the QE2 were commandeered as troop carriers and sailed at a later date. In all, over 100 ships carrying 25,000 men were sent to the Falklands.

During the first few days of the crisis my father saw very little of Margaret. She didn't need reassurance – at least not from her husband, who shared her views entirely. If it had been down to Denis, he would have dispensed with the diplomatic foreplay and evict the 'Argies' at the first opportunity. 'From the word go, I said, "Get them off!" Mark you, I knew it would be a hell of an operation with a communication line stretching 8,000 miles. I never had any doubts that we were going to win but it was just such an enormous operation . . .'

He elaborated his thoughts in a letter to John Harvey, who handled public relations for Burmah Oil and for many years was president of the Conservative Association at Wanstead and Woodford, Sir Winston Churchill's old constituency: '. . . the first job is to win for Britain . . . This Argentine Junta has invaded British territory and go they must. When, and only when, they have gone, we have to do everything possible to let them off the hook that they got themselves on . . .'

Denis reasoned that a humiliating defeat for Argentina could create future problems: 'My great cry of the time was "Get them off." [But] they had to go with some sort of dignity in the arrangement. They had to understand that we, the British, had total rights over the Falklands for ever and a day. We wanted victory but didn't want to totally devalue the Argentinians for ever.'

While Denis had time to write occasional letters, his wife was enmeshed in what she now calls 'the most totally concentrated period of my life'.

You were thinking every moment of the day about it, it was at the back of your mind no matter what else you were doing. You were thinking of what was happening down there and the decisions that had to be taken. When the telephone went or one of the duty clerks came up with a piece of paper in his hand, you always braced yourself as the thought raced through your mind, 'Is this bad news?'

I never had any doubt about the rightness of the decision. Even though we got the Task Force there, there were voices saying, 'No, don't go and land, just negotiate.' I didn't go down there to negotiate. I went down there to get the Argentinians off and if they left then we didn't need to go into battle.

It took the Task Force nearly a month to reach the South Atlantic. Meanwhile, Alexander Haig, the US Secretary of State and former military head of NATO, was commissioned to negotiate between the two sides because America was an ally of both countries. He was to try and act as an 'honest broker' between friends, which came as a disappointment to Margaret, who was counting on US support.

Haig arrived on 8 April on the first of his Atlantic shuttles. The Prime Minister made her position quite clear: 'I don't want to fight any wars; if you can get them off before we get there, you do it, but off they go.' He returned to the US Embassy afterwards and reportedly said to the ambassador, 'That's a hell of a tough lady.'

On 17 April Denis left for a business trip to South Africa with a colleague from Quinton Hazell. He never contemplated postponing his plans: his business came first whether we were at war or not. He and Ray Sollett flew to Johannesburg and from there to Durban and East London. 'I wasn't able to keep in touch except through the press, but I do remember that the one thing I did lay down [to Ray] was that under no circumstances was I going to talk to the press. "You have to make bloody sure that they don't get near me. They can take all the bloody pictures they like but I will not say a word."'

I was working for the *Daily Telegraph* at the time and would drop into Number Ten occasionally to pick up mail and hopefully see Margaret. She was rarely home, but one weekend I found her sitting on the floor in the drawing room surrounded by peace plans – one brought back by Francis (later Lord) Pym, the new Foreign Secretary, another from Al Haig; there was even a proposal from Chile. They all had a conciliatory tone, suggesting things like 'interim administrations' and 'mutual withdrawals'. The Prime Minister wasn't prepared to 'bargain away the freedom' of the Falklanders and insisted, 'I'm not agreeing with anything until they get off.'

Ever since the Task Force had left Margaret had been snatching only the odd hour of sleep, often sitting up all night listening to the World Service. The War Cabinet was meeting daily and included Francis Pym, John Nott, Willie Whitelaw and Cecil Parkinson, as well as the Chief of Defence Staff, Sir Terence Lewin and Admiral Sir John Fieldhouse, Commander-in-Chief of the fleet.

I was meant to cook for a few of them at Number Ten one day, but as I drove my battered Ford Fiesta along Birdcage Walk the engine coughed, spluttered and died. Leaping out with two Marks and Spencer carrier bags full of food, I jumped into a cab and told the driver, 'Ten Downing Street,' which is something I usually avoided – I'd say, 'Whitehall, somewhere near the corner of Downing Street,' because it prompted fewer questions.

The war chiefs were in the small dining room when I burst in, puffing madly, and declared: 'I'm sorry, my car broke down: the supply problems begin here.' They laughed.

Denis was still away when the Royal Marines retook South Georgia on 25 April and when RAF Vulcan bombers peppered the runway of Port Stanley airport six days later. He was flying back from South Africa on 2 May when he heard the news that the Argentinian cruiser the *General Belgrano* had been torpedoed and sunk by HMS *Conqueror*, the nuclear-powered submarine.

This was to be the single most controversial episode of the war. The *Belgrano* went down with the loss of 321 lives and effectively ended any last hopes of a diplomatic solution.

The cruiser was heading towards the Task Force on the edge of the Total Exclusion Zone established by Britain. Approaching from the north was the Argentine aircraft carrier, 25 *de Mayo*. It was a classic pincer movement and the admirals feared that an attack on the Task Force was imminent. They requested permission to sink the *Belgrano* and Margaret had little option but to agree: she would otherwise have been endangering the lives of British personnel against the advice of the military.

The real controversy arose later when it was discovered that, at the moment of sinking, the *Belgrano* was actually pointing away from the Task Force. It was argued that she had been turning away and therefore did not represent a major threat. The Prime Minister and the military insisted that the threat was real and the decision to fire a correct one.

Denis agreed: 'I didn't have the slightest doubt that the sinking – whatever way she was facing – was the right decision.' He sensed the tension from the moment he arrived back at Number Ten. My mother had barely slept and spent most of the night waiting for bulletins because of the time difference with the war zone.

'That was difficult,' Denis explains. 'Bad press in the morning – that would start the pressure. You can occasionally get relaxed and stand aside but you can't totally get divorced – it's impossible., We were living in a goldfish bowl, facing a new crisis each day. Sometimes in politics you can bring pressure on yourself unnecessarily by imagining a problem when one doesn't exist – this one was very real.'

On the third anniversary of Margaret becoming Prime Minister, I arrived with a bottle of champagne at about 6 p.m. Margaret tends to drink Scotch, albeit sparingly, but she occasionally has a glass of champagne to join a toast. I put the bottle in the laundry room fridge, but then word arrived that she wouldn't be back until very late. Watching television at home that night, I discovered the reason – the destroyer HMS *Sheffield* had been hit by an Argentine Exocet missile. More than twenty men were missing, feared dead.

Denis heard the news in different circumstances. A group of MPs had asked him and Margaret to dinner; the date had been arranged six months previously. The plan was to have drinks at Number Ten beforehand but, at the last minute, Jack Page got a message from the Prime Minister asking the guests to meet at her room in the House of Commons. She would be late but Denis would host.

On the way to the House Denis heard a BBC radio bulletin mentioning an 'unconfirmed report' that a British ship had been sunk. In a slightly condescending tone, the announcer began: 'British military authorities say – if they are to be believed . . .'

Denis was furious. 'I will never forget it,' he says. 'How could the bloody BBC question the integrity of the military or suggest the incident could be made up? I was livid with rage and have hated them since that day.'

Jack Page also remembers the night:

> We went to the Hispaniola, a floating restaurant, for dinner. At the table, I sat to the left of Denis, and Michael Jopling, the Chief Whip, was on his right. Everything went wonderfully until someone came and asked Michael to go to the telephone. When he returned, he whispered to me: 'There's terrible news; one of our ships has gone down. Don't mention it to anyone until the end of dinner, but tell Denis so that he knows.'
>
> I took Denis to one side: 'I'm afraid we've lost a ship. It's bad news – men are missing.'
>
> Denis shook his head and said, 'That *is* bad news.'
>
> After dinner I asked him if he wanted to come back to the House of Commons for a drink with us.
>
> 'Oh no, I'll be OK,' he said.
>
> 'I'll drop you back at Downing Street,' I suggested.
>
> 'What are you making all this fuss for?' he muttered. 'When there's a war on you've got to expect things not to go right all the time. I'll walk back to Number Ten.'
>
> I thought that if I had been husband to a Prime Minister of a country at war and such a tragedy had happened, I would have liked some company to go back to Downing Street or go on somewhere. But Denis was absolutely impervious. He decided he was going to take it absolutely calmly and was not going to be rattled.

Margaret's coolness was also astonishing. On 21 May 5,000 British troops landed in San Carlos Bay. I picked up the papers the following day and saw a picture of her smiling and waving and clutching a bouquet of flowers at a constituency function.

I walked into the flat and said: 'Crikey, why on earth did you go to Finchley yesterday? And how could you smile like that? I mean, how could you have looked so calm?'

Margaret admitted it had been an exercise in self-control. 'Of course, all my thoughts were in the South Atlantic. I was desperately worried . . . it was just so important that the landing went right. But if I hadn't gone to the function, people would have thought something was wrong – I had to carry on as normal.'

Thankfully, the landing was successful, and most of the troops reached the shore safely despite heavy air bombardment. The next two weeks signalled the start of the most concentrated and intense time of my mother's premiership. She was operating virtually on auto-pilot. I would walk into the flat and say, 'Hello, Mum, how are you?'

'Hello, darling,' she'd reply, without raising her head. Then I'd walk out again; I doubt if she even realized that I'd been there.

It was the same story at Chequers, where the War Cabinet met most weekends. One night, as I was saying goodnight to her, the telephone rang. It was ten minutes to midnight and my heart skipped. 'Please God, don't let them have sunk *Invincible*,' I thought, as Margaret disappeared to take the call in her study.

Denis did his best to puncture the sombre atmosphere when the War Cabinet came downstairs to the Hawtrey Room for drinks before lunch. Playing the host, he would keep their glasses full and talk about something other than the war. One civil servant recalls, 'We would come out of a meeting, having just had the latest situation reports. In the early stages it was nerve-racking as to whether we were going to bring it off at all, and once again it would be Denis who would entertain and take people aside, raising morale and calming nerves where necessary.'

Although an outsider, my father was trusted like an insider because he was married to the Prime Minister. He had formed his own views from the sidelines and was particularly struck by the relationship between his wife and her commanders-in-chief. 'The lasting impression I got from the service people was the enormous admiration they had for the Prime Minister. They admired her political will and determination enormously.'

There was more bad news to come. On 25 May HMS *Coventry* and a vital supply ship, the *Atlantic Conveyor*, were sunk. The latter was carrying nineteen Harrier jets and helicopters that were vital for moving troops and supplies in the land campaign. Although the jets were saved, eight helicopters and 4,500 winter tents were lost. With unconfirmed reports that HMS *Invincible* might also have been hit, Margaret later said: 'For me, this was one of the worst nights of the war.'

That day Denis had been to a Chipman board meeting in Horsham, Sussex, and stayed overnight with his golfing pal, Len Whitting. The first he knew of the tragedy was when he read the next morning's newspapers. He didn't ring Number Ten. Margaret wouldn't have told him anything on the telephone and he knew there was little he could say to console her. Instead, he carried on as planned, playing a round of golf before preparing for another board meeting the following day. He knew that life couldn't stop because of the war.

The landing force was about to set out across the Falklands, having secured the supply lines. On 28 May the first serious infantry engagement took place at Goose Green. A British force of 450 men was outnumbered four to one but won a ferocious battle. The Paras lost seventeen men, with thirty-five wounded.

It was a frustrating time for my mother. Having made the decisions and given the orders, it was out of her hands. I'm sure she would have preferred to be charging around Goose Green with a gun rather than sitting at Number Ten waiting for news. She made a conscious decision not to ring up and ask how it was going. I remember her saying, 'I wish I knew, I wish I knew,' and Denis calmly replying, 'This is how it is in a war.'

Meanwhile, she was also trying to deal with UN pressure for a ceasefire and lobbying members of the UN Security Council for support.

By 8 June British troops had 'yomped' across the Falklands because of the shortage of helicopter transport, and were closing in on the hills around Port Stanley. On 12 June Margaret was about to change for the Trooping the Colour ceremony, when the duty clerk came upstairs with a note. She almost seized it from him, expecting good news. It was disastrous. Days earlier troops of 5 Brigade disembarking at Bluff Cove for the final assault on Port Stanley had been caught by Argentinian war planes in broad daylight. Two landing ships, *Sir Tristram* and *Sir Galahad*, were bombed and set on fire. Fifty-one men, mostly from the Welsh Guards, died. Others suffered terrible burns and were airlifted from the blazing vessels. Now came the news that HMS *Glamorgan* had been struck by an exocet missile.

On Sunday night she went to Northwood to learn that the battle had moved to Mount Tumbledown on the outskirts of Port Stanley itself. For most of that night she sat up in Number Ten. There was nothing she could do, nothing that Denis could say. By the following day, however, the situation was looking much more favourable: victory was in sight. As my mother wrote, 'The speed with which the end came took all of us by surprise.'

Late that Monday night I was driving down Ebury Street when I head my mother's voice on the car radio. 'There are reports of white flags flying over Port Stanley,' she said, and I took my hands off the wheel and cheered. Slamming on the brakes and parking, I listened to the rest of the speech, feeling absolutely elated.

My main emotion was relief for my mother. Although I had seen very little of her, images of her leaving Number Ten dressed in black, on her way to give bad news to the House, showed the strain she was under.

Denis wasn't in the gallery for that statement. Instead he waited in the Prime Minister's room and they went back to Downing Street together, saying goodnight to the policemen on the door of Number Ten. 'We went inside and as we walked past the famous bulldog-pose portrait of Winston [Churchill] by Salisbury, hanging in the anteroom to the Cabinet Room, I swear the great man bowed and said, "Well done, girl."'

It was another six months before Denis and Margaret visited the Falklands. The pilgrimage began with a cloak-and-dagger operation straight from the pages of a John le Carré novel.

Because of fears of Argentinian reprisals, the expedition was kept secret. The first Denis knew about it was when a memo was sent up from the Private Office, informing him 'There will be no smoking after Ascension Island'. On an afternoon in early January he and Margaret came out of the front door of Number Ten with their suitcases, as if they were going to Chequers for the weekend. Once clear of Whitehall, the convoy headed for Brize Norton, where a VC-10 was waiting to take them on the first leg of the flight, to Ascension Island. There they transferred to a Hercules with a portacabin inside so that Margaret and Denis could at least travel in some comfort.

> The rest of us had a great fuselage with mattresses on the floor [recalls a civil servant]. We had a sort of dorm and I remember we had Black Forest Gâteau at about midnight and we all thought it was the nearest thing we'd had to a public school midnight feast.
>
> The Hercules didn't have the range, so they did a flight-to-flight refuelling operation. Denis was fascinated ... At another point I heard him say: 'Three hours, thirty-five minutes and thirty seconds to go until I can have a cigarette.'

The welcome was astonishingly warm. It seemed as if the entire population of the Falklands had come out to greet the woman they regarded as their saviour. Union Jacks were waving from every hand and Margaret and Denis felt like royalty. Governor Sir Rex Hunt met them on the runway and ushered them into his famous London taxi for the ride into Port Stanley. Later they transferred to military vehicles and travelled to San Carlos Bay, where 5,000 British troops had landed on 21 May.

> It was a comparatively small bay [Denis recalls]. I don't think from point to point it was more than a mile and a half long. The shore was rocky, although quite flat with no high cliffs. It was overcast and I looked out at the expanse of very cold water and said: 'Dear God, you didn't get the boys to land in this?'
>
> I turned to one of the military personnel who was showing us around and said, 'If this place had been defended ...'
>
> Before I could finish, the chap said: 'But it wasn't very well defended.'
>
> 'Yes, but you didn't bloody well know it then, did you?'
>
> 'No,' he said. 'We didn't.'
>
> I thought it was absolutely terrifying.

It rained when they visited Tumbledown outside Port Stanley, where the Scots Guards had come up against Argentina's finest troops who were well entrenched. The battalion lost nine killed and forty-three wounded in a bloody battle that involved hand-to-hand combat and bayonet charges. At Goose Green Denis was surprised at how flat the terrain was, with no cover for advancing troops.

Remarkably, there were few remaining signs of the conflict. Most of the troops had returned home, although a contingent had stayed and were busy building winter quarters and fortifying the islands. Minefields were fenced off and anti-aircraft guns pointed sky-wards but, as Denis explained, 'the battles weren't like Cassino or Alamein. I saw signs of war but not widespread destruction. There was barely a house spoilt in Port Stanley.'

One afternoon, as they bumped over the ruts and pot-holes, Margaret spied an empty ammunition box, discarded by the side of the road. 'What's that?' she asked Denis.

'It's an ammunition box.'

'What a terrible waste.'

Denis laughed: 'For God's sake, woman, don't get out and count them.'

A reception was held at Government House – one of the grandest occasions ever witnessed on the islands. During the celebration Denis met a couple who had driven for two days to meet the British Prime Minister, bumping along in their Land-Rover at little more than ten miles an hour. Denis was amazed at such devotion, but unsurprised by the condition of the roads. 'That's the thing about the Falklands. We sure as hell didn't go there for the real estate; it's miles and miles of bugger all.'

Not everyone was so polite. When another political delegation visited in the middle of summer – wearing six layers of clothes and still freezing – someone was overheard saying: 'Did grown men really fight over this place.'

It was an inspirational week, rated by Denis among the finest of their foreign trips. He and Margaret were visibly moved during the tour. He estimated that they had probably met three-quarters of the total population: 'Their reaction was fantastic. I remember at one point a Harrier roared overhead and I said, just for something to say – although rather tactlessly, "Those damn things are noisy." A local turned to me and smiled. "That's the sound of freedom."'

SIXTEEN

BACK ON THE HUSTINGS

'Speeches were made and they tried again to get the fire to go. I swear we were there for an hour and a half and I thought to myself, Why doesn't someone go and get some paraffin and get the bloody thing going?'

DENIS THATCHER on
Indira Gandhi's funeral in 1984

THE JOURNEY HOME from the Falklands began with an engagement to impress the environmental lobby: a spot of seal- and penguin-viewing – actually a ruse to keep the departure under wraps. However, the take-off of the Prime Ministerial party could hardly have been missed because at the first attempt it didn't happen.

Denis recalls the Hercules powering down the runway at Port Stanley and then fiercely breaking. From the cockpit came the sounds of 'Abort, abort, abort', before the jet came to a grinding halt. An engine had packed up.

We hung around for about three hours until we got another Hercules, but they didn't have time to put the Portacabin aboard because you couldn't do it in a hurry as it had to be all strapped in. So we were all at the back of this vast thing with two choices: either you could sit in the warm where it was dark and very airless so you started to nod off; or you could sit in the cold – and it really was cold – in the light. We wrapped Margaret up in as many blankets as we could. She was in the light because she wanted to read – I think she read the Franks Inquiry into the war.

The Prime Minister arrived back in Britain to find that sterling was in freefall on the foreign exchange markets. There was no time to catch any sleep or savour the Falklands triumph; she had to make our national currency worth something again.

I dropped into Downing Street that morning and found my

mother in her bedroom with hot rollers in her hair and pages of economic data stacked in front of her on the dressing table. The hairdresser was left squirting hairspray into thin air as Margaret dashed downstairs for an important meeting. For a moment it crossed my mind that she was going to attempt to physically catch sterling as she and it descended!

Denis remained unruffled in the face of financial meltdown; concerned and soothing, he sounded like a retired stockbroker contemplating his portfolio after the Footsie had taken a tumble. 'I reckon I knew more economics than some of the bloody Cabinet, I really do. I know how to calculate the rate of inflation and how quickly your money is halved. It's a very serious thing.'

A fortnight later, on 6 February, a Sunday lunch was held at Chequers in honour of Princess Margaret. Mark and I managed to squeeze onto the end of the guest list, which included Michael Heseltine, Norman Tebbit, Cecil Parkinson and their respective wives, along with Admiral Sir John Fieldhouse and Lady Fieldhouse, Antony Jay (the writer of Margaret's favourite TV programme, 'Yes Minister') and Professor Alan (later Sir Alan) Walters, the Prime Minister's economic adviser.

Chequers looked wonderful, with roaring fires in the grates and elaborate flower arrangements on every surface. Margaret had worked on her boxes in the study during the morning and came out to greet Princess Margaret when she arrived. The guests were presented in the Hawtrey Room and then the PM took her guest of honour on a tour of the house.

During lunch Princess Margaret sat between the Prime Minister and Michael Heseltine and, as we tucked into trout, roast saddle of lamb, fruit salad and cheese, the conversation turned to 'Yes Minister' and then to *Anyone for Denis*. The Princess declared that she wouldn't have *Private Eye* in her house.

We adjourned for coffee in the Long Library upstairs before Princess Margaret departed. Immediately, the atmosphere changed and the serious discussion began about election timing. The Prime Minister wanted an 'attack team' to counter what happened in the previous election when, in the middle week, 'we were very much on the defensive'.

It was fascinating to hear them talk about keeping their options open 'in case we go early', or the 'need to get regional policy sorted out', or the possibility of 'the Lords dragging their feet on the Boundary case', whatever that was. Margaret was in an ebullient mood, and teased Norman about his flat in the Barbican, saying what a cushy life bankers had – high pay, expense accounts and subsidized mortgages.

Afterwards, alone, she became somewhat maudlin: 'When I'm a private person – if we lose – I've had the best four years of one's life. You do think, perhaps I won't be here [Chequers] again.'

Suddenly she snapped out of it and became the confident, consummate politician again, mentally running through all the factors which would decide the timing of the general election:' 'You don't know what it will be like in the future. You can only make up your mind on what it's like now.' And then, as if to dispel any lingering doubts, she declared, 'I fully expect to do another term.'

Since the Falklands War her popularity had soared, and by June 1983 the Tories were thirteen points ahead of Labour in the opinion polls. Although unemployment was still high, inflation had fallen to 4 per cent – the lowest since the 1960s. Despite these positive signs. Margaret took nothing for granted and refused to be rushed into a decision.

Since returning from Australia, I'd been freelancing and working for the *Daily Telegraph*. In early April I flew back to Australia to do a series of stories, including a piece on the proposed damming for hydro-electric power of the Gordon river in Tasmania, which would drown acres of irreplaceable rainforest. On 10 May at 12.40 a.m. Margaret Willes of Sidgwick & Jackson rang me in Hobart to tell me: 'Your mother has just announced that the election is on 9 June.'

Having agreed to write a diary of daily life in Downing Street during the election, I was 12,000 miles away when the starting gun fired. I'd spoken to my mother only a few hours earlier and, typically, she'd mentioned nothing about it. I spoke to her again the next morning. 'I don't know if you've heard . . .' she said.

'Yes. Why now?'

She talked about the uncertainty and speculation being damaging and preventing international investment, which is probably exactly what she said in every interview she gave over the next twenty-four hours.

I arrived back on 13 May. On the Tube home to Chelsea I read in the paper that the latest opinion poll gave the Tories a healthy 21 per cent lead. I drove to Chequers where I found Denis on his improvised pitch-and-putt.

He was composure himself: swing-o-meters, floating voters, slogans, spin doctors and manifestos couldn't distract him from trying to perfect his short game. He knew that soon enough his regular golfing forays would be replaced with long days on planes, trains, buses and cars as he worked 'the other side of the street' (although he did manage to skive off to Scotney to squeeze in a few holes before the ordeal ahead).

We chatted about the timing of the election. I was surprised Margaret had chosen to go early. Denis thumped another wedge across the garden and said, 'I became a Juner after the horses had bolted with the carriages.' Translated, this meant that the speculation had made it virtually impossible to choose any other time.

Over afternoon tea we discussed mundane details, such as hair appointments during the campaign, how the flat would function and the food and drink arrangements. Later, when Margaret's agent Andrew Thomson and the chairman of Finchley Conservative Association, Ron Thurlow, arrived for dinner, the talk shifted to leaflets, budgets, canvassing and her election address.

One of my jobs as an 'under-dogsbody' during the election was to be the Prime Minister's fourth reserve wardrobe mistress, which meant memorizing which blouse went under which suit, which clothes were best for the telly and which shoes were used for speechmaking, walkabouts and rallies.

Although it was Denis's tenth election campaign, counting the two in Dartford, he had never got used to them and approached each one with a mixture of loathing and loyalty. 'Why we have to go through this carry-on for three bloody weeks is beyond me,' he said. 'It's either "Hello, it's me again," or "Goodbye."'

He used to tip up at the morning press conference at Conservative Central Office and stand at the back, unable to resist telling people what he thought of some of the journalists' lines of enquiry. 'What a damn silly question,' he'd mutter impatiently.

His mood didn't improve when the first electioneering foray into the countryside began with a farcical mix-up at Gatwick, where the chartered BAC 1-11 was waiting to fly the Prime Minister and her entourage to the West Country. Margaret and Denis had just settled down into their seats when they were told that airport security had failed to allow the stills photographers onto the tarmac; could they please get off the plane and pretend to get back on again.

The campaign bus was waiting for us at St Mawgan in Cornwall, and this mobile office transferred us to Padstow, a pretty fishing village. Margaret plunged into the waiting mêlée, shaking hands, asking questions, answering them, accepting good wishes. This scene was repeated again and again over the next few weeks and each time I noticed that Denis was always the last person off the bus, thus avoiding the crush.

During one particularly fierce media ruck on Dover promenade, I skirted around the back and found Denis looking like a rugby referee about to send both sides off. 'I though you were in the middle,' I said.

'No way; there's neither pleasure nor profit in this,' he retorted.

It seemed that words were irrelevant in this campaign, judging by the number of photo opportunities that were convened: Margaret was pictured in green wellies, ankle-deep in Cornish cow manure, in the back of a horse box in Norfolk, or dishing out fish and chips at a restaurant in Leeds.

One Saturday morning she strolled into a supermarket in Finchley High Street and created absolute mayhem. Photographers clambered onto freezers and shelves, snapping away while Margaret filled a trolley with provisions. Unfortunately, she was totally out of practice and had no idea what we needed in the flat. While she was grabbing Lymeswold, ox tongue, light bulbs and pâté, I dashed round behind her and collected far more vital supplies like loo paper and instant coffee. As the items were totted up by the cashier, Margaret suddenly realized that she had no money. 'Carol, please come and pay,' she said, before sweeping off and taking the crush with her.

Denis says the '83 campaign was the best run and happiest he can remember and is eternally grateful to Cecil Parkinson, the Party Chairman, who masterminded it. He would joke to Cecil that he wouldn't do his job 'for all the tea in China'.

Looking back with the benefit of years of hindsight, Cecil believes the 1979 campaign was less effective because 'I felt they worked Margaret too hard without getting full benefit from it. In '83 we deliberately took the pressure off so we could get good stuff in the can for television early and have her back in the flat in Number Ten by 7.30 p.m. I think what Denis had resented about campaigns was seeing Margaret getting absolutely exhausted.'

Although appreciative of the changes, Denis was never likely to enjoy electioneering. 'I was always rather pleased when they were over,' he says. 'I think it is the business of having to meet masses of people every single day and it isn't everyone who wants to tell you how they feel that talks sense.'

The Labour Party fought the worst campaign in its history with a left-wing manifesto that advocated unilateral disarmament, withdrawal from the EEC and wholesale nationalization. In a speech at Cardiff City Hall on 25 May, Margaret said of the proposals: 'I'm told that a member of Labour's Shadow Cabinet described it as "the longest suicide note ever penned". I can tell you this: if the British people were to put their signature to it, it would be a suicide note for Britain too.'

At each speech Denis stuck to his script with a throaty, 'Here! Here!' at precisely the right moment, geeing up the audience to applaud. When Margaret fretted over a speech, he told her, 'Look, Love, it'll be fine,' and was the first to congratulate her 'on a brilliant show' when a television interview went well. Others had moments of nerves; never Denis.

On the bank holiday weekend Margaret flew to Williamsburg, Virginia, for President Reagan's Seven-Nation Summit to discuss international economics and arms control talks with the Soviets. Meanwhile Denis headed off to Scotney for a few days of golf –

one of his few breaks, although I did catch him one evening in a hotel room in Fleetwood, Lancashire, watching the All Blacks versus the British Lions only minutes before another rally.

The campaign was going well, with the Conservative Party lead growing and the Labour Leader Michael Foot increasingly regarded as an electoral liability. Nor did voters think much of Roy Jenkins, Leader of the Alliance. Both he and Foot became phantom figures for the rest of the campaign, as Denis (later Lord) Healey and David (later Sir David) Steel were given a higher profile.

Criss-crossing the country on a whistle-stop tour, Denis rarely lost his patience, although after one walkabout at Birmingham's National Exhibition Centre he put his foot down. He and Margaret had battled through the crowds and taken their seats in the campaign bus, when someone passed in two pieces of paper with a request for autographs. My mother began scribbling, but Denis knew the floodgates would open. 'Oh, for God's sake. Come on, Love, no,' he said. 'We either sign autographs or meet people; today we're meeting people.'

After a visit to a confectionary factory in a marginal London seat, Frank Johnson wrote in *The Times*: 'Meanwhile, Mr Denis Thatcher, whose mastery of the factory-visit conversation is now the equal of the Duke of Edinburgh's, could be heard in the background working away at the firm's executives: "Do you buy your almonds from the almond people overseas? . . . I see, yes . . . you make the cherries, do you?"'

Denis avoided posing for photographs unless it was absolutely necessary, although at the Youth Rally at Wembley I persuaded him to wave an enormous foam rubber glove in the shape of a thumbs-up sign with MAGGIE'S A WINNER written across it. 'I'll look even more bloody silly than usual,' he protested. The resulting photograph appeared in most of the national dailies and thirty-five provincial newspapers.

On polling day Margaret and Denis voted in Westminster. By 7.30 a.m. they were back at the flat where the Prime Minister sat down to her first cooked breakfast of the campaign – poached egg on toast.

Denis admitted to being 'bloody bushed'. He had been more

widely recognized and more closely scrutinized than in any previous campaign – although he thought attempts to make him out to be a second Duke of Edinburgh were a 'total absurdity'.

The count in Finchley resembled a bizarre fancy dress party, starring Screaming Lord Sutch of the Official Monster Raving Loony Party attired in leopardskin, lurex and a scarlet top hat. Other candidates included Joseph Noonan (Ban Every Licensing Law), Benjamin Collingham Wedmore (Belgrano Bloodhunger), and Anthony Peter Whitehead (Law and Order in Gotham City).

The national exit polls forecast a Conservative majority of 116 seats and at 2.20 a.m. ITN flashed up a note saying the Tories needed only 15 more seats for the magic winning total of 326. Shortly afterwards, the result at Finchley was announced – Margaret had upped her majority by 1,436 and the national swing was indicating a three-figure majority in the House of Commons.

Then Margaret and Denis took the prime ministerial car down the Finchley Road past Lord's Cricket Ground to Conservative Central Office. Waving from a window to the cheering crowd in Smith Square, they made their bows alongside Cecil Parkinson.

It was getting light by the time they walked through the door of Ten Downing Street. The cleaners were wrestling with vacuum cleaners up by the Cabinet Room and Peter Taylor was in the hall. 'Welcome home,' he said – the two words my mother had been most anxious to hear for the last three weeks.

'Good night,' she smiled as the lift doors closed. The first day of her second term as PM had begun.

Denis radiated pride and admiration for her. According to Cecil Parkinson, 'The thing that he really admired was she hadn't been born with a silver spoon in her mouth. She had achieved a lot and he loved her and he was very proud of her. They weren't competitors – nothing would have made him want to be a politician – but Margaret wasn't a threat to him in his world and he was very proud of her in hers.'

Both my parents were saddened when Cecil resigned over his affair with his secretary Sara Keays during the Conservative Party Conference in Blackpool in October.

It was very early in the morning [recalls Denis]. Cecil resigned sitting on the settee in our suite in Blackpool and Margaret said to him, 'I'm very very unhappy but you've got no choice but to get out ... otherwise the press will be at you.' He agreed. Then he mentioned that he was due to open the new Blackpool heliport and unveil a commemorative plaque. Margaret said, 'Never mind that, Denis will go and do it.'

I did. I pulled the string and it had a brass plaque underneath which read, 'Opened by the Rt Hon. Cecil Parkinson'.

The next morning's newspapers carried a photograph of the plaque being unscrewed and taken away after the opening.

Denis made no comment on the scandal or the political demise of his good friend beyond saying, 'It would be easier if some members of the Tory Party could keep their flies buttoned up.'

The US invasion of Grenada, an island in the eastern Caribbean, on 25 October 1983 was another classic example of the Thatcher maxim, 'the unexpected always happens'. A pro-Soviet military coup had overthrown the island's government six days earlier, executing the Prime Minister and five of his closest supporters.

Margaret was hosting a reception at Downing Street when President Reagan rang to say he was seriously considering US military intervention. She was opposed and told him so, but later that evening he rang again to inform her that the invasion was already under way. She was dismayed and felt utterly let down, but most of all angry. It placed her in the embarrassing position of having to explain how a member of the Commonwealth had been invaded by our closest ally.

Denis heard one half of the telephone call. 'She didn't half tick him [Reagan] off on the telephone. "You have invaded the Queen's territory and you didn't even say a word to me," she said to him, very upset. I think that Reagan was a bit shocked. There was nothing gentle about her tone – and not much diplomacy either. He got a prime ticking off. I think his reasons were good enough, but to invade British territory without a by your leave or without any notice was wrong.'

At the New Delhi CHOGM several days later Margaret was

given a rough ride and had few friends among the Caribbean and African leaders. The US faced widespread condemnation, but Margaret carefully toned down her public criticism.

The trip to India was one Denis could have lived without, particularly as he was expected to troop along behind the wives of other leaders – many of them buxom African ladies in very elaborate costumes and flowing robes. One of the Prime Minister's staff sympathized with him: 'There was Denis bringing up the rear in a restrained tropical weight suit. It must have been horrific for him – stiff upper lip and all that – but he did it.'

The summit retreat was at Taj Holiday Village in Goa, where all the VIPs were housed in small separate chalets. To Denis's chagrin their immediate neighbour was Sir Sonny Ramphal (Commonwealth Secretary-General from 1975 to 1990). The administration was terrible: on the first night the telephone rang in their bedroom at half past four in the morning and a cheerful little Indian voice piped up, 'Just testing.' The lights would regularly fail, and when this happened for the umpteenth time, Denis strode out onto the balcony and declared in a stentorian voice, 'This place is very high on the buggeration factor.'

The host for the Delhi CHOGM was Prime Minister Indira Gandhi, and from the outset it was obvious that she and Denis didn't quite see eye to eye. Afterwards he declared, 'She didn't just have a chip on one shoulder; she had a chip on both.' Apparently, she had once sat next to him and launched into a long lecture on how badly she thought the British had administered India during the Raj. Eventually, it became too much for Denis, who pulled himself up to his full patriotic height and told her, 'Well, Ma'am, we did build the railways for you and without them India wouldn't be what it is today.'

Later he was also caught out during one of those inexplicable lulls in the babble of a cocktail party at Number Ten, when he was heard to put the question to several of the Commonwealth personnel: 'Who do you think is worse, Sonny bloody Ramphal or Ma sodding Gandhi?'

I met Mrs Gandhi on my mother's visit to Delhi in April 1981. At dinner I sat next to her son Rajiv and, as I looked across to where Margaret and Indira were chatting, I remarked to him: 'I would never go into politics, would you?'

'No, I'm quite happy flying planes,' said Rajiv, who was then a pilot for Air India.

Years later the conversation came back to me when he – like his mother – was assassinated while in power on 21 May 1991.

Indira Gandhi was killed by two of her Sikh bodyguards on 31 October 1984. Her death came only a fortnight after the Brighton Bombing, which so nearly took my parents' lives. When Margaret heard the news she remembered that Indira had been one of the first foreign leaders to send her a message after the bombing.

Margaret and Denis boarded the VC-10 to go to the funeral in New Delhi, giving a 'lift' to other VIP guests, such as Opposition leaders James Callaghan and David Steel. Princess Anne was already in India, visiting various Save the Children Fund projects. She would represent the Queen at the funeral.

Upon arriving in Delhi, the Prime Ministerial party was taken to inspect the funeral bier. 'There she was, all spread out,' recalls Denis. '. . . the most gory bit was a protocol official informing the Prime Minister: "You're not to be surprised when there's a loud crack of explosion when the skull pops." Your mother went bright green and I thought, "Oh God."'

The party stayed in the British High Commissioner's white-washed residence, designed by Sir Herbert Baker and built in 1917. It's an oasis of comfortably grand Britishness, with open fireplaces, chintzy decor, chandeliers, and hunting scenes on the walls. In the guest suites the only clue that you're not in the Home Counties is a note with laundry instructions and fire drill and the injunction: 'Please do not leave your balcony doors open at night as we are sometimes visited by monkeys.'

The cremation took place on 3 November on the banks of the soupy Yamuna river. Mahatma Gandhi had been cremated at nearby Raj Ghat after his assassination in 1948. The river served as a useful demarcation line between Hindu mourners on one side and Sikhs massing on the other and one could sense the tension in the solemn and shocked atmosphere.

With such a huge crowd and so many foreign dignitaries,

ABOVE Mark holds forth on getting lost in the Sahara. The misadventure spawned many jokes but Denis was not amused

LEFT Denis and Margaret in the Falklands in January 1983. With the trauma of war over, the military historian in Denis was fascinated by tours of the battlefields

RIGHT Public Denis: meeting and greeting

BELOW Private Denis: Sunday papers and a snooze in his favourite armchair at Chequers

FOOT I asked Mac to put Mark and me in as portraits when I gave this cartoon to my parents for Christmas

BELOW An early cartoon pictures a domesticated Denis armed with a tea towel. Later gin and golf became his trademarks

SUNDAY EXTRA

" What we have to ask our-selves is : ' Would you be a success as a Prime Minister's husband ? ' "

'Look dear, if it will ease the burden a little I'm quite happy to go without Christmas pudding this year'

A disapproving PM watches Denis down a beer in one

'It's about the reshuffle, Mr Thatcher, Sir – I'm afraid I've got some rather bad news …'

A dutiful round of golf with President Bush in Bermuda, despite gales and a tropical downpour. 'The worst game of golf I ever played'

However busy his schedule, Denis always tried to make time for golf – even if he had no time to change into his golf kit

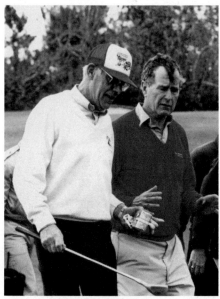

'No heels on the green, please caddie'

Politicians shake hands for the camera but Denis could enjoy a laugh with first ladies Nancy Reagan (LEFT), Barbara Bush (BELOW) and Raisa Gorbachev (BOTTOM)

Denis and his junior fans: RIGHT signing autographs, BELOW canvassing the next generation of voters

and RIGHT making a guest appearance as grandfather

LEFT Denis and Margaret at Chequers in the early days, and BELOW just before leaving in November 1990. They both adored the house and saying goodbye to it was one of the hardest parts of leaving office

Still 'Dear Bill': Denis surrounded by his family at his 80th birthday party (from left to right, Mark's wife Diane, Denis, me, Margaret and Mark). We had a cake made of the infamous *Private Eye* cover featuring him characteristically close to alcohol, clutching a Balthazar of champagne

organization was a nightmare. The top brass went by car to the velodrome, where they transferred to buses. The ensuing traffic jam of VIPs' cars, barely moving at walking pace, was surrounded by nervous security guards anxious to avoid another assassination.

Soon the buses were crowded and at least one member of the British High Commission party remembers watching more and more guests pile on board: 'I contemplated that death from crushing – by myriad heads of state – might look novel on one's death certificate.'

Denis's rickety bus was making slow progress through densely packed streets.

Down we go to this sports ground, which must have been about thirty acres, in the middle of which was the pile of whatnot [wood]. Then the funeral cortège comes in and they take the bier and put it on top of the wood and they then start to light the fire. We were about 100 yards away out in the sun and it was as hot as hell. People sort of walked around the bier and the bloody fire wouldn't go. And then they start to throw ghee on it – melted butter to you and me. Poor Rajiv got half a bucket of ghee thrown over him accidentally and it was an absolute bloody shambles.

Speeches were made and they tried again to get the fire to go. I swear we were there for an hour and a half and I thought to myself, Why doesn't someone go and get some paraffin and get the bloody thing going? The poor old girl wouldn't burn. Then suddenly they did get the fire going and that was the end of it and we left as it was spluttering away.

I was standing next to Jim Callaghan, who'd been to some of these funeral affairs before and he indicated that it was time to break for the buses so we all buggered off. The top brass returned to their cars. Anyway, we found our jalopy and to get out of the sports ground onto the road we had to negotiate a steepish slope. It was pretty much a one in six. We were the second bus and the first one got right to the top. Our bus stalled and we slid back a bit, so we were halfway up this bloody slope, then the driver has to start his jalopy on the slope with the guard of honour presenting arms. He slips back again, so there we were, going up three feet and slipping back six. Finally someone had a rush of blood to the head and said to the guard of honour, 'Someone had better push this up.'

The guard then put all their rifles down on the ground, piled behind, and they shoved the bloody thing up. It was shambolic: what with not being able to burn the body and not being able to get out of the place.

That evening we had a dinner party at the High Commission. Princess Anne was there. It was pretty hilarious because the drink came round and round and one or two people got a bit sloshed – including me.

SEVENTEEN

EVERY MINUTE IS PRECIOUS

'You have a big problem and I have a small one. If I
take my hand off this bird it'll fly away. I want you
to take it away, kill it and cook it.'

DENIS THATCHER to a waiter at a London hotel

IF MARGARET HAD IT IN MIND to reform the trade union movement upon reaching Downing Street, Denis would have favoured
outright abolition. He thought that the notorious restrictive prac-
tices they were inflicting on the economy were signing Britain's
death warrant.

At Atlas he had been a small employer and had experienced their
destructive power at first hand.

> I've never been a member of a trade union but I had to deal with
> them a bit; we had some people who were members of the Transport
> and General. I remember on one occasion the works manager fired
> somebody who was a shop steward and afterwards I said to him,
> 'Over the next forty-eight hours you're going to have to learn what
> humble pie tastes like.'
> 'Why?' he asked.
> 'Because we're going to have to take him back.'
> 'No, I absolutely refuse,' he said.
> 'Well, I think you'll find that we're in a jam.'
> The following morning, a Thursday, and the buggers were all on
> strike, sitting in Fraser Road outside the works. I waved to them as
> I drove by. Then the trade union rep turned up and said that they
> were going to stay out until this chap was reinstated. I had no choice.
> I thought about the works manager and said: 'All right, but let's
> save his face a bit, can we? This chap can come back next Monday
> morning.' The trade union rep said, 'I'll buy that.'
> The following day they all came back to work, but it taught
> me to be bloody careful when handling trade unions ... to make
> absolutely sure you know what you're doing.

The damaging three-month steel strike in 1980 was the Thatcher government's first big test in dealing with trade union might, but the Prime Minister was under no illusions: she knew that a confrontation with the miners was almost inevitable. The 1973–4 strike had precipitated the collapse of Ted Heath's government and lent credence to the opinion that the National Union of Miners had the power to make or break British governments.

Following an averted coal strike in 1981, Nigel (later Lord) Lawson, then Secretary of State for Energy, had steadily built up stocks of coal to enable the country to endure a national coal strike. The initial rumbling began in October 1983, when an NUM delegate conference voted for a ban on overtime in protest at the National Coal Board's 5.2 per cent pay offer and planned pit closures.

Ian (later Sir Ian) MacGregor, who had been Chairman of the British Steel Corporation in the wake of the steel strike, was now in charge of the NCB: he was formulating plans to bring the coal industry back to break-even point by reducing the workforce.

This put him on a collision course with Arthur Scargill, President of the NUM, and the confrontation triggered a national coal strike on 18 March 1984. Like most decent citizens in this country, Denis was appalled by the violence on the picket lines. Some of the most horrifying scenes were at the Orgreave coking plant, where 5,000 pickets tried to prevent coke convoys reaching the Scunthorpe steelworks. Nearly seventy people were hurt as bricks, missiles and darts rained down.

Denis was proud of his good friend Arthur Rees, a former Welsh rugby international and the chief constable of Staffordshire, whose men were attacked by the mob. 'Reece showed what leadership is,' he recalls.

I had no doubt that Margaret would eventually see off the miners but the strike dragged on for a year – a long time. She was totally determined. The general view was 'We'll beat the buggers,' and so she did. The miners brought down Heath's government and she wasn't going to have it happen twice . . .

Margaret saw the strike coming and we put coal stocks everywhere – an enormous quantity stockpiling. She also had to make sure that the electric generating union didn't go on strike and, thankfully, they didn't.

Denis believes the NUM ruined the mining industry. The damage was permanent: some pits had deteriorated so much they never reopened, and major customers looked elsewhere for their coal supplies. 'I don't think it did the stock market any good either,' he adds.

The strike ended almost exactly a year after it began. On the steps of Number Ten Margaret was asked if anyone had won. 'If anyone has won, it has been the miners who stayed at work, the dockers who stayed at work, the power workers who stayed at work, the railwaymen who stayed at work, the managers who stayed at work . . . all those people who kept the wheels of Britain turning . . .'

Denis greeted the end with relief and satisfaction. 'I think the great unsung heroes were the chaps at the top of the Central Electricity Generating Board because they managed to keep the power stations going.'

Denis also admired the courage of media bosses Rupert Murdoch and Eddie Shah, 'the first to say to the unions, "You're not going to run my business."' Both fought long battles in the mid-1980s to break the print unions and introduce new technology. Denis met Murdoch at Chequers: 'He is a quietly spoken man and very impressive.'

The new friends that Denis made as consort were almost invariably in industry or finance – people like Sir Denys Henderson, the chairman of ICI (1987–95), and Lord King, the chairman of British Airways (1981–93), who turned the airline around by slimming it down, improving service and giving the employees a stake in its success.

'A mighty man, John King, and a very charming chap. His success was that he handled the staff, which was monstrously overmanned. He got it fit and slowly started to make profits. He was also quite ruthless about where he bought his aeroplanes and when he believed they were sub-standard; he faced up to the government and said: 'These bloody things are no good to me." He knew where he was going and put some real management into British Airways.'

Denis loves telling the story of his little dig at John King at a lunch at Chequers one weekend. Denis remarked that he hadn't totally enjoyed his ride in John King's supersonic flagship, saying, 'The problem with Concorde is that the damn thing vibrates and it's very noisy. It's not at all comfortable, John.'

'Yes,' mused John King, unperturbed, 'but it doesn't last long.'

British Airways was an example of Margaret's grand vision of share-owning popular capitalism in Britain. British Telecom was the first state-owned industry to be sold off in November 1984. Two million people bought shares, half of them first-time shareholders. British Gas was privatized in 1986, followed by the water and electricity supply industries.

Denis was a keen advocate of the sell-offs. The strike-ridden, debt-laden and enormously wasteful nationalized industries were galling to a businessman who prided himself on what he had managed to do with a small family-owned company.

In October 1984 I was on assignment in South Korea, writing for the *Daily Telegraph*, when I called Number Ten to leave a message wishing my mother good luck in her speech to the Conservative Party Conference in Brighton that morning, and happy birthday for the following day, 13 October.

I got through to Caroline in the Private Office. 'I am sorry to give you bad news when you're so far away,' she began, 'but there's been a bomb in Brighton. Both your parents are all right and your mother is going to give her speech at the conference this morning.' She went on to tell me that Norman Tebbit was being dug out of the rubble and that several people had been killed.

Looking back, I think it was rather insensitive of me not to have been more concerned. I'd been away in the Far East for eighteen days and, like my father, rarely bothered to lift the phone to speak to the family when I was abroad. Having grown up in a political household, I had learnt not to worry about things you couldn't do anything about.

The following morning an English-edition Korean paper had a

'Thatcher Survives Assassination Attempt' report on the front page. Unable to change my ticket, I was forced to stick to my itinerary and fly back on Sunday morning. By the time I arrived at Heathrow I felt as if I was the only person who didn't know, minute by minute, what had happened.

I decided to hire a car and drive to Chequers rather than go home first. It was an Indian summer day with a blue blue sky. I was told that the Prime Minister had just come back from church and was out on the terrace. She was calm, but seemed still shaken as she said to me, 'This is the day I was not meant to see.'

Denis internalized his shock, and friends who saw him the following week remember a quieter, subdued and obviously shaken man. This was the only time during the Number Ten years that he didn't reply in his own hand to the letters he received from friends and concerned wellwishers. He had a letter printed which thanked people for their kind words about his and Margaret's well-being and – although, not a religious man – he included the line, 'I like to think God had a hand in it.'

Denis rarely shows his emotions, and neither he nor Margaret is inclined to buy each other little gifts or mementos. But after the near-miss at Brighton, he bought her a watch and wrote, in a rare note to her, 'Every minute is precious.'

Margaret gave me a full factual rundown of what had happened at the Grand Hotel. She had been in her suite working on her conference speech at about 2.40 a.m. Denis was asleep in an adjoining bedroom.

Robin (later Sir Robin) Butler, her principal private secretary, had handed her some papers and asked, 'Can I give you this to look at overnight and you can tell me by breakfast what you want done.'

> Margaret was looking at this piece of paper and a large thud shook the room and, after a few seconds' silence, another blast. Plaster fell from the ceiling. I knew it was a bomb. I thought a car had exploded outside; I didn't realise the bomb was actually above us. Glass from the window was strewn over the carpet and part of the building collapsed.
>
> Before I could stop her, she said, 'I must see if Denis is all right.'

She opened the door and plunged into the gloom. By now, the sound of falling masonry was deafening.

To my great relief, within a few minutes she came out and Denis appeared. It touched me because it was one of those moments where there could be no play-acting and her first thought was, 'I must make sure Denis isn't buried,' not knowing what might have been happening in that room.

The bathroom in the suite had collapsed and Denis recalls: 'I've never seen so much glass in my life.' He defied advice not to go back into the bedroom, declaring, 'Do be reasonable; I can't go around in my pyjamas.' He pulled on a pair of grey flannel trousers and left the hotel, inexplicably clutching a spare pair of shoes.

There was confusion but no panic. Margaret comforted one of her shaken secretaries. 'Don't worry, dear, it's only a bomb,' she said, without any notion of how serious it was. Outwardly calm, the only clue that the Prime Minister was rattled was her briefcase, which she had left beside the armchair she'd been sitting in. Normally she never moved anywhere without it.

Bob Kingston was out on a roof standing in a pile of broken glass as guests on the upper floors filed down the fire escape. After some delay firemen finally led Margaret and Denis out through a back entrance. A whole section of the Grand Hotel had collapsed and the emergency services were hunting for those trapped.

My parents were driven to Brighton police station, where Denis saw Charles Price, the American Ambassador, padding around in his stockinged feet. He gave him his spare pair of shoes, which were later returned to Number Ten with a thank-you note.

Margaret and Denis spent what was left of the night at Lewes Police College. Only when they turned on the breakfast news did they discover the true horror of what had happened and how close to death they had been. Roberta Wakeham, the wife of the Chief Whip, and Anthony Berry, MP, were dead. Norman Tebbit had been pulled, badly injured, from the rubble and his wife Margaret lay paralysed from the neck down.

The Prime Minister was determined that the Party Conference would go on and at 9.30 a.m. she walked onto the platform to a colossal ovation. She told delegates that the bombing 'was an attempt not only to disrupt and terminate our conference. It was an attempt to cripple Her Majesty's democratically elected government. That is the scale of the outrage in which we have all shared. And the fact that we are gathered here now, shocked but composed and determined, is a sign not only that this attack has failed, but that all attempts to destroy democracy by terrorism will fail.'

The Brighton bombing made headlines around the world and focused attention once again on the Irish dilemma. Less than a year earlier, on 17 December 1983, an IRA car bomb had torn through Harrods, killing five people, including two police officers.

We were at a carol concert at the Festival Hall [Denis remembers], and Bob [Kingston, one of the detectives] came up and said there'd been a bomb. We left the concert halfway through and went straight to Harrods. The place was knee-deep in glass and two of the bodies were still in their body bags. They hadn't removed them. There was glass all over the place. I'd never seen anything like it in my life.

The following day there were pressmen in Downing Street and I came back carrying Harrods' bags. They shouted at me and I shouted back, 'No murdering Irishman is going to stop me doing my Christmas shopping at Harrods. I've done it for thirty years.'

Unfortunately, his next mailbag was crammed with letters explaining that those living on the other side of the Irish Sea were not all 'murdering Irishmen'.

Denis took the view that there had been problems in Ireland for 100 years and there probably would be for another 100. The British troops and those living in Northern Ireland faced terrorism every day of their lives and didn't get enough support. He persuaded Margaret to take regular morale-raising trips to the Republic, including two on different Christmas Eves. They did walkabouts in shopping centres and visited the troops.

After the loss of Airey Neave in 1979 and then the deaths in Brighton, they had every reason to fear for their safety, but they refused to be cowed by 'common criminals'.

On Sunday 16 December 1984 my parents played host at Chequers to Mikhail Gorbachev and his wife Raisa. Word had preceded the Soviet Leader-in-waiting that he was quite different to any of his predecessors, and the chemistry between him and Margaret was instantaneous.

Neither ate much of the lunch of fish, roast beef and oranges in caramel as they sparred over the merits of their respective political philosophies and grew impatient with interpreters who were always a sentence behind.

After lunch Margaret and Mikhail continued talking while Denis introduced Raisa to the Long Library, where she browsed among volumes of English classics, showing such interest that, on a subsequent visit to Moscow, Margaret presented her with a first edition of Thackeray's *Vanity Fair*.

Some official lunches are starchy, others are tedious, but Denis quickly twigged that this one was different.

I'll never forget the lunch. It was extraordinary. This was something that the world had never seen – one of the lunches that change history. At least, I was acute enough to see it that way, although he [Gorbachev] wasn't the headman yet. At the time one doesn't say that it is 'history in the making', but I realized in my dim-witted way that this was something pretty special.

Gorbachev fell in love with her [Margaret] and I like to think that Raisa got on with me. She's a nice lady and much later, after we had been kicked out, Gorbachev came to see John Major at Number Ten and we were invited as guests. I walked in and Raisa opened her arms to me. We got on very well.

Later Raisa told me her memories of that first lunch.

The huge great fire in the hall and browsing through the library with your father, and also a discussion with Michael Jopling [Secretary of State for Agriculture] about whether your country or mine had the most recipes for potatoes.

She explained that she and Jopling then struck up a correspondence, swapping recipes until one of them admitted defeat.

I wasn't at the lunch but later wrote a piece for *Life* magazine, quoting Margaret:

I have never talked to any other Soviet leader at all like him. In the past, exchanges were very formal. They had statements typed out, they read them, and they did not answer questions which you put to them directly, if at all. It was clear to me from the first moment that

Mr Gorbachev was from a very different generation of politicians.

What was most noticeable was his tremendous self-confidence. It was a quite different experience talking to him. You don't normally enter into such a frank and outspoken debate with someone you are meeting for the first time. But we did, right from the beginning. Mr Gorbachev is a man of tremendous energy and courage. He has embarked on something historic and I just feel that the time is right for it to have a considerable measure of success . . .

Mr Gorbachev has a mischievous sense of humour and at a dinner in the Kremlin in 1991 he asked Margaret, who had brought Mark on a previous trip: 'Why hasn't Mark come this time? We've got lots of deserts for him to get lost in.'

He also joked about having read somewhere that Margaret cooked fried eggs for Denis every morning.

Their affection wasn't manufactured. After one meeting in the Gorbachev Foundation office in Moscow in 1993, my mother gave him a case of House of Lords whisky as a gift, knowing he was partial to a drop. His face lit up and he gave her a spontaneous hug.

December 1985 saw another historic occasion for Denis and Margaret – one of the most memorable evenings of their stint at Ten Downing Street. They hosted a dinner to celebrate the 250th anniversary of the house being the official home of the Prime Minister.

In addition to the Queen and Prince Philip, the guest list included a direct descendant of every incumbent of the house since Asquith, and every living former Prime Minister. Lady Olwen Carey Evans, last surviving daughter of Lloyd George; Mrs Sheila Lockhead, Ramsay MacDonald's daughter; Mrs Dorothy Lloyd, Neville Chamberlain's daughter; Lady Soames, Sir Winston Churchill's daughter; and Earl Attlee, the son of Clement Attlee were there.

Although I wasn't invited, I managed to gatecrash the pre-dinner drinks. I went straight up to the flat via the lift and was greeted by Joy Robilliard hopping from one foot to another.

'You're cutting it a bit fine,' she said, tapping her wristwatch.

'Sorry.'

'I've got some good news – you're in for the dinner. You're Mrs David Steel; she can't get down from Scotland.'

The State Dining Room looked magnificent – a far cry from Margaret's first official dinner for Helmut Schmidt. Eight enormous gold candelabra lit up the horseshoe-shaped table, which was dotted with displays of pink carnations and orchids. It was photographed and used on the Prime Minister's Christmas card that year.

The Queen's speech was delightful: she quipped that by this stage in her father's reign he'd been a guest at Number Ten far more often. 'I was beginning to wonder what I'd done wrong!'

Afterwards, over coffee in the Pillared Room, I chatted to Harold and Mary Wilson. In a room full of women wearing brand-new evening dresses, Mrs Wilson took justifiable pride in her own choice – the very same dress she had worn the last time the Queen came to dinner in Number Ten, for her husband's resignation dinner in 1976.

Many of the elderly guests had spent some of their childhood in the house and grew moist-eyed as the memories came flooding back. Dorothy Chamberlain had attended her father's dinner for King George VI and Queen Elizabeth in 1939. 'It was very formal – white tie and decorations and lots of tiaras. The King and Queen had to have their own chairs. Two beautiful red velvet ones were brought over from Buckingham Palace, and because the Queen was so small there was a matching footstool for her to rest her tiny legs on.'

Lady Olwen, a marvellously extrovert ninety-three-year-old, related how Lloyd George had insisted on her demonstrating the culinary skills she'd just learnt on a cooking course by preparing a dinner. The kitchen staff were forbidden to help. 'I thought the meat looked a bit rare and when I went up to join them for coffee, father had penned a verse: "Now the meal is over we sigh with longing grief for the mealie tatties and the bloody beef."'

Lloyd George did it again when he wanted to see what his daughter had learnt from a language course in France. 'He got me in to translate his meeting with the French Munitions Minister. I fared quite well until they started to discuss "barbed wire entanglements".'

It was a magical evening, adding another page to the history of this remarkable house, of which Lady Violet Bonham Carter once said: 'If walls of brick and stone can hold, for all time, some intangible deposit of the great events which once took place within their span, no human dwelling should have a richer heritage than Number Ten Downing Street. It is a "house of history" in which the past is a living presence not to be put by.'

My father turned seventy in May 1985, a milestone that was not to pass unnoticed like so many birthdays in our family. Margaret insisted that it had to be special and should take precedence over her own sixtieth five months later.

John Wells slipped out of his 'Dear Bill' role to pen the following tribute to Denis in the *Evening Standard*'s *ES* magazine: 'To sight Denis, unencumbered by security of any kind, smiling like a cherub, with hat at a devil-may-care tilt after a good lunch, as I have done, is an experience that only dedicated ornithologists could understand. A rare bird is Denis, and we wish him a very happy birthday. Lord Forte and Lord Barber [a former Chancellor of the Exchequer] were among the guests who were greeted by the PM encouraging everyone to relax with "It's Denis's party."'

An enormous buffet was laid out in the dining room, with cold platters of Scotch salmon, roast rib of beef, roast turkey and baked gammon, and hot casseroles of paprika chicken and lamb curry, followed by strawberries, fruit salad and lemon soufflé – all washed down with Mâcon Chardonnay 1982, Château Beychevelle 1971 and Bollinger Special Cuvée.

The Great Hall resembled the car park at Twickenham, as my father's rugby pals downed champagne poured from a salmanazer. Peter Yarranton was standing at the buffet table with another international referee when Margaret scolded, 'Two rugby players standing there pecking at the food! Have this . . .' and doled out ladles of curry and turkey, ribs and vegetables until their plates groaned; they needed both hands to carry them back to their table.

Peter's wife admonished him: 'How could you?' and he swiftly replied, 'The Prime Minister gave me all this.' Denis defended him, 'Yes, I saw her.'

Denis talked himself out of making a speech. 'Well, we had a wonderful day. I don't recall anyone proposing a toast probably because I said to Margaret, "For God's sake, don't let's have any speeches because then I've got to get up in front of all the best speakers in the world and that's the last bloody thing I want to do."'

In fact Denis was being modest: his speech-making skills had improved enormously since his nervous early attempts. His fund of amusing anecdotes was growing daily, and for sporting audiences he could always fall back on old standbys from his refereeing years.

A favourite was a story about refereeing a game up in the Midlands, where the teams took no prisoners and were inclined to let him know when they disagreed with a decision.

> The language was really very bad and I thought, Well, Thatcher, if you're going to get to referee at Twickenham you'd better get command of this.
>
> I ordered a set scrum and the hooker cried out as the ball goes in, 'Why the blankety blank can't we have the blankety thing in straight.' This was my opportunity to get a real grip of the game so I blew my whistle, broke the scrum and said to the hooker, 'What did you say?'
>
> The hooker turned to the prop forward and said, 'The old sod's deaf as well.'

The change in my father was remarkable to see. He had been a serious child and, up until the point he retired, a serious adult, but in Number Ten he found a sense of humour which had remained hidden behind shyness and the weight of business responsibilities. He is the first to admit that it helped him to survive. 'I suppose if you are thrown into that sort of goldfish bowl, unless you develop what you've got, no one is going to do it for you. If you didn't, you'd go barmy, wouldn't you?'

One of Denis's great eccentricities involved food; it was often not cooked to his taste. When he and fellow board members of Quinton Hazell went out to dinner and ordered steaks, the waiter took the details as follows, 'Rare, medium, well done – and, for Denis, case-hardened' (engineering jargon meaning that the surface of metal or timber was made impenetrable).

For a man who had travelled the world, my father was very narrow-minded about food – his years at boarding school probably had something to do with it. He regularly came unstuck in France where, by his standards, every piece of meat placed in front of him was simply à la tartare. To make the point to a despairing chef, he would prod the tournedos with his fork, while emitting an exaggerated mooing.

While dining with friends at a very grand château on the Côte d'Azur, he gambled and ordered lamb chops, requesting emphatically that they be well done. They arrived looking decidedly bloody and hadn't left the waiter's hand before Denis sent them back to the kitchen, muttering, 'I'll still be able to taste the wool.'

The chops came back, still very pink, and he refused to touch them. Meanwhile his friends were staring sadly at their congealing dishes. 'I really must insist you start without me,' said Denis.

They had all finished when his chops materialized, after their fourth session under the grill, looking black and twisted. Unfortunately they came with a basil sauce; Denis, most apologetically, said: 'I've got to have mint sauce.' The sight of an Anglais munching charcoal soaked in vinegar and mint leaves was too much for the poor waiter.

Denis's close friends grew accustomed to his habits. On one golfing holiday, the regular foursome borrowed a villa near Cannes; Len Whitting's wife, Barbara, went along to cook. Len told her on the first night that unless Denis actually saw the smoke billowing from under the kitchen door he wouldn't believe the food had been cooked. To the party's astonishment, Denis cleared his plate, boasting with a naive pride, 'If my woman [Margaret] could see this, she wouldn't believe it.'

The number of dishes Denis will even contemplate ordering is so limited that there is no point handing him a menu in a restaurant. When we took him to the Hotel Walserhof in Klosters, a great foodie haunt of the Prince of Wales and the Duchess of York, Denis spotted *émince de veau* on the menu. Herbert, the maitre d', described the dish and it duly arrived. Denis hardly touched it.

'Was anything wrong?' enquired Herbert.

'Nothing,' Denis assured him. 'It just wasn't mince!'

To give him credit, my father is a mince connoisseur. At a banquet at Number Ten Denis was seated next to a crown prince who had been educated at a British public school. Roast beef was on the menu, which Denis avoided because it was too rare. Instead he quietly ordered mince. When it arrived, the Crown Prince asked, 'What have you got there?'

'I've got mince,' said Denis.

'Oh, I've always liked mince.'

Being the perfect host, Denis said, 'Would you prefer mince to roast beef?'

'Yes, as a matter of fact I would.'

So Denis handed over the plate and asked for another. Unfortunately, the message came back from the kitchen. 'Mince is off.'

With such a total lack of culinary adventurousness, it is remarkable that Denis regularly arranges business dinners in the penthouse of one of the Park Lane hotels. Among the guests there is usually an ambassador, a government minister and three or four PLC chairmen.

On one occasion they served partridge, which were so pink that Denis called the waiter over and said, 'Would you please bring me a cheese roll?'

Ten minutes later the waiter returned, bearing the crusty cheese roll on a silver tray. Denis put it on his plate, squashed the top down with his hand, cut it in half and promptly set about eating it while the rest of the guests looked on in disbelief.

But perhaps the best tale comes from a dinner at a top London hotel, when Denis considered his poussin to be undercooked. Putting his napkin over it and placing his hand on top, he solemnly summoned one of the staff. 'You have a big problem and I have a small one,' he said, charm-plating his complaint. 'If I take my hand off this bird it'll fly away. I want you to take it away, kill it and cook it.'

EIGHTEEN

LOVE AND LOYALTY

'I looked round and Margaret had gone – chin on
chest, fast asleep. Bernard Ingham was slumped on
the table snoring, Charles Powell fast asleep with his
eyes open. But they didn't get me; I used the old army
trick – finger touching roof of mouth and if you fall
asleep you're either sick or wake up.'

DENIS THATCHER on a marathon speech by
President Banda of Malawi

MENTION THE REPUBLIC OF SOUTH AFRICA to Denis and
he's likely to murmur, 'God's own country.' For him it's been
blessed ever since he first visited in 1949. On following stays he
extensively toured the game reserves, made many friends and
developed a deep admiration for the country. He often waxes
lyrical about the beauty of the Cape and the eternal grandeur
of the veld and was more familiar with the national geography
than many of those who used to whinge about the country's
politics.

When he heard left-wing critics mouthing off about South Africa,
Denis would rarely argue back. Sitting on a sofa in the Number
Ten drawing room, he would glare at the television and simply
challenge a few fundamental facts: 'Bet you don't even know
whether Simon's Town [the country's premier naval base] is east
or west of Cape Town!'

Denis has never supported apartheid and has patiently and tire-
lessly corrected those who were under the misapprehension that
Margaret's stance against sanctions meant she was pro-apartheid.
'Of course she was against apartheid and so was I. Not only was
it wrong, but economic idiocy as well. When I worked for Castrol
we managed to beat the system in our South African operations:
we employed black men in quasi-managerial positions – foremen

and that sort of thing – which we weren't supposed to do. We got away with it.'

Throughout the 1980s the Commonwealth Heads of Government Meetings were dominated by the fierce debate over sporting and economic sanctions against South Africa. By 1985 Margaret had become increasingly isolated in opposing such measures, not just within the Commonwealth but in Europe and America; even President Reagan had introduced a limited package of sanctions. At the same time foreign banks had refused to renew credit, tourists cancelled holidays and South African goods were left on supermarket shelves.

At the 1985 Nassau CHOGM Margaret fought a long battle, refusing to accept even a partial boycott, which angered the black African leaders and Australia's Prime Minister Bob Hawke.

Denis was also wholly opposed to sanctions, although he now acknowledges that 'to an extent' those taken against South Africa did work. 'The point about sanctions is that someone always breaks them. I was only a kid when the League of Nations imposed them against Italy after the invasion of Abyssinia and they were pretty ineffective then. The only sanctions that I saw get near to working were those against Rhodesia put on by Harold Wilson' (imposed when Prime Minister Ian Smith made a Unilateral Declaration of Independence in 1961).

Denis was familiar with the commercial scene in Salisbury (now Harare) because Atlas had done business there. After the imposition of sanctions he was able to see the French – 'who were always up-front at sanction breaking' – doing very nicely, thank you, out of busting the embargo any and every way they could.

A member of the Prime Minister's CHOGM team says of Denis: 'He had very crisp beliefs on the political views expressed about the British and South Africa, but he kept them to himself on the whole and played his role rather nobly I think.'

However, sometimes he found it impossible to stay silent. After listening to a scathing attack on Britain and her Prime Minister from the leader of a leading Commonwealth country, Denis was seething. At the conclusion of the session he wove his way through

LOVE AND LOYALTY

the milling delegates, reached the Prime Minister's side and coolly advised her, 'I'll tell you exactly how to deal with this, Sweetie Pie: cancel all their aid and he can work out how much each minute of that bloody speech cost his country.'

But he reserved his real venom for the topic of sporting relations with South Africa. 'I was totally opposed to the Gleneagles Agreement [1977], which Harold Wilson signed because he was anti-South Africa. Why should they be excluded from international sport? Sport and politics should not be mixed.'

Not surprisingly, F. W. de Klerk was one of the world leaders that Denis most warmed to: he had the utmost admiration for what he was trying to achieve in South Africa. They first met at a lunch at Chequers on 19 May 1990, three months after Nelson Mandela, the ANC leader, had been released from twenty-eight years of imprisonment. With progress being made towards restructuring the constitution and dismantling apartheid, Denis and Margaret knew that her position had been vindicated.

After the official talks de Klerk and his wife Marika joined the other guests for lunch. He and Denis found they had much in common and spent most of the meal discussing great Springbok players of the past, game parks and their favourite places in the Republic. Their friendship was to continue long after Margaret had left Number Ten. 'I'm very fond of de Klerk,' says Denis. 'He is a super chap – a Christian gentleman – and his wife is lovely. We see him a lot – every time he comes over.' Similarly, when my parents visited South Africa in 1991 they spent a weekend camping at Mala Mala with the de Klerks.

Denis, however, is realistic about the many hurdles that still have to be overcome in South Africa.

Whether they can hold the thing together as a unitary state one can't tell. I've met Chief Buthelezi [the Zulu leader] twice in South Africa and once in London at Laurens van der Post's flat in Chelsea. He's a strange man, very emotional and inconsistent, although quite personable and always roaring with laughter.

The threat to South Africa is that the Zulus want to be independent of the government of Pretoria and Cape Town; and naturally the government isn't going to let that go for nothing. If they do, then you've got a federated state and not a unitary state. That is the substantial danger because they're tribal.

Denis also maintained an interest in Hong Kong, another international pressure point. He accompanied Margaret when she went to China in December 1984 to sign the Joint Agreement handing Hong Kong back to the Chinese in 1997.

Although he wouldn't claim to be an expert, Denis had been to Hong Kong several times on business, and it was difficult to spend much time in Number Ten without being aware of the profound dilemma facing Britain.

> We had a very bad hand to play. They [the Chinese] had the legal right and all we could do was our best. Some will say, of course it was mishandled, particularly those who were anti-Margaret, and that it was left to Geoffrey Howe [the Foreign Secretary] to sort it out, but that I don't believe.
>
> The negotiations were about the sort of country we were going to leave behind and how they were going to handle it. We're not out of that particular wood yet by any means. The Chinese are more interested in politics than economics.

On the home front, Denis survived the daily crossfire in Number Ten by keeping his head down. If he ventured along the corridor past the Cabinet Room to check the paper cascade of wire service reports outside the Private Office, he was less likely to be in search of political wisdom than the stock market results or the latest score. He would certainly never stick his head round the door and ask those who were running the country for the latest news.

So when Michael Heseltine flounced out of a Cabinet Meeting in January 1986 and resigned, Denis never quite caught up with what was going on. That's one of the problems with Number Ten – if you miss an episode or try to reconcile what happens inside with what's reported outside, you are lost; no one ever has time to start explaining it all to you.

In fact the drama had its origins in a disagreement during the last months of 1985 between the Department of Trade and Industry and the Ministry of Defence over whether an American or European rescue package was the best solution for Britain's ailing helicopter company, Westland. Eventually it led to the resignation of both ministerial protagonists, Leon (later Sir Leon) Brittan and Michael Heseltine, and drew Downing Street into the row.

'To this day, I haven't got a clue what it was all about. One day I'll read it up in *The Downing Street Years*,' says Denis. Yet in the aftermath he rallied to patch up the party, making a speech in Leon Brittan's seat of Richmond, Yorkshire:

> The party has had something of a pounding in recent months, but in the words of Shakespeare, are we to 'suffer the slings and arrows of outrageous fortune, or to take arms against "a sea of troubles".'
>
> From where I sit I see no reason for depression nor defeatism. We might be bruised a little in the minor skirmishes like Fulham and elsewhere. When the real battle comes we will all up and fight and like the soldiers at Agincourt cry, 'God for Margaret, England and St George.'

The Westland affair had barely left the front pages, when another crisis was signalled by the sound of fighter planes flying overhead. In April 1986, after a tense weekend in Number Ten, the Prime Minister allowed US bombers to fly out of British bases for an air strike against Colonel Gaddafi in Libya.

The strikes followed a string of terrorist attacks by Middle Eastern terrorists on American targets in Europe, including the shooting of seventeen people in Rome and Vienna airports and the bombing of a discotheque in Berlin. Intelligence reports indicated a Libyan link and President Reagan needed the support of Western allies to attack targets in Libya, using US jets based in Europe. The French refused to allow American jets to fly over their air space, but Margaret gave her consent.

The Saturday before the raid Margaret ducked out of the wedding of Sir Peter and Lady Yarranton's daughter Sandy and left Denis to make her apologies. She had to see General Vernon Walters to discuss the list of targets on the bombers' itinerary.

Denis, meanwhile, remained calm and composed until he arrived at the wedding reception when, his thoughts being elsewhere, he collided with a huge flower arrangement, made two brilliant attempts at catching it, and finally managed to put it back on its stand. He then excused himself, saying, 'Got to get back, there's a lot going on.'

'The Americans thought Margaret was the Virgin Mary after that,' he says of the bombing. 'At the Embassy when we were dining a month later, I remember they thought she was absolutely wonderful.'

However, it caused an outcry within the government: ministers accused the PM of taking decisions without proper consultation or debate. Coming as it did so soon after Westland, the affair gave Margaret's personal and party popularity a huge knock. Secret opinion polls showed that only one in five people approved of the job she was doing and the Tories trailed both Labour and the Alliance.

Journalist and author Rodney Tyler wrote in his book, *Campaign! The Selling of the Prime Minister*:

> Whether the government had lost its grip or not and whether, at its head, the Prime Minister had lost control of her Cabinet or not, was in many ways irrelevant. What was important was that it was perceived in that way by many Tory backbenchers, party workers, the media and public at large. Some put it down to 'mid-term blues', others saw it as a natural reaction to the enormous strains of the 12-month-long miners' strike the year before; whatever the reason, the loss of confidence by, and in, her was palpable.

For the first time since the difficult early years, there was speculation that Margaret might have to go – either by falling on her sword or being pushed. The 'Falklands factor' was a distant memory.

Denis regarded such conjecture as pointless rubbish, fostered and fertilized by the press.

Remarkably, in eleven and a half years, he never once attended the Tuesday and Thursday sessions of Prime Minister's Question Time in the House of Commons. It wasn't that he opposed public access – on the contrary, he wholly disagreed with Margaret over the televising of Parliament when she voted against the proposal on 20 November 1986. (It was carried by only twelve votes.) Nor did he lack devotion or interest. 'I took the view that it was bad enough for her to be in the House and I didn't want her to look up and see me – after all, I thought she'd got other things to do.'

In truth, Denis hated seeing Margaret attacked or ridiculed. Daily lampooning in the press was part and parcel of political life, but during the bad spells it bruised him more than it did her: he actually read the papers; she deliberately avoided them. When anyone asked her whether she'd seen a particular leader or feature, she'd say, 'I never read the papers because I can't afford to have my judgement warped by what they say.' Denis, however, read what her critics were saying and his loathing and contempt for the press increased almost daily.

In 1985 the Hebdomadal Council, Oxford University's ruling executive, discussed giving the Prime Minister an honorary degree. She was the eighth post-war PM to be nominated, but the dons refused to grant the degree by 738 votes to 319. Margaret took the snub in her stride, saying, 'If they do not wish to confer the honour, I am the last person who would wish to receive it.'

Denis, however, was profoundly upset. 'They kicked her out,' he lamented with tears in his eyes, totally unable to comprehend why anybody could be so rude to his wife. This was one of the many drawbacks to being the husband of a Leader who inspired love and loathing in equal measure.

Many of the men who worked with Margaret quipped that they fell in love with her energy and her political conviction and were overawed by her achievement. Denis loved all these things; he saw his wife as a heroine.

When Crawfie was seeing them off to the garden party at Buckingham Palace one year she said to him: 'Mr Thatcher, don't you think the Prime Minister looks fantastic in her new blue suit?'

'Crawf,' declared Denis, 'she's been looking beautiful for thirty-five years.'

Watching my parents together, I could see the subtle change in their relationship. Having led a rather separate life ever since they married, Denis increasingly began to dote on Margaret. When they first married, he had given her the space, financial security and freedom to pursue her career and raise a family; after all, he was rarely home. Now he saw that he could make his support more tangible. He had the confidence of experience and age, along with all the discipline, loyalty and love that were in his make-up.

Often, towards the end of business dinners, when the conversation inevitably got round to Margaret, a mellow Denis would ignore the political discussion and look doe-eyed at the very mention of his beloved wife.

They retained a fundamental closeness which was the backbone of their partnership. Each would express concern for the other. 'Did you enjoy your holiday in Switzerland, Prime Minister?' someone would ask.

'Well, you know, Denis loves being in the mountains,' would be her reply.

Similarly, when Mark's less-than-universally-approved business antics made headlines, Denis would worry because 'Margaret gets upset'.

She was also fiercely protective of him, describing his love as 'a golden thread, which runs through the days, through the weeks, through the months, through the years'.

Having already proved so popular on 'Thatcher Tours', Denis was now a seasoned member of the PM's entourage. He rarely had cause to communicate with the travelling media in the prime ministerial VC-10, and they tended to give him a wide berth. According to Bernard Ingham, the press developed a sneaking respect for him because he lived life on tour rather harder than most of them. 'Fleet Street was dramatically reformed over the 1980s, converted almost from a perpetual piss-up into the peace pledge union. The dramatic change that overcame journalists was quite remarkable and I think they had a sneaking respect for Denis – a man who was old fashioned, old style, good old bonhomie, who didn't compromise and who was keeping up the traditions they had abandoned.'

In Kandy, Sri Lanka, Denis found himself caught up in a scene that would have been implausible had 'Dear Bill' concocted it. Charles Powell witnessed the incident.

We were having a lovely picnic lunch on the Governor's lawn and this ceremonial elephant, aged ninety, was there. It was suggested that the Prime Minister might like to feed it but she knew a thing or two about politics and knew not to get tangled with any elephants.

So Denis advanced on the beast, banana in hand, to feed it, but he hadn't studied the physiology of elephants very carefully in his lifetime and as it stuck out its trunk he took the banana and tried to force it up its trunk instead of giving it so it could curl its trunk around it ... The ancient elephant rather took offence at this – especially having a large banana stuck down its nose ... and started to squeal. Everyone fled for cover – including Denis, banana in hand and looking rather angry. There was only one TV crew there – from the Sri Lankan government info service – and as they left the BBC sort of fell on them crying, 'We'll pay anything for this tape.'

On another overseas trip with the Prime Minister, Denis visited Egypt and Jordan. In Cairo Margaret held talks with President Mubarak about a Jordanian proposal for an international peace conference on the Palestinian question. While she was occupied with world affairs, Denis's programme took him to Egypt's most basic 'attractions'. It featured not a glimpse of the Sphinx or a pyramid, but still managed to fill the senses.

MR DENIS THATCHER'S PROGRAMME

(when not accompanying Prime Minister)

TUESDAY 17 SEPTEMBER

8.45	Leave Tahra Palace accompanied by Mr Lello
9.45	Arrive Motherwell Bridge site [composting plant]
10.35	Leave Motherwell Bridge
10.40	Arrive Chloride factory, Abu Rawash
11.30	Leave Chloride factory
12.15	Arrive Barclays Bank
12.45	Leave Barclays Bank
13.00	Arrive Ambassador's Residence for a small lunch
14.30	Leave Residence
15.00	Arrive Ameriya [wastewater pumping station site]. Meet Chairman Cairo Wastewater Organization, senior staff of AMBRIC and contractors. Presentation of plans etc.
15.20	Tour site
15.45	Leave site
16.00	Arrive Shaft 6 site
16.45	Arrive Residence
17.00	Reception at Residence (followed by dinner given by President Mubarak at Kubba Palace)

Denis had toured shipyards, factories and enterprises all over the globe; he had become so expert at planting trees that his leafy handiwork had only one option: to flourish. But it was Cairo's sewers that really captivated him. Years later he would bang on about the city's wastewater system, quoting statistics such as the fact that a London bus could drive through the widest part of the main pipe.

In March 1988 Denis found himself in Africa again, zigzagging through Morocco, Zimbabwe, Malawi and Namibia. The itinerary included a nostalgic stopover in Harare, one of Denis's old haunts from the days when he'd stay in the jacaranda-fringed Meikles Hotel.

Unfortunately, on this trip, the accommodation was decidedly below par. He and Margaret unpacked in a villa whose architectural style was tactfully described as 'African Over the Top', and Denis turned on a hot water tap.

'There's no water,' he yelled to Crawfie.

'We'll find some,' she said, totally unfazed by Third World plumbing.

Crawfie's discreet enquiries revealed that the guest house hadn't been used for eight years: the boiler had been put on full blast two days previously and had blown up.

Water was carried up from the cellar in dustbins and heated on gas rings in the kitchen. Having performed basic ablutions, Denis helpfully gave a little demonstration of how he'd managed to shower by throwing water in the air and niftily dodging into its downward path.

Darkness fell rather suddenly when all the lights gave out. Denis's cry rang out again, 'Beloved, Crawf – no electricity.'

'We'll improvise,' she said, and swept into housekeeping to scrounge some candles.

The next stop was Blantyre in Malawi, the private fiefdom of Dr Hastings Kamuzu Banda, who'd been in office since 1963 and in 1971 had declared himself President for Life. He enjoyed a universal reputation as a despot and tyrant, famous for his three-piece suits, homburg hat, shades and the constantly flicking fly-swatter. His autocratic style had won him the nickname of 'One Man Banda'.

On 30 March he hosted a state banquet for the British Prime

Minister and her party in the New State House – one of the most
bizarre follies ever constructed in post-independence Africa. It has
300 rooms and a banqueting hall that seats ten times as many
guests as the State Dining Room in Downing Street.

After dining on what Denis described as 'some rubber chickens
and cheap wine – left by the Germans, I guess', Dr Banda, resplendent in tribal dress, rose to address the guests and launched into a
dissertation on 'My Life and Times'.

After three quarters of an hour he'd reached the age of forty.

Denis recalls: 'I looked round and Margaret had gone – chin on
chest, fast asleep. Bernard Ingham was slumped on the table snoring, Charles Powell fast asleep with his eyes open. But they didn't
get me; I used the old army trick – finger touching roof of mouth
and if you fall asleep you're either sick or wake up.'

The only destinations which truly filled Denis with foreboding
were Communist countries. He saw nothing to recommend China
in 1982, and disliked the shoddy workmanship and the repressed,
totalitarian atmosphere. He skipped Margaret's phenomenally successful visit to Moscow in March 1987, and on the June 1990 trip
to Kiev – to support a 'British Days' exhibition – he saw no reason
to alter his opinion of the Eastern Bloc.

An evening performance by the English National Ballet was
arranged and during the interval an official whispered in Crawfie's
ear that Mr Gorbachev wanted Mrs Thatcher's party to stay overnight in a VIP dacha in the forest. Crawfie vanished to pack the
overnight bags and went ahead to a rather gloomy Tsarist week-
ender in the middle of nowhere. When the rest of the party turned
up they found the dining-room table groaning under a vast spread
of caviar, smoked fish and dark bread. Feeling peckish, they sat
down and tucked in.

So far so good, until Denis felt in need of a nightcap. 'Is this a
dry house?' he inquired and Crawfie rose to the challenge, hunting
down some none too refined vodka and the PM's party had an
entirely appropriate nightcap, drinking the stuff neat!

The following morning Crawfie asked the staff what time breakfast would be served and met with blank, rather embarrassed stares.
Finally, she enlisted the help of an interpreter, who translated the

housekeeper's terse reply. 'There isn't any breakfast. You ate it last night.'

No Prime Minister this century had secured a third mandate in succession from the electorate and, in the middle of 1986, Margaret's chances appeared unpromising. Many thought that the Conservative government was badly split and running out of steam. Margaret was also laid up temporarily after an operation on her hand at the beginning of August. She went to recuperate with the Wolfsons in Cornwall, and her doctor was horrified by front-page photos of her being hauled along the beach by the Wolfson's hyperenergetic dog Polo.

Although the Westland row and Libyan bombing had inflicted some damage on the Prime Minister's popularity, by the end of the year the economy showed signs of improvement, with inflation down to 3 per cent and manufacturing output up.

We gathered for our eighth Christmas at Chequers. The family usually arrived on Christmas Eve. We'd dump presents under the huge floor-to-ceiling Christmas tree in the Great Hall. The wood panelling was patchworked with hundreds of Christmas cards; only the top cards (from British and foreign royalty) were displayed on the grand piano so that guests could comment on the signatures and the family photos on the covers.

Mark arrived with Diane Burgdorf, an extremely glamorous blonde from Dallas, where he'd been living for several years. He prattled away excitedly about their wedding plans for the following Valentine's Day.

There were three guest lists for Christmas, covering forty-eight hours through to Boxing Day. The first was for a cocktail party in the Great Hall: the fifty guests included Lord and Lady Carrington and their house party, and a sprinkling of MPs who lived reasonably close by – George Walden, Michael Portillo, Ray Whitney, John Patten, and their wives.

Margaret and Denis always attended a service on Christmas morning. Ellesborough church was the nearest and when at Chequers my parents attended it so regularly that Denis claims, 'We were told by the C. of E. Mafia that we'd been more often in two years than all the previous prime ministers since 1945 put together.'

Denis trained the vicar to shorten his sermons, telling him, 'Padre, most of us know what the Sermon on the Mount is all about, we don't need you to explain it to us. Twelve minutes is your lot.' Subsequently, no sermon ever exceeeded this time limit.

One Christmas Denis took the Roman Catholic contingent to the Catholic church in Great Missenden. It was a welcome change from Ellesborough church, largely because it was so beautifully warm. Denis returned to Chequers and, over lunch, mischievously suggested converting to Catholicism.

After returning from church, the Prime Minister tended to stay in for a few days because she wanted to release her detectives to spend Christmas with their own families. Twenty-two of us sat down to Christmas lunch in the dining room, the emphasis very much on the family and close friends. The menu never ever varied from absolutely traditional fare: chilled melon, roast turkey, bread sauce, roast potatoes, brussels sprouts, garden peas and carrots, followed by Christmas pudding, brandy sauce, cream and mince pies.

Jack Page, a regular Christmas guest since 1980, would rise towards the end of lunch and deliver some verse he'd composed for the occasion. The first time this happened, I was detailed to ask Margaret if Jack could address the guests.

'So long as he's finished before the Queen,' she said crisply.

Jack began:

> For Denis is the perfect host
> he gives us wine we like the most
> he's wise and cheerful, never ill
> (and only wants to fight Dear Bill)
> and is a perfect loving mate
> to the captain of our Ship of State.

Afterwards, we adjourned to the Hawtrey Room to watch the Queen's Christmas broadcast on television. There was always a ritual fussing by the PM to ensure that the box was plugged in correctly (as if it wouldn't be in a house where the staff turned the TV guide to the current page) and that everyone had a seat.

After the broadcast Margaret insisted on taking some fresh air before tea, which usually meant a route march down to the police post at the side entrance to Chequers, where we'd view the grounds through the security monitors while handing the guards a spare Christmas cake the PM had been given.

Lord and Lady McAlpine often stayed overnight, and supper in the dining room was a cold buffet and caviar from a gift hamper. The only time I ever visited the kitchen at Chequers was when, needing more toast for the caviar, Margaret, Romilly and I attempted to locate bread and breadboard.

On Boxing Day the staff would lay out the buffet tables in the Great Hall for lunch. The guests included the Ambassador of the United States and his wife, Lord and Lady King, Jeffrey (later Lord) Archer and his wife, and Duke Hussey and Lady Susan Hussey. Everyone was off-duty, so these were usually relaxed, rather amusing parties. I always attributed this success to the low quota of politicians but Denis was probably nearer the mark when he put it down to the fact that, 'they're all the great and the good so you don't have to introduce anyone. They're all friends and our friends.'

As the New Year dawned the Prime Minister was already gearing up for another general election campaign – one in which she needed every omen of good luck. Her eventual re-election on 11 June 1987 came at the end of a campaign that Denis describes as being 'in perpetual danger of becoming a cock-up'.

Rod Tyler wrote in his book, *Campaign! The Selling of a Prime Minister*, 'Everybody knows it all very nearly went wrong, everybody has a favourite horror story, everybody names a different guilty party . . . That they managed to keep it working throughout what was probably the most politically fraught month of their lives, was a miracle.'

A slow start, poor communication, and a defensive rather than aggressive approach, were all to blame for a terrible first week of the campaign, during which the Labour Party did all the running.

Neil Kinnock, the Labour Leader, had invigorated his party with a new red rose logo and a perceived 'moderate' image, but the shadow of the 'loony Left' still haunted him. The Alliance were a greater threat, seeking to win over disaffected Tory voters.

The day before the election was announced Denis celebrated his seventy-second birthday at Chequers. He had gone to the Rugby Sevens at Twickenham and arrived home in a jolly mood. The kitchen staff had prepared his favourite meal – salmon steak with chips and peas, followed by steamed sultana pudding.

Afterwards, the Prime Minister spent the evening discussing election tactics with Tim Bell. She had an understandable desire to surround herself with the same people who had helped her to success in the past – people like Tim and Gordon Reece. She saw no reason to change a winning team.

Norman Tebbit, the new Party Chairman, was a very different operator to his predecessor Cecil Parkinson. Cecil was smooth and charming, while Norman had already earned himself the nickname, 'the Chingford Strangler'. He called himself the 'lightning conductor' and launched attacks on, among other things, the BBC's political coverage, which he considered biased.

Denis agreed entirely. He loathed the BBC, regarding them as a bunch of leftie, pinko socialists, overmanned, overpaid and unpatriotic. Everyone has something which makes them erupt and for Denis it was the BBC – whether it was the licence fee or the hue of their political reporting.

On the other hand, he had a great deal of time for Duke Hussey, who became the corporation's chairman in 1986, which is again evidence of how rarely he visited his prejudices upon individuals. Once, however, he struck up a conversation with Peter Jay, former economics editor of *The Times*. Denis, thinking he was still at the newspaper, asked him about several of the writers on the business pages. Peter Jay twigged and updated him: 'Oh, I'm no longer at *The Times*; I'm now economics editor of the BBC.'

Denis clicked his heels together and turned to leave, informing him tartly, 'Never watch it.'

He had strong opinions on the power of the visual media not only to entertain and inform but also to corrupt. He summed these up in a speech at Buckingham University in November 1987, when he rewrote William Blake's Songs of Innocence:

> The TV mast from street to street
> Shall weave old England's winding sheet.
> The trouble comes out lives to curse,
> But television makes them worse.
> The box exerts its baleful charm
> And brings our children's minds to harm.
> The powers of Government are shrinking
> As television does our thinking
> And courts of law are superseded.
> A TV probe is all that's needed
> A trend's set is beyond revision
> The country's ruled by television.

Following the Brighton bombing, security during the campaign was stepped up, but despite warnings, Margaret continued to meet and greet the people during walkabouts.

On assignment in Jordan during that first week, I was horrified by what friends and contacts were telling about the Tory campaign. Labour was better organized, better at handling the press, better on TV and had better advertising. I rang Margaret with this view, 'You'd better get your act together or start packing.'

After a dreadful rainy day touring Finchley and other North London constituencies, she returned to the flat looking more upset than I could remember for a long time. Denis was there as we sat with a small group that included Lord Young (Secretary of State for Employment) and Tim Bell. I kept the drinks topped up while the experts tried to get the campaign back on the rails. Denis occasionally joined in, urging his wife to listen to what she was being told.

Going on the attack, Margaret turned the campaign around. Answering Labour's claims that Tory policies promoted greed, she argued that people shouldn't feel guilty for doing well; only by encouraging people to succeed could everybody enjoy a better life. At her last major speech in Harrogate on 9 June, her barnstorming finish electrified the crowd, which rose to its feet when she closed with: 'We are a forward-looking people, a lion-hearted nation, ready to confront the twenty-first century and reach out for greatness again. Let us continue our task on Thursday.'

On the way back Denis poured champagne and mingled with the sixty travelling photographers and journalists at the back of the plane. Now a household figure in his own right, he commanded respect and affection from enormous numbers of people he met on the campaign trail.

He had also become more forthright. Two days after polling day, when the Tories had been returned with a majority of 101, Denis was at the traditional reception for Commonwealth high commissioners following the Trooping the Colour ceremony. He turned to Sir Sonny Ramphal, Commonwealth Secretary-General, a man whose views were diametrically opposed to his own, and with the utmost courtesy said to him, 'You've got us for another five years so you'd better start being nice.'

NINETEEN

TEN YEARS AT NUMBER TEN

'The usual combination of the "ambitious coupled
with the disaffected" and "disappointed" is nothing
new – indeed when we passed ten years I have long
foretold it.

DENIS THATCHER on Black Monday,
October 1987

DENIS WAS BACK in Downing Street – a house my parents would
occupy for longer than any other during their married life. The
election campaign had been enormously draining and he had seen
enough of the swings and roundabouts of politics to know that the
euphoria of electoral victory evaporates in a flash. We were both
in the flat one evening, soon after polling day, watching Margaret
shaking hands and acknowledging cheers from a crowd. Denis
turned to get himself a refill and said, 'In a year she'll be so unpopular you won't believe it.'

These were prophetic words. Although the economic boom of
the mid-Thatcher years was bubbling along nicely, there were signs
that the economy might be overheating. In August 1987 the
Chancellor, Nigel Lawson, raised interest rates by 1 per cent – the
first increase in several years. Then, on 19 October, the boom years
were stopped in their tracks by 'Black Monday'. Dow Jones fell 23
per cent in a day; London lost 15 per cent and the markets in Hong
Kong and Tokyo tumbled in turn.

Denis was in Downing Street when the news broke. However
bad the political news, he always attempted to find some redeeming
feature. 'It wasn't that bad – it wasn't like Heath's crash in 1973,'
he says. 'Quite a bit was wiped off but when Burmah went down
the swanny the Footsie went very low indeed.' (The 'Heath Crash'

was limited to the property market and the secondary banking sector rather than the global financial markets that were hit on Black Monday.)

Denis, of course, was viewing the financial carnage through the eyes of a semi-retired investor. 'There was no panic. Not for me. I've always had a good list [of personal investments] and I took the view that it would come back. If you're one of these people who can see these things coming – and don't forget that the stock market is always a matter of timing – you can liquidate everything, when the market comes crashing down you've got cash. You can sit for a bit, see the first signs of recovery and you're in. Then it goes up and up and there's your capital gain. Cash is king.'

The domino effect of the international markets used to annoy Margaret. She would listen to the radio first thing in the morning and hear that the Far East markets had fallen and sigh, knowing that when the Stock Exchange opened London would toboggan after them, followed by New York five hours later.

One morning, totally exasperated as always when faced with something she was powerless to do anything about, she said: 'I really think everyone should be on Greenwich Mean Time – it would stop all this.'

I said: 'That's splendid, Mum, you've just condemned half the globe to living in the dark.'

Denis saw her frustration and reminded her, 'You always have to remember a market is exactly that. They're just like sheep; a leading sheep goes through the gate saying "Baa" and all the others follow; and then the leader turns around and goes back and all the silly sods go with him.'

But Black Monday was no mere blip. The immediate reaction was to cut interest rates, out of a fear that we faced a depression like 1929, but the economy continued to overheat: too much money was being taken out on credit and loans. House prices soared as banks and building societies offered attractive mortgages and customers felt they must get onto the housing ladder. Meanwhile inflation was rising ominously.

Ignorant of the economic turmoil ahead and fresh from a

stunning electoral victory, the Conservative Party Conference in October was an exuberant affair. After three election victories in a row, it seemed like a party born to rule.

The conference showed widespread support for an idea first aired at a meeting at Chequers of Department of the Environment ministers in March 1985. The plan was to abolish the system of council rates levied on property owners and replace it with a flat rate paid by every adult resident – from the dustman to the duchess, as the saying went. It was to be called the Community Charge, but became better known as the Poll Tax.

Margaret had always been profoundly unhappy with the old rating system, which penalized homeowners at the expense of everyone else, and had committed herself to its abolition as long ago as the mid-1970s. But when the Community Charge was introduced, its critics quickly tagged it the most unpopular tax levied in Britain since the Middle Ages.

Despite reservations within the Cabinet, the Poll Tax was made a centrepiece of the election manifesto. After the Tory Party Conference, there was no more talk of phasing it in slowly to soften the blow: in November 1987 it was announced that the tax would come into operation in Scotland on 1 April 1989 and the rest of the United Kingdom on 1 April 1990.

Denis fully supported the plan. He deplored the unfairness of rates. 'I thought the Community Charge was a very very good Act of Parliament and I still do. It made everyone contribute and made the local authorities accountable. When you consider the vast expenditure of these terrible socialist local authorities without regard for money something had to change.'

Unfortunately, neither he nor Margaret could foresee just how unpopular the new tax would become.

In January 1988 Margaret overtook Asquith and became the longest serving Prime Minister this century. Her supporters had even more reason to celebrate in March, when the Budget cut the standard rate of income tax to 25 per cent and the top rate to 40 per cent. Denis raised a gin and tonic and reminded us all, 'When we came in it was 83 per cent on earned income and 98 per cent on unearned.' The size of Margaret's achievement and the obstacles she'd overcome was not lost on him.

His own diary was still remarkably full and one week saw him jetting off for business meetings in Miami and Connecticut. On his return, he and Margaret accepted a regular invitation to dine at Windsor Castle ('Dine and sleep Windsor' says the diary entry); the following Saturday Denis found himself at the 134th Cambridge versus Oxford Boat Race.

His widely recognized love of gin made him an obvious choice to present the Beefeater Gin Trophy to the winning president. 'They were all so exhausted they just grabbed their medals and shoved off,' he recalls.

Such sporting presentations were the kind of engagement that Denis willingly accepted and thoroughly enjoyed. He gave a lot of time and energy as a governor of the Sports Aid Foundation, was involved in the Sports Aid Trust and the Lords Taverners, and was also life vice-president of the London Society of Rugby Football Union Referees. 'I'd worked up a bit of a reputation for being interested in sport,' he admits, with typical understatement.

One of his finest memories is from 1989, when he was asked to present golf's Ryder Cup at The Belfry. In a thrilling finish, the scores were tied, allowing Europe to retain the trophy.

It was a great day. I've been on many a better golf course but the Americans like The Belfry. It's rather treeless but has some very very exciting holes like the tenth over the water. They like it because they get a lot of people watching at The Belfry, which creates enormous excitement.

The great thing about the Ryder Cup is that while professional golf is the best disciplined and sportsmanlike game, in these contests they play for nothing; there's no money.

Fair play has always been paramount to Denis, who summed up his 'lifetime in sport' during a speech to Buckingham University on 12 November 1987, attacking what he saw as the lack of sportsmanship and blatant cheating that was creeping into sport at all levels.

That television has had an enormous effect on sport in this country over the past twenty years needs no emphasis. Millions of people, and particularly young people, watch a wide variety of sport every day – racing, football, cricket, tennis, golf, snooker and even darts.

This has meant that the television companies pay vast sums to the governing bodies, as they are called, for the right to broadcast the events . . . Without this income a number of our sports would cease to exist in the form we know them.

These long hours of television have brought what we know as sponsorship . . . very successful sportsmen and women enjoy large incomes not only for the winning performances but from their endorsement of manufacturers' equipment, clothing and other activities. No one begrudges them their earnings, for the life of a top sportsman is by definition short – but, it is a far cry from the days when a Wimbledon champion got a £25 voucher for Lillywhites.

However, human nature being what it is, these vast sums of money have engendered not only greed but, in nearly every sport, an over-riding requirement to win at any cost. That manifests itself in bad behaviour in varying forms and outright cheating.

The disgraceful performances by some tennis players at Wimbledon are well known.

We have test cricketers insulting the umpires who are paid a pittance compared with their own earnings, and even in rugby union football – an amateur game – thuggery on the field of play is sometimes appalling . . .

Worst of all is the Association Football game. The hooliganism in football grounds requiring large contingents of police, both uniformed and plainclothes, culminating in our national humiliation in the Heysel incident . . . did not start because of unemployment, or inner city deprivation. We had much worse of both in the thirties, and large crowds watched the games in enjoyment and in safety. No, it starts on the field of play, when players deliberately break the rules of the game and even deliberately set out to injure their opponents . . .

There are millions of youngsters under the age of sixteen watching their so-called sports heroes acting and behaving in this manner and, in their watching, believe that this is the right way to play and behave. It is not. It is an affront to the Christian ethic and a prejudice to our British way of life. As far as children are concerned, it is not easy to correct, for too many of our state schools have given up organized games for a variety of reasons, most of which I find bad.

The solution to the problem of outright cheating and bad behaviour is not as easy as it may appear and I will not dwell on the reasons, but if the government bodies concerned and/or the players association concerned would really grasp the nettle an enormous improvement could be made.

Denis went on to talk about the rise of drug use in sport, particularly athletics. Wrong-doers, he said, should be banned for life from competitive sport at any level. Summing up, he said; 'I believe that sport, any or all sports, from bowls to boxing from coarse fishing to cricket, is an essential factor in our national life. I am a passionate supporter of competitive sport for our young people, bringing as it does exercise and discipline, companionship and character.

'The desire to win is born in most of us, the will to win is a matter of training, the manner of our winning is a matter of example. If we fail in the latter we do so at our peril.'

On 17 November 1988 the whole family was invited to Washington to say farewell to President Reagan, who was due to retire after his second term. Not even their disagreement over the invasion of Grenada had dented the relationship between Ron and Maggie, which Denis acknowledged was a private mutual admiration society.

After we arrived at Andrews Airforce Base, there was an elaborate White House ceremony and Mrs Reagan hosted a coffee morning in honour of Denis in the Green Room. The farewell banquet the following evening was probably the most dazzling I have ever attended. I kept a copy of the menu:

Baby Lobster Bellevue
Caviar Yogurt Sauce
Curried Croissant
Roasted Saddle of Veal Périgourdine
Jardinière of Vegetables
Asparagus in Hazelnut Butter
Autumn Mixed Salad
Selection of Cheese
Chestnut Marquise
Pistachio Sauce
Orange Tuiles and Ginger Twigs

Eleven circular tables were decorated with thousands of pink roses arranged in giant balls like scoops of strawberry ice-cream. The marine band, resplendent in red tunics, played as we all trooped in. Denis had Nancy Reagan on his table, along with Mrs Bob Hope, an extremely cheerful and chatty lady, Dr Billy Graham and the late Malcolm Forbes, then publisher of *Forbes* magazine.

Celebrities were dotted among the guests, although Denis wouldn't have recognized them. He's not a follower of fashion or TV series, so Loretta Swit (Hot Lips Houlihan from *M*∗*A*∗*S*∗*H*), Tom Selleck and Mikhail Baryshnikov were probably unknown to him. At Ten Downing Street functions he would have cast an eye over the official briefing, which gave a rundown on the guests. This, of course, avoided the predicament of mental blocks or asking someone exceedingly famous what they did for a living.

George Bush had won the Republican nomination and was duly elected as the next President. Denis got on very well with Bush, who was a familiar face after his two terms as Vice-President to Reagan. His wife Barbara is a jolly soul and good for a laugh. I remember standing next to her in a queue waiting to go into a lunch when, exasperated, she turned and complained that, 'politics consists of rushing and then waiting'. Denis would have agreed; he'd spent years being made to wait or having to dash off at a trot to keep up with Margaret. Of Barbara Bush, he says, 'She's a great chum and very nice. She says in her book that I was rude to her, but she's retracted that elsewhere. Sitting next to her was no hardship.'

(In her memoirs, Mrs Bush had written, 'When George and I first met the Thatchers, George was still in Congress and Margaret came to Houston to give a speech. I was so impressed with her knowledge and presentation but Denis I found rather rude, especially when he made several disparaging remarks to me about Americans. But I learned over the years that he has a wonderful sense of humour and is steady as a rock, plus, he's a good sport. Many times he found himself the only male in a room full of "spouses".')

Back in Britain the countdown to Margaret's tenth anniversary in Number Ten had already begun. HERE'S TO THE NEXT 10 YEARS trumpeted the *Daily Mail*.

Privately, Denis had made up his mind after the 1987 election victory that he didn't want Margaret to fight again. In his heart and head he wanted out.

> I was beginning to think that we can't win the next general election, not just because of the performance of the government, but there always comes a time when it's time for a change. I thought that it was going to be very difficult because of the 'time for a change' momentum.
>
> I certainly wasn't thinking of myself. I always said quite early on, 'When we go – hopefully next Tuesday – we'll miss Chequers' because I loved it and still do.

Margaret was sometimes annoyed when he expressed these thoughts, according to Denis – but they summed up his feelings, also unwittingly echoed by 'Dear Bill': 'Quite honestly, Bill, I've taken a decision about a Third Term . . . I told the Boss it was all very well for her to go on and on, but some of us were getting a bit long in the tooth for that kind of thing, and I'd also spent a lot of money on the insulated liquor store at Dulwich [their house]. When, I asked, rhetorically as it turned out, was I going to get a chance to enjoy the fruits?'

Finally he did something he had never even contemplated in all his years as a loyal consort. At Chequers, in the company of two of Margaret's closest friends, Gordon Reece and Tim Bell, he broached the subject of Margaret's retirement. 'I thought that we'd been there too long. The thought of another election really appalled me – and the possibility of losing, too,' he explains.

Tim recalls the occasion: 'He thought Margaret ought to retire after ten years. He thought that she really ought to go and Gordon was suggested as the man to convey the message because she relied on him and trusted him.'

Turning to Gordon, Denis said, 'She trusts you, you tell her.'

'I can't do that,' he said.

'Why not?'

'Well, because I love her.'

'Steady – she's my wife, you know,' said Denis.

In his heart my father knew that if anyone was able to convince Margaret that now was the time to bow out, it was him. She had always listened to him: it was he who calmed her down and delivered unpalatable news. 'Political aides, on the whole, who are enjoying a good run are the last people to say, "You should pack it in and hand it over to someone else." It would be putting themselves out of a job.'

Denis doesn't remember exactly when he talked to Margaret, but I think it was probably at Christmas 1988, several months before the tenth anniversary on 4 May 1989.

I told her that I didn't want to fight another election but if she wanted to, of course, love and loyalty, I'd be beside her all the way. I think it may well have crossed her mind and her reaction was by no means that she wouldn't consider it at all.

But look at the possible scenarios. If she didn't go at the time of her choosing, she could be defeated at a general election. I didn't want to see her lose. I wanted her to go out at the top. She could say that she never lost – she was never defeated or humiliated; with her reputation entirely intact and after ten years she would hand it on to the next person.

Politically, it was also a good time to go; the new leader would have time to get established before the next election.

He really thought he'd managed to convince Margaret that ten years was long enough. She had broken several records, won three general elections and made her mark on history. 'She'd made up her mind not to do another election. She'd made up her mind to go. She got as far as looking for convenient times to go and see the Queen.'

So what happened to change her mind? 'What stopped her was that she went to see Willie Whitelaw and he said, "You can't do that, there'll be blood on the walls when choosing your successor. It will split the party."'

In truth, Denis knew that she didn't really want to go. After all, she didn't want to go eighteen months later. She loved being Prime Minister; she knew she was good at it, and there was still a lot that she wanted to do. He gave in gracefully: 'I didn't pursue it any more. I thought this is a wise man [Willie Whitelaw] and if that was his gut feeling as a great politician then that was that.'

Margaret doesn't enjoy celebrating anniversaries but has always accepted that other people like making a fuss. For her, milestones were unnecessarily sentimental and often simply fuelled speculation about the future.

She hosted a lunch at Chequers on the nearest Sunday to the anniversary. Most of her closest friends and political colleagues gathered in the Great Hall and toasted her with champagne. The gung-ho mood was summed up by a Jak cartoon in the *London Evening Standard* on Friday 5 May, portraying the Prime Minister as Mona Lisa, holding a front page of the *Standard* with the headline, TEN MORE YEARS? Only the question mark was inappropriate.

A month earlier the Community Charge had been introduced in Scotland and was proving highly controversial. Not only were whole new groups of people paying the tax for the first time, but the actual charge was in most cases far higher than expected. As would happen in England a year later councils had increased their spending to coincide with the introduction of the tax, knowing that all the opprobrium would fall on the government.

A MORI poll in May showed that Labour had overtaken the Tories for the first time since 1987, and led by 2 per cent. By June a Harris poll gave them a lead of 14 per cent. The figures got worse and worse, and by November the Prime Minister was the most unpopular leader since records began.

Her position wasn't helped by the deep divisions in the Cabinet on whether to move towards closer union with Europe – specifically, whether to go forward with economic and monetary union, which Britain's partners wanted by the mid-1990s. Margaret was against it and had the support of Nick Ridley (Trade and Industry) and Alan Walters. However, the majority of the Cabinet were in favour of joining the European Exchange Rate Mechanism to stabilize exchange controls.

The ERM became a huge bone of contention and opened up a rift between the Prime Minister and the two men who had served her as Chancellor of the Exchequer, Nigel Lawson and Geoffrey Howe.

In June 1989 the 'Madrid ambush' saw Howe and Lawson

threaten to resign on the eve of a European summit meeting in Madrid unless the PM made a commitment to join the ERM at a later date. This betrayed serious conflicts at the heart of government and eventually led to Lawson's resignation on 26 October. Denis and Margaret had come back overnight from Kuala Lumpur and Denis later went to a private dining club. Even though he was 'among friends', he never commented on crises and resignations. He'd been around long enough to know that politicians were prone to disloyalty because they all wanted his wife's job. He believed she deserved far better from her party.

As the pressure began to mount, Margaret was seen as increasingly isolated. Reading the newspapers every day, Denis realized that the press were becoming more and more hostile; colleagues were sniping from the backbenches. The sense of invulnerability that had greeted her third electoral success had evaporated. Of course, there'd been mid-term blues and patches of unpopularity before. After all, she'd survived the crisis of confidence in the early 1980s, and again in 1986. But this time it looked different.

The discontent among her own benches was such that, for the first time since she became Leader in 1975, she was challenged for the job by Sir Anthony Meyer, MP for Clywd North West in North Wales. Sir Anthony, no political 'heavyweight', stood as a stalking horse candidate. His challenge was not a worry because both Howe and Heseltine, potentially far bigger threats, had already ruled out contesting the leadership.

In the ballot on 28 November Meyer gained 33 votes against the Prime Minister's 314. There were 24 spoilt papers and 3 abstentions.

Although in *The Downing Street Years* Margaret says the result was 'by no means unsatisfactory', the warning bell had been sounded. I remember saying to her, 'Oh well, that's over then.'

'Oh no,' she said, 'that's just the beginning.'

The Meyer challenge had set a precedent and she knew that there was nothing to stop another challenge the following year from a more serious candidate. Denis also registered the telltale cracks: 'We had too many people voting against her.'

*　　*　　*

Christmas at Chequers was a welcome relief from the pressures of the previous few months. The day after Boxing Day Denis drove himself to Ashridge golf course, a few miles from Chequers, and met Cecil Parkinson and two friends on the first tee. 'We had the most tremendous match and Denis and I went round in some amazing score like seventy-eight,' recalls Cecil. 'He said he had never played better golf. Afterwards, we arranged to have a return match the same day next year. Sadly, it was not to be.'

The combination of golf and politics doesn't always guarantee success on the fairways. In April 1990, when the Prime Minister flew to Bermuda for weekend talks with new US President George Bush, Denis found himself called upon to play golf in some of the most atrocious weather the island has ever seen.

Bernard Ingham was glad it wasn't him. 'The forecast for the following day was absolutely abominable and George Bush said to Denis, "You'll be playing golf with us tomorrow, Denis, won't you?" Denis had heard the weather report and said, "Oh, I'm not a very good golfer at all, I'm not a good golfer."

'"That's exactly the kind we want," said Bush,' thereby closing Denis's last escape hatch.

By breakfast the following morning the Atlantic storm was in full force, with rain slanting sideways and palm trees arching. Charles Powell recalls Denis looking absolutely shattered as he sat down to breakfast at Government House: the sea was a stormy blur.

The President was due to ring with the golfing arrangements but Denis took one look outside and cheered up. 'Of course, the President *can't* want to play golf today,' he said.

The telephone rang and was handed to Denis. 'Yes, Mr President. What? Golf today? Are you sure, George? Is this wise? All right, I'll be there.'

Never one to duck anything, Denis set off for the exclusive Mid-Ocean Club, the best course in Bermuda and one of the top fifty in the world. 'There we were, waiting for the great man to arrive on the first tee, dressed up in waterproofs and a fellow in the crowd told me that his family had been in Bermuda since 1823 and it was the worst day they'd ever seen.'

The plutocratic colonial-style mansions overlooking the course almost disappeared in the dense rain, but the soggy presidential foursome played on.

> We got to the end of the first nine holes – including some perilous dog-legs ringed with hazards, and I had water pouring down my neck. The entire experience was most uncomfortable and unpalatable. We were ushered into a brick clubhouse and my spirits rose in the hope of being offered a black coffee and a couple of slugs of brandy. Surely the ordeal was over, I thought, and I could be off to a hot bath to facilitate recovery.
>
> What did I get? A glass of Coca-Cola and the President chivvying us, 'Come on . . . off for the next nine holes.' It was the worst game of golf I've ever played.

Denis realized that, at the age of seventy-five, his golfing days were numbered. Before flying in August to Aspen, Colerado, where President Bush was making a speech at the Aspen Institute's fortieth anniversary, Denis investigated the possibility of having a game.

Henry Catto, then American Ambassador to Britain, had asked Denis if there was anything he could do for him in advance. 'Yes,' he replied, 'could you rent me a set of left-handed clubs?' Lowering his voice, he added, 'Women's clubs, because I'm so god-damned old I can't swing men's clubs any more.'

Margaret was scheduled to deliver the closing address at the Institute and it looked, on paper, like a relatively relaxing few days in the American Rockies. She, Denis and Crawfie stayed in a chalet-style guest house on Henry Catto's ranch on a mountain near Woody Creek, about twenty minutes north-west of Aspen. The chalet was nicknamed 'Parliament House' after a couple of owls the Cattos had noticed standing sentry on their first visit. Henry's wife Jessica had decided to leave it simply furnished and curtain-free and, until the British PM and accompanying security men arrived, the only thing likely to appear in the windows was a wandering bear.

This setting should have been idyllic but the forests were thick with American Secret Service agents and Denis found it impossible to sleep at that altitude (Aspen town is at nearly 8,000 feet).

The calm was shattered on 2 August, when Iraq invaded Kuwait.

With President Bush staying in the Cattos' main house, just a few minutes down the road, it probably seemed a perfect opportunity for two prominent world leaders to chorus their disapproval. Unfortunately, it nearly turned into a *Carry On* farce. The chalet had only one telephone line, so Crawfie found herself cooking breakfast while answering the phone to the likes of Prince Bandar bin Sultan, the Saudi Ambassador to the US, and other international heads desperate to talk to the British Prime Minister. And Margaret couldn't even reach President Bush because the overzealous security men had closed the road.

Amid the chaos Denis remained totally aloof, engrossed in a novel he'd brought along for such an eventuality.

The fate of Kuwait was just one of the worries that confronted the government at home. Almost every new economic and market indicator delivered bad tidings, and on 18 October came the crushing news that Ian Gow's seat of Eastbourne had been lost to the Liberal Democrats. Gow, Margaret's first principal private secretary and a good family friend, had been killed by an IRA car bomb on Monday 30 July.

Many backbenchers were anxious about their own seats and this gloom deepened when Geoffrey Howe resigned from the Cabinet on 1 November, unable to resolve his differences with the Prime Minister over a single European currency. This triggered speculation about another possible leadership challenge, particularly when Howe made a dramatic resignation speech in the House of Commons, inviting Michael Heseltine to stand.

The following day, Wednesday 14 November, Cranley (later Sir Cranley) Onslow, the Chairman of the 1922 Committee, telephoned the Prime Minister to say that he'd received formal notification of Heseltine's intention to challenge Margaret. This time it was no stalking horse candidate: Heseltine was seen by some in the party as the person who could restore the government's popularity.

It's a measure of how astutely Denis judged the danger that a week earlier he'd written a letter to John Harvey, a friend and colleague from Burmah Oil days, summing up his feelings about the criticism of his wife.

The usual combination of the 'ambitious coupled with the dis-affected' and 'disappointed' is nothing new – indeed when we passed ten years I have long foretold it.

Sad for our party and even more sad for our country with Kinnock and co in power.

One gets both philosophical and realistic at our age.

Not Margaret's fault: one wonders what the great Churchill would have said of those who wish to 'sell' the House of Commons to Brussels; and what he would have said of Heath, the latter day appeaser of a latter day Hitler.

TWENTY

'SHE'S DONE FOR'

*'Congratulations, Sweetie Pie, you've won; it's just
the rules.'*

DENIS THATCHER

WHEN WE SAT DOWN TO DINNER at Chequers on Saturday 17
November 1990 there was no particular feeling of unease about
the Tory leadership ballot in three days' time. It was unusual for
the Prime Minister to entertain on a Saturday night, but she was
surrounded by friends, including Alistair McAlpine, Gordon Reece,
Kenneth Baker, Tim Bell and the late Sir Peter Morrison.

Denis was in fine form, although suffering from writer's cramp
after spending the morning signing Christmas cards. It always took
my parents about two days to sign the thousands of cards sent out
to friends, colleagues and party members.

I sat down next to Peter Morrison, Margaret's campaign
manager, and asked him about Tuesday's leadership ballot. 'I
don't expect to deliver anything other than good news,' he said
reassuringly.

Margaret was due to fly to Paris the following day for the CSCE
Summit on Monday. Some of her closest advisers thought she
should stay in London until the ballot, marshalling her supporters
to guarantee herself a comfortable victory.

She wouldn't hear of it. She was the Prime Minister and felt her
place was at the summit. This is what people expected of her and
she refused to let her enemies within the Conservative Party divert
her from her duty.

After dinner we retired to the Great Hall and, as the guests began
leaving, Margaret asked Alistair McAlpine and Gordon Reece to
stay behind.

Peter Morrison had told Margaret: 'I've done a trawl and I think you'll have a majority of forty. Make an allowance for the fact that perhaps fifteen of them are just telling me that and you'll have a comfortable majority. It won't be that comfortable but it'll be all right.'

Turning to Gordon, Margaret said ruefully: 'Where have we heard all that before?'

'We've heard that before Ted Heath in 1975,' he replied, 'and the fact is that people tell stories to representatives of leaders of parties because they don't want to block themselves out for future promotions.'

'Yes, exactly,' she said.

Gordon also wanted her to stay in London rather than going to Paris. 'A few telephone calls from you personally tomorrow could swing the day because if you lose you're not going to lose by many – you're only talking about ten, even if all these figures are completely out.'

'No,' said the Prime Minister, her mind already made up.

The following morning I was up early, preparing to return to London. I left my bedroom at the very top of the house and walked down and along the gallery overlooking the Great Hall to my mother's dressing-room, where she was doing her boxes. I didn't want to keep her and simply said goodbye and good luck.

Surrounded by files, she looked at me and replied: 'I might lose, but I don't think I will.'

I left with the impression that she truly believed it would be all right on the night, while I began to have doubts about her position. Many of my journalistic contacts had been warning me all week that my mother's campaign was pathetic and that she was in danger of losing.

I went back upstairs, collected my things and walked out to my car. One of the staff came out to say goodbye and said in utterly neutral tones, 'Goodbye, Miss Thatcher, I hope we see you again soon.' It was as if she was tactfully distancing herself – ready for the next occupant.

As I drove out of the inner gate onto the drive, I took a long look at Chequers through the rearview mirror. Almost without thinking, I said to myself, 'I'll never come here again.'

If I was profoundly uneasy about the outcome of the vote, my father was positively pessimistic. On Sunday night, as Margaret was about to leave for Paris, Crawfie found Denis in the drawing room of the flat and said goodbye.

'By the way, Mr Thatcher, where will you be when we get news of the first ballot?' she asked.

Denis didn't answer and seemed lost in thought as he nursed a large gin. Finally he whispered, 'Crawfie, she's done for.'

The magnitude of what he was saying barely registered – as if, somehow, it was all happening to someone else. Years later he would call it a 'gut feeling that she would lose'. That is so like my father who, despite his analytical accountant's mind, often makes decisions or gives advice on the basis that it 'feels right'. It might not be scientific or factual; he might not be able to list his reasons or argue the case, but he was rarely wrong.

The following afternoon Denis was watching TV in the flat when he heard the result of the first ballot – Thatcher: 204 votes; Michael Heseltine: 152; 16 abstentions. She was only two short of overall victory under the rules stipulating that the winner must have a majority of at least 15 per cent of those entitled to vote.

Fifteen years earlier, in the boardroom of Burmah Oil, Denis had been handed a piece of paper with the result of another leadership ballot. Back then he hadn't taken much notice of victory margins and majorities – he claimed to have little understanding or interest in them. But, as a statistics man, he knew what this result meant. It confirmed not only the Conservative Party's capacity for treachery, but also his own presentiments of doom.

The telephone rang and he picked it up. Margaret was calling from Paris. It was only a short conversation because she was due at a summit banquet in Versailles hosted by President Mitterrand.

Denis was fabulous: 'Congratulations, Sweetie Pie, you've won; it's just the rules,' he said, as tears trickled down his face. He was crying for her, not for himself. Margaret did well to hide her disappointment, telling him that she'd decided to fight on in the second ballot.

A friend who was with Denis says, 'He put the phone down, turned to me and said: "We've had it. We're out."'

That night my father dined with Mark, who was visiting from Dallas, and a friend at Buck's Club, in Clifford Street. Mark did his best to be jolly, telling him, 'Don't worry, she'll win next round.' Margaret was still in Paris but had publicly announced that she would definitely stand in the second ballot.

When I got home that evening there were a lot of calls on the answering machine. Most of them were from semi-political friends and journalists who were saying, 'Yes, she really can still win. She should fight on – knuckle down for the next twenty-four hours and start grubbing around for votes.' People were saying that if you lose by two it is perceived as carelessness but if you lose by twenty, pack your bags – your time is up.

Margaret was back at Number Ten by lunchtime, still vowing to fight on, but Denis had already made up his mind. He took Peter Morrison to one side and said, 'Please, please do everything you can to persuade her not to stand in the second ballot.'

More than anything else, he was desperate not to see her humiliated. He loved her, perhaps more now than at any time during their life together, and he couldn't bear to see her hurt. He had always told her to quit while she was ahead, to go out at the top – all those sporting clichés he loved to use. He hoped against hope that she'd listen.

I had a call from Charles Powell, who had been with her in Paris. 'Everyone is absolutely gung-ho to go for the second ballot,' he said, 'except your father.'

'What about Dad?' I asked.

'He seems quite anxious – I don't think he wants her to stand again.'

Margaret was spending the evening in the Cabinet Room working on her speech for the No Confidence debate the next day. 'She's only having sandwiches for dinner,' Charles told me. 'Will you do something with Denis?'

'Of course,' I said. 'I'll ask Alistair if he can come and dine with us.' A group of us were due to have dinner with Alistair McAlpine at Mark's Club in Charles Street, Mayfair.

That afternoon the Prime Minister went to the House to report on the Paris summit, and on a tour of the tea rooms, discovered how demoralized her supporters were. Still determined to fight on, she immediately secured the support of Douglas Hurd and a slightly reluctant John Major for the second ballot.

Then she saw the Cabinet one by one. Almost to a man, they said the same thing: if she did stand, they would support her. However, in order to avoid 'humiliation' (their favourite word), she should resign and let someone who could win (i.e. someone from the Cabinet) stand against Michael Heseltine. The tide was running against her, and departure looked inevitable.

Norman Tebbit recalls seeing the Prime Minister in the House: she told him that she was going to draft her resignation. He urged her: 'You mustn't do that until you've seen Denis.'

All afternoon my telephone rang and I was pleased to have an excuse to get out of the house. The *Evening Standard* had asked me to judge their 'Pub of the Year' competition and, as I closed the front gate, I thought, 'Thank God I don't have to worry about Mum for the next few hours.'

One of the pubs on the shortlist was virtually my local, the White Horse on Parson's Green. Two of my fellow judges were Angus McGill from the *Standard* and Willie Rushton, who are always a laugh. I had already had a glass of wine before I left home and, as I walked into the pub, they poured me another large one.

Willie looked up and said: 'Carol, by the way, I'm thinking of standing for the second ballot and Angus might even throw his hat into the ring too.'

I grinned and suddenly relaxed. Not surprisingly, by the time I got to Mark's Club I was well-wined. Everyone was sitting down at the table. Alistair immediately ordered a large bottle of champagne. 'Right, you lot,' he said. 'Everyone in the place knows who we are so we all have to look frightfully up.'

I slurped down a bit more champagne - already feeling 'up' - and looked across at Denis. I could tell he was struggling to be jolly.

'Well, how are things?' I asked Alistair in a quiet moment.

'Come into the bar and I'll tell you.'

He looked downcast. 'She's seen the Cabinet and they have defected one by one. She's decided she is going to resign.'

I couldn't believe it. 'But yesterday, in Paris, she said she would fight to win. It's not like her; she doesn't back down.' The enormity of Alistair's news took time to sink in. I wanted her to go on, but then I wasn't exactly seeing it from her perspective.

Alistair said, 'Ah, Carol, you're not the one having holes shot in you.'

He was right, of course. I hadn't seen it that way.

At the end of the evening Alistair said, 'You have my car and take your father home.'

The chauffeur headed towards Downing Street but, knowing that TV cameras and photographers would be massed outside Number Ten, I asked him to drop us on Horse Guards Parade. I got out and started walking with Denis across the parade ground towards the base of the Foreign Office steps. It was dark and windy so Denis wrapped himself in his phantom-like Nelson cape. We were arm in arm as we trudged across the wet gravel and ahead I could see the eerie glow of TV lights lighting up the exterior of Number Ten.

Halfway across Horse Guards Denis stopped and turned to look at me. He pushed up his glasses and I could see tears in his eyes. 'Oh, it's just the disloyalty of it all,' he whispered and we hugged. It was the only time I have ever seen him cry.

'Look, Dad, what really matters now is Mum. It's going to be a hell of a shock and we have to support her,' I said, fighting back the tears. 'We have to do everything we can to make it easier.'

We trudged to the policebox at the back of Number Ten. The policeman came out and I said: 'Please will you see my father up the steps.'

As Denis left, I told him, 'Goodnight, Dad, let's all be strong and see what tomorrow brings.'

Denis went straight up to bed, but I doubt if he or Margaret got any sleep that night.

At my home in Fulham I found a message on my answering machine from Richard Ryder, MP for Mid Norfolk, who had worked for Margaret in Opposition and had married Caroline

Stephens in 1981. I had known both of them a long time and they were very good friends. 'Whatever time it is, ring me,' he said on the tape.

I knew Richard was someone who could tell me what had really happened. He explained how the tide had turned against Margaret. 'Look, Carol, you have to understand ... there just isn't the support. The defections were all over the place.'

I thanked him for being so honest and said how much I appreciated that he and Caroline had thought to call me. At least now we have an ending, I thought.

It was just after 8 a.m. when Denis rang me. He began, 'There have been all sorts of consultations and your mother ...'

I interrupted, 'I know, Dad.'

There was silence and we finally said goodbye. There was nothing more to say.

About mid-morning I rang Number Ten and spoke to Joy Robilliard, who told me that Margaret was OK, 'although a bit weepy and liable to break down if anyone says anything nice to her'.

'I'm not going to speak to her because I think I might cry,' I said.

'She's not taking any calls at all,' said Joy. 'And she's not seeing anyone until she makes her speech this afternoon.'

Bernard Ingham and Charles Powell went in to see Denis, who was breakfasting in the dining room. Bernard thought 'he looked relieved in a quietly subdued way. He could see that this whole long interminable saga was over. I think he was sad about the circumstances and he might even have been quietly seething underneath at the way in which it was done, but I don't think he was actually sorry that it was over.'

Afterwards, Denis left with Peter Morrison to go to Elizabeth Douglas-Home's memorial service, and got his first taste of the public reaction: 'I think a lot of people were slightly surprised to see me there. I remember Ken Baker came up to me and said, "The whole country is outraged."' He had lunch with Pools tycoon Paul Zetter at Mosimann's before returning to Number Ten to watch his wife's speech in the House.

That morning I let the machine pick up most of my calls, but answered one – from a journalist at the *Evening Standard*. 'There is a strong rumour that your mother is going to resign,' he said.

'Thank you, I shall turn on the telly,' I replied, hanging up.

The announcement was brief and explosive: a one-line statement at 9.25 a.m. signalling the end of Margaret Thatcher's eleven and a half years as Prime Minister. She would not stand in the second ballot; she was stepping down as party Leader and would resign as Prime Minister when her successor had been chosen.

All day the telephone rang and flowers arrived at the door. Friends from around the world were asking, 'How could this happen?' I even had a call from Saudi Arabia from a press photographer covering the Gulf War; he was incredulous: 'When will she be reinstated?' he asked. Many were angered by the utter injustice of it all; my mother had won three general elections for the Conservative Party and this is how they repaid her.

However furious I was, I told myself that it wasn't for me to say anything to the journalists waiting outside the house. But as I went out, I turned to one and said: 'After all she's done, I think this is an act of gutless treachery. As far as I'm concerned Tory is now a four-letter word.'

I could hardly bear to watch the televised No Confidence debate: the thought of Margaret breaking down and not being able to get through it was dreadful. When she rose to address the House at 4.50 p.m., I kept turning the TV on and off until I was sure she was OK.

I knew that she'd make it after Dennis Skinner, the acid-tongued Labour MP for Bolsover, interjected and suggested she should become the first governor of a proposed Central European Bank.

The Prime Minister replied: 'What a good idea, I hadn't thought of that . . .' the House erupted in laughter '. . . I shall consider the proposal from the honourable Member for Bolsover, now, where were we? I am enjoying this.'

I was amazed. How on earth could she pull this off?

Back in the flat, Denis was watching it with a friend and several drinks. He was bursting with pride, and, when Margaret returned, he leapt up, moist-eyed and said, 'That was wonderful . . . brilliant . . . magnificent.' Then he reminded her, 'If your view had triumphed and the House of Commons had not been televised, millions of people would not have seen it. . .'

The Prime Minister was on a high. It might not have been her greatest speech, but I doubt if she has ever delivered one more brilliantly. As she sat down, she joked, 'Wasn't Dennis [Skinner] wonderful? I wonder if when the Resignation honours come out he'd accept one. How about Baron Skinner of Bolsover.'

I hadn't spoken to my mother since eight o'clock on Sunday morning, so after her Commons speech, I rang Joy and said, 'I'd really like to speak to her this evening; let me know when I can.'

'You can now, she's just come in.'

I wasn't prepared. I was hoping to plan what I was going to say.

'Hello,' said Margaret.

'Oh, Mum, it's me. I think you're a heroine.' And then I burst into tears. 'I don't know how you made that speech. It's just so awful what they've done – your party are complete shits.'

She calmly replied, 'Well, they've done what the Labour Party didn't manage to do in three elections – defeat me.' Unable to hide the bitterness in her voice, she told me that at the end of her speech she had seen Conservative members cheering and waving their order papers – members she knew had voted against her. Self-controlled yet elated, she was still on a high after her speech to the House and had not yet contemplated the future, but she rang off saying, 'Carol, I think my place in history is assured.'

She was right. One day another woman might become Britain's Prime Minister and maybe she would win three consecutive general elections, but she could never be the first to do it. Nor were there enough years left for anyone to become a longer serving Prime Minister this century. Her records would be intact long after the lesser men who had deposed her were forgotten.

That night Denis went to Harrow for the Churchill Centenary Songs. He had been invited by Robin Butler, Cabinet Secretary and head of the Home Civil Service, who was a governor of the school. No one would have blamed Denis for not turning up, but he didn't want to let Robin down. They were firm friends and my father admired him enormously, not least because he was an Oxford rugby blue, a head boy at Harrow and a man who had fast-tracked his way to the top of the Civil Service at a young age.

At the end of the evening the audience gave Denis a standing ovation, a remarkable gesture which summed up the guests' feelings of shock and disbelief.

The next morning the *Daily Mail* front page announced: SHE'S TOO DAMN GOOD FOR THEM.

Reading the extravagant tributes, I almost felt as if she'd won rather than lost.

Over the next few days, Denis vacillated between relief that their time in Number Ten was over and fury at the treachery. He appeared shaken, almost numb, becoming tearful when he saw Margaret's hurt.

Thankfully, my mother had very little time to ponder the fact that she was out of the top job. The following weekend was dominated by the leadership struggle, as Michael Heseltine, John Major and Douglas Hurd battled to win the favour of Conservative MPs. There is no doubt that one of the reasons Margaret resigned was to stop Heseltine becoming Prime Minister. She immediately threw her support behind John Major, who had gone through more jobs in a shorter space of time than any known politician: – over the previous three years he had been Chief Secretary to the Treasury, Secretary of State for Foreign and Commonwealth Affairs, and Chancellor of the Exchequer.

The weekend was chaotic. Crawfie, Joy and others were scrambling around the flat, trying to mark what stayed, what moved to the house in Dulwich and what went into storage. 'I'll come in and move my junk out,' I told them and suddenly found myself involved in a full-scale operation.

It was incredible how much stuff my parents had managed to accumulate in what was basically a rented furnished flat. The floor was covered with books, clothes, lamps, porcelain, over-flowing wastepaper baskets and half-filled garbage bags.

The TV cameras and photographers were still camped outside, doing their 'pieces to camera' and prattling on about history being made. If only they had known that inside, Margaret was standing in her stockinged feet surrounded by mobile wardrobes and tea-chests, deciding whether to wrap the knick-knacks in two layers of paper to prevent breakage or whether one would do.

All day Saturday Denis's battered Ford Cortina ferried stuff up and down to Dulwich. I was doing the same in my Mini Metro, taking my gear from Downing Street to Fulham.

Mark arrived setting new records for transatlantic travel. He had been in London for the first ballot and had flown back to Dallas after having dinner with Denis. When he heard the news, he took the next plane back again.

Margaret was incredibly busy as she tried to juggle moving with her political duties. During a live broadcast for the 'Frost' pro-gramme from the steps of Number Ten, I was asked if my mother would be writing her memoirs. 'Right now, she could pen a very good hand-book on how to do a fast move,' I said.

In many ways it was a strange hiatus – the future was too far off to consider and Margaret was still Prime Minister until the new leadership ballot on Tuesday.

On Saturday afternoon someone shouted, 'George Bush on the phone.' Margaret got up, moved packing cases, edged around bags and finally picked up the receiver. Suddenly she snapped straight back into prime ministerial mode and began discussing the Gulf War.

Later that afternoon she asked me, 'Do you want to come to Chequers, Darling? It'll be the last time.'

'No. I said goodbye to Chequers last weekend.'

Knowing how much they adored the house, I wanted them to have their privacy. Their final lunch with two friends at the small window table where they'd had their first meal at Chequers was a miserable one. No one knew what to say. Margaret broke a long silence, staring out of the window at the rose garden and com-menting, 'Look, there's a late rose.'

According to one of the guests, 'They were walking hand in hand in tears along the gallery that overlooked the Great Hall.' They were absolutely heartbroken at leaving the house they had lived in for eleven years.

* * *

Having the house in Dulwich was a godsend. When Ted Heath lost the general election in 1974, he had nowhere to go. Eventually, they had to give him Chequers for the weekend, and then the Duke of Westminster provided him with a house in Chapel Street.

After that, Denis had said, 'Look, we should never be homeless. You don't know with politics; we might have to move in a hurry and we must have somewhere to go.'

Dulwich wasn't their first choice. They found a property near Regent's Park but it needed quite a lot of work. Margaret hadn't time to supervise a building site and Denis didn't want to take it on. Then they were invited to spend a Saturday with Robin Butler, who had a lovely old house in Dulwich village, and they saw quite a bit of the area.

On hearing of their house-hunting, Robin said: 'Ah, but just over there is a remarkable new estate, very upmarket. Why don't we go over and have a look?'

Off they went, with Prime Minister in tow. There was a poor fellow plastering a ceiling and Margaret looked up and said, 'Gosh, that looks interesting, how do you do that?'

The chap looked down, saw who it was, and nearly fell off his ladder.

My mother loves instant solutions and said firmly, 'We'll have that one over there.' It wasn't quite finished so they made a few modifications to the plans and, Hey, Presto! – instant house.

Dulwich was considered a marvellous idea, not least because it backed onto a golf course, an obvious selling point for Denis. In reality he rarely played there: the course didn't impress him greatly, although he remembers one hole during a game with Robin Butler with particular fondness. 'It was at a short par three, about 140 yards, and I took a six-iron and hit it sweetly. Robin and I strolled up to the green and there was the ball sitting on the edge of the cup. "That's got to be a hole-in-one." I suggested, tongue-in-cheek.

'"Sorry, Denis," said Robin. So I knelt down, pressed my face to the green and blew the ball into the cup.'

Even now, Denis is still frightfully proud of the fact that he nearly hit a hole in one. In fact, mention Dulwich, and he'll talk about the sweet six-iron before he even gets round to the house.

With the packing completed, there were still the goodbyes to be said. On one of the last evenings at Number Ten, Margaret held a farewell party for her staff. She made an impromptu speech, taking off her shoes, standing on a chair and declaring, 'Life begins at sixty-five.'

Andrew Turnbull, the Prime Minister's PPS, also said a few words and ended by thanking Denis for all he'd done, adding: 'He's taught some of us around here how to be a gentleman.'

Denis replied with his usual modesty: 'I hope I've never been unkind to anyone.'

On Tuesday 27 November the final leadership ballot saw John Major emerge with 185 votes, Heseltine 131 and Hurd 56. Although my mother was no longer Prime Minister of Great Britain, she had ensured that her chosen successor would follow her into Downing Street.

Now simply the Rt Hon. Margaret Thatcher, MP for Finchley and Friern Barnet, she prepared to leave Number Ten. The staff lined up along the corridor and into the entrance hall, many sobbing uncontrollably. They started applauding and Margaret could no longer hold back her own tears. When she stepped outside into the glare of the television lights, she looked quite bewildered.

Confronting a bank of microphones, she summed up what she had changed during her premiership and then looked forward to her successor's administration. 'Now it is time for a new chapter to open and I wish John Major all the luck in the world. He will be splendidly served and he has the makings of a great Prime Minister, which I am sure he will be in a very short time . . .'

The car was waiting and Margaret got in. As the camera flashguns lit up the darkened interior, it was clear that she was crying. These photographs were bounced around the world and became the most poignant image of her final days.

The car swept away and headed south across the Thames towards Dulwich. My parents said very little. Their lives had been turned upside down in a matter of days, and it would take Margaret, in particular, a long time to recover.

For my father it was perhaps a chance to finally relax. Having delayed his retirement for so long, I think he harboured a slight hope that he would now live a more normal married life and perhaps see more of his beloved wife. At the very least, he thought, they would go back to the way they were before she became Opposition Leader.

Such dreams were quickly shattered. As the car arrived at the house in Dulwich, a journalist shouted out to Margaret, 'What are you going to do now?'

She turned, hooked her handbag over her arm and said: 'Work. That's all we have ever known.'

TWENTY-ONE

SIR DENIS THATCHER

'For forty wonderful years I have been married to one
of the greatest women the world has ever produced.
All I could produce – small as it may be – was love
and loyalty.'

DENIS THATCHER

THE FIRST TIME I saw my parents after they left Number Ten
was the following Sunday at their house in Dulwich. I went into
the sitting room and found my mother reading the Sunday papers
with the aid of a magnifying glass. This might not seem unusual,
but in the previous eleven and a half years she had rarely lifted a
Sunday paper off the neatly laid out selection on the sideboard at
Chequers. 'I must keep in touch, keep up with the news. I must
stay informed,' she explained.

Her demotion was brought home to her when President Bush
rang soon after they moved. Margaret had carefully prepared her
comments on the Gulf War, but was very disappointed and
wounded when the call turned out to be less politically substantial
than she'd been expecting.

Margaret's resignation had also removed the clockwork of her
daily existence. Along with the job, she had lost her status, VIP
treatment, staff, home (Number Ten) and weekend residence
(Chequers). And, as if that wasn't enough, she was discovering
daily that apparently loyal colleagues had really been plotters.

Even the small things were revealing. Here was a woman who
had shown that she could juggle a career and a family, who had
matched her intellect and determination against those of the most
powerful political figures in the world; yet now, stripped of power,
she had difficulty making a simple telephone call.

She hadn't had to dial a number since 1979 – in Number Ten

everything is done through the switchboard: you simply lift the receiver, ask for somebody and the operator organizes the call. Margaret had spent so long in this environment that she had forgotten all about dialling codes or redial buttons. She didn't even own an address book. When she wanted Crawfie one weekend, she had to go to the garage, where the new police post had been established, and ask them for her number. She dialled and Crawfie picked up the phone. 'It's Margaret from the garage,' she said, her voice hoarse from a head cold.

Crawfie immediately thought, Have I put my car in for a service?

'Ah, I think you may have the wrong number,' she said.

'It's Margaret.'

'Margaret who?'

'Margaret Thatcher.'

More evidence of the confusion could be found in the sitting room at Dulwich, which was littered with phone numbers written on 'post-it' notes. At one point I rang Margaret and asked why she never called me (although we didn't exactly have a tradition of chatting on the telephone).

'Because I haven't got your number, dear,' she said. Until then she'd simply asked the operator to 'Please get me Carol.'

At other times I rang to see if I could help with things like buying food, which hadn't been part of her life either; I couldn't imagine her wheeling a trolley up and down the aisles of the local Sainsbury's.

'Can you manage the supermarket shopping?' I enquired.

'Good heavens, yes, dear, I've opened enough of them,' she said.

By contrast, Denis's routine was barely disrupted by the upheaval. He carried on with his business engagements and luncheons – although he soon discovered that suburban Dulwich was incredibly inconvenient. Without the traffic jam-hopping benefits of the Prime Minister's car, the journey to Trafalgar Square took far longer than the previous time of seventeen minutes.

Denis didn't change his lifestyle one iota; he merely conducted it from a different address – or, more accurately, several of them in quick succession. After deciding that Dulwich was a mistake, they moved into an apartment in Eaton Square, borrowed from an American acquaintance.

One of his priorities was to find an office, which the Small Business Bureau provided for him in Buckingham Palace Road. Then he focused on preserving his own sanity by keeping all his appointments and carrying on as usual. The only engagements crossed out in his diary related to his former role as Prime Ministerial consort – 'To Chequers', for instance, or 'No. 10 Xmas Party'.

On leaving Downing Street he had said, 'Of course, no one's going to want to have lunch with me now,' yet if anything, his number of invitations increased: his telephone rang non-stop because so many of his friends and acquaintances had waited until it was all over to pat him on the back and congratulate him on the fabulous job he'd done as consort.

But Margaret's diary was at first virtually blank. For much of their married life she had pirouetted around the sitting room in a long dress at 7 p.m. before dashing off to make a speech or attend a dinner. Now it was Denis who, clad in dinner jacket, would prepare to go out while Margaret enquired, 'What time will you be home, dear?' and faced an evening alone eating poached egg on toast.

My father's friends stayed with him, rain, hail or shine; Margaret's stopped with politics. She would be the first to say that when you're at the top you have lots of friends, but as soon as you go they inevitably gravitate – like bees to the new honeypot – to the next occupant of Ten Downing Street.

Margaret had to reorganize her life totally and therefore needed an office. Alistair McAlpine generously loaned her his house in Great College Street, in a maze of streets between Smith Square and Westminster Abbey. She moved in with Crawfie, Amanda Ponsonby, who'd been diary secretary at Number Ten, and her detectives. Joy worked from the House of Commons where, as a backbench MP, Margaret was entitled to a desk.

She received an enormous number of letters. Sackloads of mail arrived every day, most of it from voters who wanted to vent their outrage. It was impossible for Margaret's skeletal staff to answer all the correspondence, and eventually she put a notice in *The*

Times to thank people and apologize for not being able to answer every letter personally.

I, too, received letters from absolute strangers expressing their shock at Margaret's betrayal. 'This letter should be edged in black,' one of them wrote. Another said he was 'ashamed to be British after the dastardly and cowardly way my own party have treated the Prime Minister'. An elderly voter said: 'I can remember George VI dying, and of course Churchill's death, but I cannot remember such spontaneous sadness and anger ever before.'

People from every walk of life could only sympathize. I'd been working for several years at TV-am and my boss there, outgoing Australian Bruce Gyngell, and his wife Kathy had invited me to dinner, along with David (now Sir David) Frost, his wife Lady Carina and several others. When Margaret was so unexpectedly forced out, Bruce telephoned me to ask if she'd like to come too.

Rupert Murdoch and Sky TV supremo Sam Chisholm also joined the party at the Gyngells' Chelsea home. Margaret had to leave at ten o'clock for a vote in the House and, after she'd left, I asked Rupert Murdoch, 'How do you think she is?'

'Absolutely shell-shocked,' he said, 'but if I'd lost everything, so would I be.'

It would be years before the gales of bitterness softened into breezes of reminiscences for Margaret and sometimes, when her car drove down Whitehall and she was working in the back, she'd look up when they overshot the turning to Downing Street. Why hadn't they turned in? Then she remembered – she didn't have a job there any more. Similarly, she'd hear something on the news and reach for the phone to get it sorted out before seeing that her hand wasn't on the hotline.

Denis didn't have these dispiriting daily reminders and he was able to look back on the resignation more philosophically: 'the manner of our going could not have been better. God was good to us. We had the world's sympathy.'

Having left Number Ten a month before Christmas, my parents had to un-invite all the people who were due to go to Chequers and then arrange an alternative venue – a room at the Dorchester.

Denis treated himself to another Rolls-Royce, having been denied the pleasure for so long. 'After Margaret resigned, I asked her if she'd mind me getting another one. She couldn't understand my passion but agreed. After all, it wasn't her money I was spending. So I got another. I don't drive it much any more – only to board meetings in the country – not around London.'

Others felt that Denis deserved a far more valuable and long-lasting reward. On Friday 7 December 1990 the Queen bestowed on Margaret the Order of Merit – one of the nation's highest honours – and gave Denis a hereditary baronetcy making him Sir Denis Thatcher Baronet of Scotney in the County of Kent. He chose Scotney because he was born in Kent and served in a Kent regiment and felt the years we lived in the county had been especially happy ones.

The hereditary baronetcy was a remarkable honour – the first to be granted since the 1960s – particularly as it was given to a recipient with a male issue.

When she resigned, Margaret – along with a number of others who lobbied discreetly – had been extremely anxious that Denis should be recognized for the role he had played. She also wanted Mark to inherit the title eventually: she believed that the press had hounded him out of the country.

On the day the honours were announced Tim (now Sir Tim) Rice was speaking at a lunch of the Saints and Sinners Club at the Savoy in honour of Ronald Reagan. He congratulated Sir Denis and the whole dining room erupted into thunderous applause. The following morning the *Daily Mail*'s leader echoed these sentiments: 'The baronetcy given to her husband has been well-earned. Always cheerful and supportive, yet unobtrusive, he has been the perfect Prime Minister's spouse.' The *Daily Telegraph* wrote:

The simultaneous award to Mr Denis Thatcher will give the public, if anything, even greater pleasure than that to his wife. His contribution to Mrs Thatcher's long span of office has been remarkable. It is wholly appropriate that he should receive what has become a singular honour. All politicians' husbands or wives are called upon to be more long-suffering than any, enduring great responsibility without the compensations of office or power. Had Denis Thatcher put a foot wrong during the last decade, both he and his wife would have suffered heavily. Most of the world has come to see that his support for his wife has been indispensable.

Denis felt extraordinarily honoured, yet he'd always been proud of the fact that it was *his* name that his wife, as Prime Minister, made world famous.

He had a great deal of fun choosing the design for his coat of arms, which features two golden Chevrons resembling roofs to symbolize a thatcher's skills. Also, in the upper part of the shield, two Fleur-de-Lys and a Mural Crown are set in azure blue, the former an emblem of the parish of St Mary, Uffington, where my father's forebears were established over 300 years ago. A demi-Lion is the central figure in the crest, representing strength and energy, and holding a pair of thatcher's shears and a New Zealand fern.

Following his long-established policy, Denis rarely went to Margaret's office in Great College Street. He had never interfered in her professional life and wasn't going to suddenly start now that she was out of office. He took the view that she had to establish a new place for herself and a role in which she felt comfortable.

In truth, he expected that her resignation might encourage her to retire. 'I had no idea how busy we were going to be,' he says, admitting with hindsight that it was never on the cards.

My mother found it desperately difficult to take her foot off the accelerator and to shift out of the fast lane into the slow lane of a backbencher. She undertook a succession of 'farewell tours' at the invitation of foreign hosts who wished to salute her achievements as a world leader.

The highlight was in Washington in March 1991, when President George Bush awarded her the Medal of Freedom, the highest honour a foreigner can receive from the US government. The atmosphere was so relaxed that the President quipped to Crawfie before the dinner, 'If we go on meeting like this people will think we're going steady.'

About sixty guests attended the dinner in the Yellow Oval Room of the White House – among them Vice-President Dan Quayle, Katharine Graham and David Frost. During the meal various guests stood up and shared impromptu reminiscences of the Thatcher years. Barbara Bush eventually goaded Denis into saying a few words. He rose, cleared his throat and said, 'Like Caesar going into Cleopatra's tent, I didn't come here to talk.'

There were shrieks of laughter, although Margaret wasn't impressed. 'I think she thought it was a bit vulgar,' explains Denis. 'I suppose it is really, but you've got to say something and make them laugh. It's not really Margaret's style; it's my style.

'I remember my old grandma, who was the last of the Edwardian snobs, saying to me, "Gentlemen can be coarse but never vulgar." I don't know whether she would think I was coarse or vulgar that evening in the White House.'

After eleven and a half years, Denis left Downing Street with a rich accumulation of anecdotes and experiences. In one post-resignation speech, to the Captains of Cambridgeshire Golf Clubs, he told his audience, 'I am now asked of my experience of the years at "Ten". Well I'll tell you: we were booed in Blackburn, bamboozled in Blantyre – bitched, buggered and bewildered in Bombay, and bombed in Brighton. When I tell you this happened every year for eleven years through every other letter of the alphabet, you will appreciate we had a wonderful time.'

He displayed great modesty in his acceptance speech at a dinner hosted by the Jurade St Emilion at the Carlton Club on 26 November 1992. 'I have in recent years received certain honours which I have not deserved and far less earned. It is therefore a great honour – as usual unearned – to be intronized into this ancient and illustrious Jurade of St Emilion and to have my own piece of ermine and thus keep pace with my wife – if that were possible, which it is not.'

Although Denis didn't foresee the sheer volume of his wife's engagements, he showed no signs of trimming his own hectic schedule. He was often out five nights a week at various meetings, dinners and ceremonies. The pace would have exhausted a man half his age.

He seemed to savour his role as the elder statesman of consorts and occasionally passed on the benefit of his experience to others. A classic is his reply to 'Mr Connecticut', an American who asked for advice on how he should approach the role of consort; his wife had just been made president of the local riding club.

Dear Mr Connecticut,

Thank you for your letter of 6 May which I return for easy reference. I am unsure whether there is a similarity of scope or scale of being the spouse of the President of a Riding Club with that of being the spouse of the Prime Minister of the United Kingdom.

The following guidelines which are not in order of priority may be of operational assistance to you.

a) Never ever talk to the Press, Local or National. A smiling 'Good Morning' will suffice. Remember that it is better to keep your mouth shut and be *thought* a fool than open it and remove all doubt. Avoid telling them to 'sod off'; it makes them cross.

b) Never ever appear *speaking* on TV. This is the short road to disaster.

c) Never make speeches longer than four minutes, and prepare them very carefully to ensure that there is no possible quote. This results in the Press not ever reporting you were there at all.

d) When visiting or opening factories, i.e. horse shoe manufacturers, saddle makers, animal feeds, etc., take the elementary precaution of reading their last Annual Report so you know what sort of corporation it is and whether it makes any money, then you can ask moderately intelligent or tactful questions.

e) When Members of the Club approach you with complaints and suggestions as to the conduct thereof, listen attentively and then say 'I will pass on your excellent comments,' and *then* forget it.

f) Avoid the small function whenever possible. The Annual Picnic for the Stable Boys on Lincoln's Birthday can be deadly. Carry a hipflask so you can lace the Coca-Cola but *don't* get caught doing it.

g) Avoid any possible 'run in' with the Police or FBI as this tends to attract unfavourable comment.

The price of keeping moderately trouble free is everlasting vigilance and the strict observance of the above rules of the game.

Good Luck and good wishes . . .

DENIS THATCHER

It was advice that he felt many others could benefit from – particularly the younger royals, who seemed to court the media spotlight rather than avoid it. At a dinner Denis found himself sitting next to the Duchess of York, who had recently been monopolizing the headlines.

'Oh, Denis, I do get an awful press, don't I,' she whined.

At which point Denis leaned back, pinched his thumb and forefinger together and made a theatrical zipping motion across his lips. 'Yes, Ma'am. Has it occurred to you to keep your mouth shut . . . ?'

This was the key to his success and in his view required no great skill. 'There's no secret – a lot of people should learn that. You take Fergie: she parades herself in *Hello* magazine crying poor or complaining. No wonder she gets an awful press. She should have learned a long time ago to keep her mouth shut.'

Another who could learn the lesson, he thought, was Hillary Clinton, who set out to break new and controversial ground as America's First Lady by taking an active role in policy decisions and campaigning. Denis predicted the result. 'If you open your mouth in this business then you're dead. Look at Hillary Clinton; she's not doing the US government any good.'

Even before the publication of Margaret's memoirs, *Downing Street Years* and *The Path to Power*, her every public utterance created a headline. Eager to manufacture stories, the media set out to look for direct or implied criticism of her successor in Downing Street. Margaret was accused of 'sour grapes' or criticized for 'damaging the party'. Some of her detractors likened her to Ted Heath, who spent years sniping at Margaret from the backbenches, much to his own discredit.

Denis's views of the media had not mellowed upon leaving Number Ten. The memories of what he regarded as the 'absolutely lunatic criticism of my woman' were still too fresh in his mind. His attitude hardened as he read the reporting of her rare public utterances. Such was his anger that he broke his own rule of silence and defended his wife during a speech he made to Archie (later Sir Archibald) Hamilton's constituency of Epsom and Ewell before the 1992 general election.

I have carefully avoided saying anything at all which could be construed as expressing a personal view on any subject on the current political scene – well knowing that someone somewhere was lying in wait for me 'to put up a black' for next morning's newspaper or, inevitably, the BBC's 'Today' programme. This evening I am going to depart from my rule and doubtless will live to regret it.

Chairman, it seems to me that the right of free speech which our country has embraced for centuries is now denied to one good and intensely patriotic citizen – namely the last Prime Minister.

Every time Margaret makes a speech or gives a TV interview at home or abroad on any subject she earns vicious obloquy from the media, who misrepresent what she has said. Worse, she is accused of disloyalty to the Prime Minister and dividing our party.

This is neither true nor fair. Are the many present problems at home and abroad any less important than they were a year ago? Why is it now wrong when a backbench MP with thirty-two years' experience in the Commons, to say nothing of twenty years of knowledge as a cabinet minister and junior minister, expresses her opinions on matters which affect the future of our country both at home and abroad.

He then went on to attack the real enemy – socialism. It was an extraordinarily fighting speech, which showed his depth of feeling for his 'beloved wife'.

He often despaired at the press coverage of Mark's business affairs, saying dejectedly on one occasion, 'I never thought I'd see my family name on the front page of the *Sunday Times* associated with fraud.'

Margaret left the House of Commons at the 1992 general election and accepted a Life Peerage, becoming Baroness Thatcher of Kesteven in the county of Lincolnshire. Denis was absolutely pro her becoming a life and not a hereditary peer, because he says pointedly, 'We're not that sort of people.'

On 11 November 1993 he gave one of the most impressive and important speeches of his life, revealing his philosophy of life to an unprecedented degree. He was addressing the Baronets Dinner in London.

Now, in the evening of my days, I am here to speak in this noble and historic Grocers Hall in the City of London which has – over the centuries – hosted the greatest orators of our country. Which hall, dare I say, is specially adorned by Michael Noakes's portrait of the second greatest Prime Minister of *this* century. I am told – you miss her . . .

One has to be humble. After a long life I have now concluded that one *never* reaches the top of the greasy pole.

One arrives, you will recall, at a prep school – small, frightened, insignificant and very, very junior. An experienced and wise child, at least ten years older, tells you, 'You don't get beaten here so long as you don't say anything.'

After four years, able to read and write, a member of the eleven, possibly a prefect and, therefore, locally important, one believes one has climbed a foot or two up the pole . . .

One moves then to the army – as many here did – and one is the Junior Subaltern. The reception on that first evening in the Mess is, if anything, worse than on the previous occasions. The Senior Subaltern speaks as though God to Moses, saying, 'I am the Senior Subaltern, you call me Sir. I do not want to hear a word from you for six months, and do exactly what your Troop Sergeant tells you.'

The few years move on and comes war. With only slightly more brain-power but even more cunning, the climb up the greasy pole starts again and one arrives to be the Brigade Major, perhaps even a local lieutenant-colonel. Important, you are now, and to a lot of people, for one is expected to guide the Brigade Commander *not* to make silly decisions like getting people killed, if only in one's own self interest.

After some years peace breaks out and one seeks a new career in industry – and, by luck – a job as an assistant works manager (you can't be more junior than that).

The reception does not change. A terrifying works director says, 'Good grief, not another ex-officer! Take over the chemical plant. Do what the foreman tells you and for God's sake don't say anything and cause a strike.'

The years go by and, with even more cunning, one climbs the pole – getting greasier by the year – but some small success comes.

An appointment to the Board – the Junior Director. The reception this time is slightly more civilized. The Chairman receives you with effusive kindness – barely knowing your name – saying 'Glad to have you, my boy.' And then with an arm round the shoulder goes on, 'Don't take up the time of the Board – if I need your view I'll ask for it.' The message is familiar.

The years roll on and one arrives – vicariously – at Downing Street. The top of the pole – now inches thick in grease – is within reach. The reception there is deferential, smooth if perhaps mooted.

The message does not change and is, perhaps, even more explicit. 'Don't say anything,' they said and please (that was a change), 'don't do anything.'

After a lifetime of saying nothing and doing nothing, the following twelve years presented neither challenge nor problem.

It seems, however, I was half-successful, for Our Liege Lady and Gracious Majesty – probably against Her better judgement – appointed me to your Noble Order. The top of the pole one thinks is now within touching.

As befits the noblesse oblige of beloved Toby Clarke my reception to your number has been, of course, generous, kindly and welcoming. *But* I am now – so help me – the Junior Baronet – back where I was on that first day at prep school sixty-odd years ago.

It seems that in this classless society I am likely to remain in this rank. This time, Mr Chairman, as the new Junior here I have *not* received the usual message, *but* I have given myself one – culled from *Henry VI Part II* where the King says, '. . . in thy face I see the map of honour, truth, and loyalty' . . . which message goes on to my son and grandson who will follow me, as the Second and Third Baronet of Scotney.

On that note, Mr Chairman, My Lord, Ladies, Gentlemen and Brother Baronets – with humility I invite you to join me in the Toast of the Baronetcy.

May we prosper, root and branch.

Although the 'Dear Bill' letters were no more – having been discontinued when the Thatchers were no longer resident at Number Ten – their legacy continued and occasionally allowed Denis to live up to the persona that had been created for him.

When Gordon Reece was in hospital, Denis and Margaret came to visit him. 'I managed a rather sick hello and said, "Very kind of you to come and see me, Denis. Thank you very much." His bedside manner was typically unsympathetic: "My dear Reece, you can rely on me to come to your deathbed anytime."'

Denis even managed to get a little of his own back on his nemesis Richard Ingrams, the former editor of *Private Eye*, who later founded the *Oldie* magazine and gave Denis the Glengoyne Oldie of the Year award. At the celebratory lunch at the Savoy Denis rose to speak:

This is a luncheon, with Mr Ingrams here, to which I have long awaited an invitation. Sad – I am – that Boris isn't here. In the middle of 1990 they carted him off to Siberia on the grounds of his being politically incorrect. A gross injustice. There were more people coming in and out of Number Ten in that year who were more politically incorrect than poor Boris is ever likely to be.

Sorry too that the Major isn't here. As you know, he recently dropped dead on the tenth green after a surfeit of tinctures at lunch.

I feel I am owed a lunch by Mr Ingrams, for *Private Eye* published my letters to 'Dear Bill' for many years and I have long felt that such deathless prose required some small acknowledgement. Several cases of gin at Christmas would not have come amiss so that Bill and I could be maintained with that full ration of tinctures to which we have long become accustomed, and on which we were both weaned.

However, like the taxi drivers say to me, 'All is forgiven – come back, Guv.' *Not while I'm alive!*

My mother's lifestyle remained just as programmed and planned as it became in 1975 when Margaret won the Tory leadership contest. Her itinerary is known weeks in advance; every arrival is an 'entrance', the security men having done a recce, and each step is choreographed.

Denis and Margaret still lead remarkably separate lives – passing each other on their way to various engagements. Denis doesn't look at his diary and say, 'Well, she's coming all the way around the world, it would be awfully nice if I was there and perhaps we could spend a quiet evening catching up.' It will never happen.

I invited him and his sister Joy over to my house in Fulham for a Sunday lunch party recently while Margaret was overseas. He didn't winge about the rather casual level of hospitality but joined in the fun. As he left, he said to my friends, 'My place at noon tomorrow; I've got a magnum of champagne in the fridge.'

'Oh, do you know when Mum's coming back?' I asked.

'Haven't got a clue.'

In 1995, when Parliament was recalled to discuss the Bosnian crisis, I was in her office when Margaret arrived home from a visit to Tokyo. She said hello to her husband, who promptly announced,

'I'm going to dinner at the Royal Academy,' and went straight off to change.

As I left, I said to Denis, 'Do make sure Mum gets some sleep – she must be shattered. Don't let her go on and on about Bosnia.'

'Oh yes, Christ, she can't rule the world,' he said in an exasperated voice. What he really meant was, 'I haven't got a hope – she'll do exactly what she wants to – but I'll try.'

Five years out of Number Ten, a great part of my parents' lives is still quasi-official. The invisible disciplines that come with Special Branch protection are still there and they go to more official functions than private parties. They don't go to church as often as they'd like on a Sunday because it means getting the detectives out on a Sunday.

Margaret is still in constant demand as a speaker, particularly in Japan and America, and although the lectures are lucrative, a more important factor is her passion for politics. She has too much drive and ambition to stop working. She loved being Prime Minister more than anything else in her life and knows she was good at it. She also knows that, as an admired elder statesperson, her experience, opinions and influence are in demand and can perhaps make a difference.

In some ways, very little has changed. There are still the regular wrestling bouts over speeches as she rewrites, striving to get it right for an overseas audience. Similarly, she keeps herself amazingly well-informed. Recently, I mentioned to her that I was doing a radio slot on the Bosnian crisis and she whipped down to her study and returned with the UN Resolution, along with a thesis on the arms embargo written by an academic.

She was back at the Aspen Institute in Colorado in August 1995 – the fifth anniversary of the speech she made there when Iraq invaded Kuwait. She left London on Thursday and was back on Sunday afternoon after spending a night in New York. Less than a fortnight later she delivered two Rajiv Gandhi memorial lectures in India – one in New Delhi and the second in Bangalore – and was out and back on two overnight flights in little more than a long weekend.

Twenty years after he first tried to retire Denis is still likely to find himself having an evening cocktail at home with Margaret's portrait for company, but companionship has hardly been a theme of their marriage.

On consort duties, such as the VE or VJ celebrations, Denis is faultless and he chats up the veterans and tells them with charm and courtesy how pleased he is to see them while they beam at meeting him. Never putting a foot wrong, he has become a role model for consorts, male or female, and has given them a first-class demonstration of how to conduct themselves. In Washington DC there is even a Denis Thatcher Society for husbands of powerful women.

Nor has he lost the knack of injecting some calm into the occasional panics that still beset his wife. Recently, when he was with her on a visit to the Harry S. Truman Institute Library and Institute for National and International Affairs in America, Margaret suddenly and unexpectedly had to make a speech. Speaking off the cuff rarely worries her when on her own territory, but down in Independence, Missouri, inspiration failed her. As she walked down a gravel path beside Denis, she frantically tried to think of what she could say about Truman.

'Very easy, dear, he was the architect of freedom,' said Denis.

She had her cue.

Eighty years of age is as good a time as any for someone to look back on their life. Anyone can walk on eggshells for a short time, few people manage it for eleven and a half years.

Denis provided Margaret with an important link with the real world – something appreciated by many of those around her. John Major recognized this in a thoughtful and generous speech he delivered on Margaret's seventieth birthday at a party held for her at Number Ten in October 1995. 'You cannot think of Margaret without thinking of Denis,' he said. 'There comes a time when every Prime Minister needs someone to give him or her the unvarnished truth and, in Denis, Margaret had just that.'

Sir Charles Powell goes further.

I think he was a lot of things – the single most important was that he was the great balancing factor, bringing stability and calmness into her [Margaret's] life. Whether it was on foreign trips or sitting up in the flat, he was the man who produced the, 'Let's get relaxed, keep it calm, let's think carefully, don't let's get over excited.' He was the constant reassuring presence, absolutely the rock of the Prime Minister's life. I think that was absolutely invaluable.

The truth is that he became rather a national institution, in the best possible sense. People came to adore Denis; he was just part of national life like the Tower of London, the Beefeaters and the Changing of the Guard.

But in this era of high-profile co-partner consorts, Denis prefers to describe his walk-on part as 'always present, never there'.

I think I was guided by two things. I said so on one occasion – certainly when we got to Number Ten, if not before – that 'God gave me a job to do, do it as best you can.'

I remember somebody saying, 'Why do you work so hard at it?' And I said, 'I'm not sure I can rationalize it, but if you want a sentence it is love and loyalty.' Those two things have guided my efforts, good or bad as they may have been.

I suppose it sounds terribly pompous but I really believe it. For forty wonderful years I have been married to one of the greatest women the world has ever produced. All I could produce – small as it may be – was love and loyalty.

I enjoyed Number Ten. After all, you've only got one life to live.

Few could argue that Denis has done a quite extraordinary job. It's remarkable that such a quiet, unassuming and once painfully shy man should now be regarded with such respect and affection.

It's ironic that if he hadn't been married to the first woman Prime Minister, he would probably have been very lukewarm about voting for one. He's certainly still obdurate on the possibility of women one day being allowed to blow the whistle at his beloved Twickenham. When the London Society of Rugby Football Union Referees was discussing the issue of female rugby referees, Denis rolled his eyes, pursed his lips, shook his head and said to the President, 'Sir, I don't understand what they're talking about. There's no such bloody thing. It's barmy.'

INDEX

Alexander, Andrew, 97
Allen, Penny, 15
Alliance party, 208
Alliss, Peter, 172
Anne, Princess, 212, 214
Anti-Aircraft Defence, School of, 37
Anyone for Denis, 145–8, 203
Archer, Jeffrey, Lord, 242
Archer, Mary, Lady, 242
Arnold, Matthew, 104
Aspen, Colorado, 258–9
Asquith, Herbert Henry, Lord Oxford
  and Asquith, 223, 248
Atkins, Humphrey, 10
Atkins, Maggie, 116
Atlantic Conveyor, 197
Atlas Marine Engineering Service, 33
Atlas Preservative Company: in New
  Zealand, 18; established at Deptford,
  21; Jack's management, 29, 31;
  Denis starts work, 31; Erith
  premises, 31, 33–4; Denis as works
  manager, 34–5; Jack's death, 39;
  Denis as general manager, 50, 51–
  2; Denis as managing director, 52,
  162; African market, 53, 67, 84;
  success, 66–7, 84, 91; product
  range, 67; Denis as chairman, 84;
  Torrey Canyon disaster, 87; sold to
  Castrol, 93–4, 168; trade unions,
  215
Attlee, Clement, Lord, 223
Attlee, Martin Richard, Lord, 223

Baker, Sir Herbert, 212
Baker, Kenneth, 261, 267

Baldwin, Stanley, Lord, 9–10
Ballesteros, Seve, 170–1
Banda, Dr Hastings Kamuzu, 238–9
Bandar bin Sultan, Prince, 259
Bandaranaike, Sirimavo, 124
Barbara (nanny), 70–2
Barber, Anthony, Lord, 225
Baryshnikov, Mikhail, 252
Bates, Arthur, 14
BBC, 243, 284
Beefeater Gin Trophy, 249
Belcher, Elizabeth Ann
  (great-grandmother), *see* Thatcher
Bell, Sir Tim: Tory advertising, 115,
  146, 148; *Anyone for Denis*, 146,
  148; 1987 election campaign, 243,
  244; MT retirement question, 253;
  party leadership election, 261
Belmont School, 85
Benn, Tony, 174
Bermuda, 257–8
Berry, Anthony, 220
Bhutto, Benazir, 151
Bird, Kathleen (mother), *see* Thatcher
Bird, Louisa Alice (grandmother), 23,
  27
Bird, Thomas (grandfather), 23
Black Monday, 246–7
Blair-Wilson, Colonel, 122
Blake, William, 244
Blofeld, Henry, 135
Boat Race, 249
Boat Show (1980), 160
Bonham Carter, Lady Violet, 225
Bossom, Alfred, Lord, 63, 65
Bradman, Donald, 26

Brighton bombing, 212, 218–21, 244

British Airways, 217–18

British Gas, 218

British Telecom, 218

Brittan, Sir Leon, 232–3

Brown, George, *see* George-Brown

Brownlie, Cyril, 26, 76

Buckingham Palace Road office, 277

Buckingham University, 244, 249

Burgdorf, Diane, *see* Thatcher

Burmah Oil Company: DT's role, 1, 5, 95–6, 168; DT's retirement, 1–2; Castrol takeover, 95; financial difficulties, 101–2, 246; leadership ballot, 263

Bush, Barbara, 252, 281

Bush, George, 252, 257–9, 271, 275, 280–1

Buthelezi, Chief Gatsha, 231

Butler, R.A., 93

Butler, Sir Robin, 77, 219, 269–70, 272

Caines, William, 18

Callaghan, Audrey, Lady, 123, 124

Callaghan, James, Lord, 116, 123, 212, 213

Cargill, Sir John, 7

Carr, Robert, 3

Carrington, Iona, Lady, 240

Carrington, Peter, Lord, 124, 150, 189, 191, 240

Carter, Amy, 179

Carter, Jimmy, 179

Carter, Rosalynn, 179

Castle, Barbara, Lady, 96

Castrol Oil, 94–5, 229

Catto, Henry, 258–9

Catto, Jessica, 258

Chamberlain, Annie, 126

Chamberlain, Neville, 223

Charles, Prince of Wales, 227

Chequers, 129–32, 186, 191, 197, 204, 205, 240–2, 253, 255, 257, 261–2, 271, 272

Chipman Chemical Company, 108, 116, 198

Chisholm, Sam, 278

Christie, Agatha, 66

Churchill, Sir Winston: 1945 election defeat, 45; 1950 election, 62, 64; Madeira visit, 65; death, 93, 278; quoted, 126; Chequers tree planting, 130; constituency, 192; portrait, 199; daughter, 223

Clements, Dick, 145

Clinton, Hillary, 153, 283

Colley, Arthur, 84

Commonwealth Heads of Government Conferences (CHOGMs), 149–52, 174, 176, 210–11, 230

Community Charge (Poll Tax), 248, 255

Conqueror, HMS, 194

Conservative Central Office, 205–6, 209

Conservative Party: leadership election (1975), 2–9, 101, 103; 1975 Conference, 111–12; 1979 election, 119–20; 1983 election, 208; 1983 Conference, 209; 1984 Conference, 218–20; 1987 election, 242–5; 1987 Conference, 247–8

Cook, Peter, 138, 143

Coombe, Kim, 51, 164

Court Lodge, Lamberhurst, 107, 113

Coventry, HMS, 197

Crabbe, Ken, 39–41

Crawford, Cynthia (Crawfie): Wolfson personal assistant, 117; arrival at Number Ten, 123; life at Number Ten, 127, 155, 162, 186, 235, 263; overseas tours, 238, 239, 258–9, 280; leaving Number Ten, 270, 276; MT's office, 277

CSX, 163

Curzon, George Nathaniel, Lord, 9–10

Daily Mail, 46-7
Daily Telegraph, 193, 204, 218
Davies, Pat, 96
Deedes, William (Bill), Lord: Denis's admiration for, 104; Schmidt dinner, 124; on Denis's role, 137-8, 144, 175-6; on Denis's relations with press, 158; golfing with Denis, 168-71
Deedes, Jeremy, 142
de Klerk, F.W., 231
de Klerk, Marika, 231
Dempster, Nigel, 46-7
Dodds, Norman, 61-2
Dormers, Farnborough, 77-8, 81, 95
Douglas-Home, Sir Alec, Lord Home, 9, 95
Douglas-Home, Elizabeth, Lady Home, 267
Downing, George, 129
Downing Street: life at Number Ten, 125-9; 250th anniversary dinner, 223-4
du Cann, Sir Edward, 4
Dulwich house, 253, 272-4, 275, 276-7

Eaton Square, 277
Edinburgh, Prince Philip, Duke of, 208, 209, 223
Edwards, Nicholas, 160
Edwina (daily help), 127
Elizabeth II, Queen, 155-6, 223, 223-4, 241
Elizabeth, Queen Mother, 156, 224
Elkington, Archie, 28
European Community, 100
Evans, Eric, 75
Evans, Lady Olwen Carey, 223, 224
Evening Standard 'Pub of the Year' competition, 265

Falklands, 188-201
Farrell, Nick, 147-8
Fergusson, Ewen, 76-7
Fieldhouse, Sir John, 194, 203

Fieldhouse, Margaret Ellen, Lady, 203
Finchley constituency, 78-9, 196, 205, 206, 209, 244
Flood Street, Chelsea, 1, 7, 12, 99, 101, 103, 105, 119, 123, 125-6, 183
Foot, Michael, 174, 208
Forbes, Malcolm, 252
Forte, Charles, Lord, 225
Fox, Robert, 145, 146
Franco, General Francisco, 111
Fraser, Malcolm, 152
Frost, Lady Carina, 278
Frost, Sir David, 278, 280

Gaddafi, Colonel Muammar, 233
Gadney, Cyril, 54, 74
Galtieri, General Leopoldo, 191
Gandhi, Indira, 124, 211-14
Gandhi, Mahatma, 212
Gandhi, Rajiv, 211-13
Garnier, Jean, 183
General Belgrano, 194-5
George VI, King, 224, 278
George-Brown, George, Lord, 140
Gerda (nurse), 70
Gilbert and Sullivan, 26, 30-1, 38
Giles, Mick, 133
Gilmour, Ian, Lord, 173
Glamorgan, HMS, 199
Goldsworthy, Russell, 19
Gorbachev, Mikhail, 221-3, 239
Gorbachev, Raisa, 221-2
Gow, Ian, 259
Graham, Billy, 252
Graham, Katharine, 182, 280
Green, Kent, 30, 64
Grenada, US invasion, 210, 251
Gulf War, 271, 275
Gyngell, Bruce, 278
Gyngell, Kathy, 278

Haig, Alexander, 182, 193, 194
Haig, Patricia, 182
Halfords, 108
Hamilton, Sir Archibald, 283

Harrods bombing, 221
Harvey, John, 192, 259
Hawke, Bob, 230
Healey, Denis, Lord, 208
Heath, Sir Edward: party leadership,
    2, 9, 10, 95, 101, 107; Prime
    Minister, 99–100, 123, 138, 216;
    election (1974), 272; 'Heath
    Crash', 246–7; leadership election
    (1975), 2, 4, 101, 262; attitude to
    MT's leadership, 104, 283
Henderson, Sir Denys, 217
Henderson, Mary, Lady, 182
Heseltine, Anne, 203
Heseltine, Michael: 1983 election
    campaign, 203; resignation, 232;
    Westland affair, 232; leadership
    question, 256; leadership challenge,
    259; leadership election, 263, 265,
    270, 273
Heston, Charlton, 182
Hickman, Sir Howard, 47
Hickman, Margot, Lady (née
    Kempson, Denis's first wife), 46–
    51
Hobbs, Jack, 25–6
Holyrood School, Bognor, 25
Home, see Douglas-Home
Hong Kong, 232
Hope, Bob, 182
Hope, Dolores, 252
Howe, Derek, 183
Howe, Geoffrey, Lord, 7, 124, 232,
    255–6, 259
Hunt, Sir Rex, 200
Hurd, Douglas, 265, 270, 273
Hussein, King of Jordan, 176
Hussey, Marmaduke, 122, 242
Hussey, Lady Susan, 122, 242

IDC group, 160
India, 211–14
Industrial Welfare Society, 32
Ingham, Sir Bernard: on Denis's public
    image, 137; *Anyone for Denis*, 146;
    on Denis's press relations, 157–8,

236; Mark's rescue, 184; Malawi
    visit, 239; Bermuda visit, 257; MT's
    resignation, 267
Ingrams, Mary, 143
Ingrams, Richard, 138, 140, 142, 145,
    286–7
Invincible, HMS, 197, 198
IRA, 221, 259
Isle of Wight, 79

Jacklin, Tony, 171–2
Jackson, Jim, 94–5
Jamieson family, 31
Jay, Antony, 203
Jay, Peter, 243
Jenkins, Roy, Lord, 173, 208
Johnson, Frank, 208
Johnson, Johnnie, 75
Jopling, Michael, 196, 222
Joseph, Helen, Lady, 3
Joseph, Sir Keith, 3, 108, 124
Junor, Sir John, 110
Jurade St Emilion, 281

Kaunda, Kenneth, 152
Keating, Frank, 75
Keays, Sara, 209
Kempson, Leonard, 49
Kempson, Margot, see Hickman
Kennedy, Jimmy, 37–8, 48, 50
Kilner, Phyllis, 5, 7, 12, 33, 108
King, Isabel, Lady, 242
King, John, Lord, 217–18, 242
Kingston, Bob, 105, 220, 221
Kinnock, Neil, 242, 260
Kipling, Rudyard, 20, 27
Klosters, Hotel Walserhof, 227
Kuwait, invasion, 258–9

Labour Party: 1945 election, 45; 1974
    election, 2; SDP relations, 173–4;
    1983 election, 207, 208; 1987
    election, 242–3
Ladbrokes, 4
Laing, Hector, Lord, 183
Law, Andrew Bonar, 10

Lawson, Nigel, Lord, 216, 246, 255–6
Lawton, Frederick, 71
Lee of Fareham, Lord, 130
Lee-Potter, Lynda, 47
Lenzerheide, Switzerland, 89–90, 93
Levin, Bernard, 104
Lewin, Sir Terence, 194
Libya, US bombing, 233–4, 240
Life magazine, 222
Lloyd, Dorothy, 223, 224
Lloyd George, David, 130, 223, 224
Lockhead, Sheila, 223
London Society of Rugby Football Union Referees, 54, 60, 68, 74, 158–9, 249, 290
Lords Taverners, 249

McAlpine, Alistair, Lord, 242, 261, 264–6, 277
McAlpine, Romilly, Lady, 242
MacDonald, Ramsay, 223
Macfarlane, Sir Neil, 172–3
McGill, Angus, 265
MacGregor, Sir Ian, 216
Macleod, Iain, 95
Macmillan, Harold, Lord Stockton, 9, 130–1
McPherson, Bob, 73
McWhirter, Ross, 105
Madeira, 65–6
Major, John, 222, 265, 270, 273, 289
Malawi, 238–9
Mandela, Nelson, 231
Marcos, Imelda, 140
Margaret, Princess, 203
Marseilles, 42–4
Marsham Street, Westminster, 95
Mastriforte, Sue, 6, 9
Meir, Golda, 124
Menuhin, Yehudi, 99
Meyer, Sir Anthony, 256
Mill Hill School, 29–32, 51, 88
Millar, Sir Ronald (Ronnie), 111, 112
Miller, John, 57, 61, 64, 77
Miller, Phee, 61, 64, 77

Mitchell, Leslie, 75
Mitterrand, François, 177, 263
Moi, Daniel Arap, 134
Monk, Ron, 168
Monte Cassino, 42, 201
Montgomery, Bernard Law, Lord, 40, 44, 54–5
Moore, Henry, 129
Morley, Robert, 144
Morris, Vivian, 15
Morrison, Sir Peter, 261–2, 264, 267
Morrow, Ann, 122
Mossie (daily help), 127
Mount, The, Lamberhurst, 96–7
Mubarak, Hosni, 237
Murdoch, Rupert, 217, 278
Murray-Wood, Bill, 30
Muzorewa, Abel, 149
Mymwood School, 85

National Coal Board, 216
National Paint Federation, 52–3, 61
National Union of Miners (NUM), 216, 217
Neave, Airey, 6, 10, 118, 221
News of the World, 46, 146
Nicklaus, Jack, 171–2
Noakes, Michael, 284
Noonan, Joseph, 209
Nott, Sir John, 191–2, 194
Nunn, Trevor, 124

Old Millhillians' Club, 51, 54, 60, 68, 88
Onslow, Sir Cranley, 259
Operation Baytown, 41
Operation Husky, 40
O'Reilly, Tony, 77
Ormonde, SS, 39
Owen, David, Lord, 173
Owen, W.T., 18

Page, Sir John (Jack), 186, 195–6, 241
Paint Materials Trade Association, 53
Palmer, Arnold, 171

Pao, Y.K., 172–3
Parkinson, Ann, Lady, 203
Parkinson, Cecil, Lord: political
  career, 124, 210; friendship with
  Denis, 124, 210; golfing with Denis,
  172–3, 257; Falklands crisis, 194;
  1983 election campaign, 203, 207;
  resignation over Sara Keays affair,
  209–10; style, 243
Patten, John, 240
Pellatt, Tom, 78
Perón, Eva, 124
Peyton, John, Lord, 7
Philip, Prince, Duke of Edinburgh,
  208, 209, 223
Picarda, Noel, 143
Pile, Stephen, 161
Poll Tax, see Community Charge
Ponsonby, Amanda, 277
Portillo, Michael, 240
Powell, Sir Charles: memories of Denis
  at Chequers, 132; memories of Denis
  on overseas tours, 178, 236; Malawi
  visit, 239; Bermuda visit, 257;
  leadership election, 264, 267; on
  Denis's role, 289–90
Price, Charles, 220
Prior, James, Lord, 7
Private Eye, 138–45, 148, 174, 203,
  286–7
Pym, Francis, Lord, 194

Quayle, Dan, 280
Queen's Own Royal West Kent
  Searchlight Battalion, Royal
  Engineers, 36
Queenswood School, 85
Quinton Hazell, 108, 116, 133, 193

Ramphal, Sir Sonny, 211, 245
Reagan, Nancy, 182–3, 251–2
Reagan, Ronald: Presidential
  progress, 178; London visit (1969),
  179–80; MT's visit (1981), 180–2;
  assassination attempt, 183;
  relationship with MT, 179–82,

186, 210, 233, 251; Seven-Nation
  Summit, 207; Grenada invasion,
  210; South Africa sanctions, 230;
  retirement, 251; Savoy dinner, 279
Reece, Sir Gordon: press handling of
  Denis's first marriage, 46; memories
  of Denis, 106, 110; on Denis's role,
  113, 153; 1987 election campaign,
  243; MT's retirement question, 253;
  leadership election, 261–2; illness,
  286
Rees, Arthur, 216
Rees-Mogg, William, Lord, 104
Reid, John (great-grandfather), 17
Reid, Margaret Ann (grandmother),
  see Thatcher
Reid, Margot (great-grandmother), 17
Rice, Sir Tim, 279
Ridley, Nicholas, 255
Robbins, Peter, 75
Roberts, Alfred (father-in-law), 57,
  59, 64
Roberts, Margaret, see Thatcher
Roberts, Muriel (sister-in-law), 57, 62
Roberts, Suzanne, 165–7
Roberts, Vic, 165–6
Robilliard, Joy: constituency
  secretary, 126; life at Number Ten,
  126, 127, 155, 190, 223; MT's
  resignation, 267, 269; moving out
  of Number Ten, 270; at House of
  Commons, 277
Rodgers, William, Lord, 173
Roe, David, 33, 34, 50, 61
Rolls-Royce, 99
Rowe, Joseph, 16
Rowlands, Edward, 190
Royds, Sir Percy, 74
Rushton, Willie, 265
Ryder, Caroline, see Stephens
Ryder, Richard, 114, 266–7
Ryder Cup, 249

Saatchi and Saatchi, 115, 146
Sanders, Sandy, 75
Saudi Arabia, 151

Scargill, Arthur, 216
Schmidt, Helmut, 124–5, 224
Scotney Castle, 113, 123, 140, 205, 207
Selleck, Tom, 252
Shah, Eddie, 217
Sheffield, HMS, 195
Shelton, Sir William, 6, 9, 10, 104, 105, 107
Shields, Susie, 10, 12–13
Sicily, wartime, 39–42
Sidgwick & Jackson, 204
Sieff, Marcus, Lord, 124
Sir Galahad, 199
Sir Tristram, 199
Ski Club of Great Britain, 89
Skinner, Dennis, 268–9
Skinner, Reuben, 64
Smith, Ian, 230
Soames, Mary, Lady, 223
Social Democratic Party, 173–4
Sollett, Ray, 193
South Africa, 229–31
Soward, Stan, 56, 58
Sports Aid Foundation, 249
Sports Aid Trust, 249
Steel, Sir David, 208, 212, 223
Steel, Judith, Lady, 224
Stephens, Caroline, 150, 218, 266–7
Sutch, Screaming Lord, 209
Sutcliffe, Herbert, 26
Swan Court, Chelsea, 66, 70, 77, 103
Swit, Loretta, 252

Taylor, Peter, 124, 190, 209
Tebbit, Margaret, Lady, 11, 203, 220
Tebbit, Norman, Lord: on Denis after leadership election (1975), 10–11; political career, 124; friendship with Denis, 124; 1983 election campaign, 203–4; Brighton bombing, 218, 220; party chairmanship, 243; MT's resignation, 265
Tennyson, Laura, 123
Thatcher, Carol (daughter): relationship with father, 87, 97, 134, 266, 287; relationship with mother, 5, 6, 11, 85–7, 89–90, 98–9, 115, 205, 206–7, 247, 269, 276, 278, 288; birth, 69–70; childhood, 70–2, 77, 81–2, 85–7, 90; family holidays, 79, 89–90, 97; education, 81, 83, 98; law studies, 6, 8; mother's election as party leader, 8–9, 11; career, 115, 118, 146, 193, 204, 218, 222, 265, 278; in Australia, 15, 115, 117, 204; at Number Ten, 122–3, 124, 126; at Chequers, 129–30, 203, 240–2, 261–3; White House visit, 179–82; return to Britain, 183; brother's Sahara exploits, 183–7; memories of Falklands crisis, 189–99; memories of sterling crisis, 202–3; 1983 election diary, 203–6; Brighton bombing, 218–19; 1987 election campaign, 244; 1990 party leadership question, 261–6; mother's resignation, 266–9, 278; leaving Number Ten, 270–1
Thatcher, Sir Denis: family background, 15–23; birth, 23; childhood, 24–9; education, 24, 25–6, 29–33; career plans, 31; shorthand course, 32–3; career at Atlas, 33–5, 50, 51–3, 60, 66–7, 84, 87, 91–4; girlfriends, 34; war service, 36–45; father's death, 39; in Sicily, 39–42; in Marseilles, 42–4; military MBE, 44; first marriage, 46–51; *Accounting and Costing in the Paint Industry*, 53; African business trips, 53, 78, 84, 91–3, 178, 193, 229, 238; first meets MT, 56–60; political career, 57–8; courtship and engagement, 61–4; wedding and honeymoon, 64–5; fatherhood, 68, 69–72, 79, 97; Farnborough house, 77–8, 95; MT's Finchley selection, 78–9; family holidays, 79, 89, 97; 1959 election campaign, 79–82;

Thatcher, Sir Denis: family *cont.*
husband of MP, 83; sells Atlas to Castrol, 94–5; Marsham Street flat, 95; career at Burmah Oil, 95–6, 101–2, 229; Lamberhurst house, 96–7; Flood Street house, 99, 101; Corsican holiday, 101; attitude to party leadership election, 3–8; wife's election as party leader, 7–13, 104; life with Leader of the Opposition, 105–17; retirement from Burmah Oil, 1–2, 108, 154–5; non-executive directorships, 108,163; no-interview policy, 110, 156–7; 1979 election campaign, 118–20; at Buckingham Palace, 121–2; arrival at Number Ten, 122–3; position as PM's husband, 123–5; life at Number Ten, 125–9, 232; at Chequers, 129–32; 'Dear Bill' letters, 138–45, 148, 184–6, 253, 286–7; *Anyone for Denis*, 145–8; overseas tours and visits, 149–52, 174, 176–82, 211–14, 232, 236–9; son's Sahara exploits, 183–7; Falklands crisis, 188, 192–9; Falklands visit, 199–201, 202; 1983 election campaign, 203–9; Mrs Gandhi's funeral, 212–14; Brighton bombing, 218–21; Gorbachev visit, 221–3; seventieth birthday, 225–6; Christmas at Chequers, 240–2; 1987 election campaign, 242–5; seventy-second birthday, 243; Black Monday, 246–7; wife's retirement question, 253–4; party leadership question (1990), 259–60, 261–5; wife's resignation, 266–71; leaving Number Ten, 270–4; Dulwich house, 272; lifestyle after Number Ten, 276–7, 281–9; office, 277; baronetcy, 279–80; achievement in consort role, 289–90

lifestyle: appearance, 1, 28–9, 49, 133, 174, 208, 225; cars, 34, 60, 63, 132–3, 279; common sense, 5, 153–4; 'Dear Bill' letters, 138–45, 148, 184–6, 253, 286–7; domestic skills, 106; drinking, 40, 42–3, 44, 109, 127, 137, 143, 148, 174, 214, 249, 287; factory visits, 109, 208, 237; food, 1, 226–8; health, 2, 73–4, 83, 91–3, 115, 171, 176; left-handedness, 25, 147, 258; letter-writing, 128, 160; overseas tours and visits, 149–52, 174, 176–82, 211–14, 232, 236–9; political views, 58, 96, 100, 152–3, 215, 217–18, 229–31, 234, 284; religion, 86, 240–1; security, 132–3, 225, 244, 287, 288; shyness, 24–5, 30, 37, 108, 135, 226; smoking, 125, 287; speeches, 158–60, 164, 244, 249–51, 284–7; temperament, 12, 24–5, 28–9, 203, 211, 226

relationships: daughter, 87, 97, 134, 266, 287; friends, 165–71, 210, 216, 217–18, 277; media, 104, 110, 137, 157–8, 206, 236, 243–4, 249–50, 283–4; son, 87, 183–7, 284; wife, 113, 219, 234–6, 253–4, 264, 287–90; wife's career, 8, 66, 68, 78, 79–80, 83, 91, 92, 98–9, 104, 106–7, 115–16; world leaders, 175–7, 211, 231, 245

sports: cricket, 24, 25–6, 30, 67–8, 87–8; golf, 31, 97, 107, 113, 132, 168–72, 205, 207, 249, 257–8; riding, 26; rugby family tradition, 15, 24, 26; rugby at school, 26, 30; rugby at son's school, 87–8; rugby refereeing, 54–5, 68, 73–7, 97, 226, 290; sailing, 2, 26; skiing, 89; South African politics, 231; sportsmanship, 249–51

Thatcher, Diane (*née* Burgdorf, daughter-in-law), 84, 240

Thatcher, Doris (aunt), 21, 26, 31, 84, 91, 92

Thatcher, Edith (aunt), 16, 19, 31, 91, 92

Thatcher, Elizabeth Ann (*née* Belcher, great-grandmother), 16

Thatcher, Elizabeth Helen (grandfather's first wife), 16

Thatcher, Jack (father): birth, 18; childhood and education, 19–21; career, 21, 22, 26, 29, 39; marriage, 23; fatherhood, 24–6, 30–1, 59, 76; freemasonry, 25, 27, 29, 34; Gilbert and Sullivan, 26, 30–1, 38; sailing, 2, 26; Kipling Society, 27; shorthand, 32–3; ill-health, 33, 34, 38; politics, 34; New Zealand trip (1936), 35; wartime experiences, 38–9; son's wedding, 50; death, 39

Thatcher, John (great-grandfather), 16

Thatcher, Joy (sister), 24, 26, 28–9, 33–4, 35, 45, 49, 88, 91, 108

Thatcher, Kathleen (*née* Bird, mother), 22–3, 24–8, 31, 35, 45, 88, 91, 92

Thatcher, Margaret Ann (Madge, *née* Reid, grandmother), 17, 19, 23, 27–8

Thatcher, Margaret, Baroness (*née* Roberts, second wife): appearance, 7, 61, 64, 128, 152, 203, 205; temperament, 12, 90–1, 121, 147–8, 151, 153–4, 178; first meets Denis, 56–60; Dartford candidate, 56–8, 60, 62, 63–4, 77, 81; courtship and engagement, 61–4; wedding and honeymoon, 64–5; law studies, 68, 70, 71; motherhood, 68, 69–72, 80–1, 85–7, 97; in chambers, 71; Orpington candidature attempt, 72–3; tax law, 73; health, 73, 93, 240; interest in rugby, 76; on safe seat candidate list, 77; Farnborough house, 77–8; Finchley candidate, 78–9; family holidays, 79, 89–90, 97; 1959 election, 79–82; maiden speech, 83–4; family life, 85–7, 97; Parliamentary Secretary, 90; 1964 election, 93; in opposition, 95, 100–1; Minister of Education, 97–9; Corsican holiday, 101; party leadership election (1975), 2–9, 101, 102; Leader of the Opposition, 9–13, 103–17; speech-writing, 105, 111, 288–9; 1975 Party Conference, 111–12; Iron Lady, 114, 148; Far East tour, 115; 1979 election, 118–20; meetings with Queen, 121–2, 155–6; arrival at Number Ten, 122–3; Schmidt dinner, 124–5; life at Number Ten, 125–6; at Chequers, 129–32; *Anyone for Denis*, 146–7; Commonwealth Heads of Government Conferences, 149–52, 210–11; SDP successes, 173–4; relationship with Reagan, 179–82, 186, 210, 233, 251; son's Sahara exploits, 183–7; Falklands crisis, 188–99; Falklands visit, 199–201, 202; 1983 election, 203–9; US invasion of Grenada, 210–11; Mrs Gandhi's funeral, 212–14; trade union relations, 215–16; miners' strike, 216–17; Brighton bombing, 212, 218–20, 244; Gorbachev visit, 221–3; husband's seventieth birthday, 225; sixtieth birthday, 225; South Africa policy, 229–31; Westland affair, 232–3, 240; Libya bombing, 233–4, 240; Oxford honorary degree snub, 235; Christmas at Chequers, 240–2; 1987 election campaign, 242–5; Black Monday, 246–7; Community Charge, 248, 255; tenth anniversary as PM, 252–5; retirement question, 253–4; ERM issue, 255; leadership challenge (1989), 256; Kuwait invasion, 258–9; leadership challenge (1990), 259, 261–5;

Thatcher, Margaret, Baroness *cont.*
resignation, 266–70; leaves
Number Ten, 270–4; Dulwich
house, 272, 275; lifestyle after
resignation, 275–8, 287–8; office,
277, 280; OM, 279; farewell tours,
280–1; memoirs, 283; life peerage,
284; speaking engagements, 288–9;
seventieth birthday, 289
Thatcher, Margot (*née* Kempson, first
wife), *see* Hickman
Thatcher, Mark (son): temperament,
9, 78; birth, 69; childhood, 69–72,
77, 78, 86, 90; health, 79, 93; family
holidays, 79, 89, 97; education, 81,
83; relationship with father, 87–8,
284; life at Flood Street, 105; at
Number Ten, 10, 122–3, 124, 126;
at Chequers, 129–30, 203; driving,
129, 183–7; business exploits, 183,
236, 284; rescued from the desert,
183–7, 223; Gorbachev visit, 223;
marriage,240; mother's leadership
question, 264, 271; Number Ten
departure, 271; future baronet,
279
Thatcher, Thomas (grandfather), 14,
15, 16–22
Thistle, 26
Thomas, Peter, 111
Thomas, Vera, 131
Thomson, Andrew, 205
Thorndike, Dame Sybil, 66
Thurlow, Ron, 205
Trinder, Tommy, 38
Truman, Harry S., 124, 289
Truman, Margaret, 124
Tuck, Basil, 66, 91
Turnbull, Andrew, 273
Twickenham, 76, 87–8, 164–5, 175,
225, 243, 290
Tyler, Rod, 46–7, 234, 242

Uffington, Wiltshire, 15–16, 21, 27
United States, 178–82, 210–11,
233–4

Vanderbilt, Gloria, 182
van der Post, Laurens, 231
Verney, Charlotte, 183

Wakeham, Alison, Lady, *see* Ward
Wakeham, John, Lord, 220
Wakeham, Roberta, 220
Walden, George, 240
Walters, Sir Alan, 203, 255
Walters, Barbara, 182
Walters, Vernon, 233
Wanganui, New Zealand, 14–15,
16–20, 26
Ward, Alison (*later* Lady Wakeham),
46, 101, 111, 117
Watson, Tom, 171
Wedmore, Benjamin Collingham,
209
Wells, John, 138–40, 142–3, 145–7,
186, 225
Westland affair, 232–3, 240
Westminster, 5th Duke of, 272
White House, Washington, 178–82,
251–2
Whitehead, Anthony Peter, 209
Whitelaw, William (Willie), Lord, 4,
7, 194, 254
Whitney, Ray, 240
Whitting, Barbara, 227
Whitting, Len, 168–72, 198, 227
Willes, Margaret, 204
Williams, Diana, 168
Williams, George, 93–4, 98, 168
Williams, Johnny, 75
Williams, Shirley, Lady, 173, 174
Wilson, Harold, Lord: 1974 elections,
2, 100, 101; 1964 election, 93;
1966 election, 95; 'Mrs Wilson's
Diary', 138; Number Ten
anniversary dinner, 224; Rhodesia
sanctions, 230; Gleneagles
Agreement, 231
Wilson, Mary, Lady, 124, 138, 224
Wogan, Terry, 145
Wolfson, David, Lord, 117, 240
Wolfson, Susan, Lady, 240

Yarranton, Mary, Lady, 233
Yarranton, Sir Peter, 133, 158–9, 165, 225
Yarranton, Sandy, 233
York, Sarah, Duchess of, 227, 283
Young, David, Lord, 244

Zardari, Asif, 151
Zetter, Paul, 267
Zia Ul-Haq, Mohammed, 176
Zimbabwe, 238

25 de Mayo, 194

In Search of Churchill

Martin Gilbert

'A fascinating account of tireless and resourceful detective work...
Gilbert's zeal in pursuit of every scrap of evidence on Churchill's
life is an example to all biographers. The work he has done puts all
historians of the twentieth century, and all students of Churchill,
incalculably in his debt.'   JOHN GRIGG, *Sunday Telegraph*

Martin Gilbert's biography of Churchill is probably the longest
biography ever written, and in the opinion of many one of the
greatest. *In Search of Churchill* is the story of Gilbert's thirty-year
quest for his subject. He reveals the staggering extent of his historical labour and shares with the reader some of the great moments in
his pursuit. It is also the story of those who have helped Gilbert
along his way, as they had earlier helped Churchill on his.
Secretaries, assistants, diarists, correspondents, soldiers, politicians, civil servants; the eminent and the humble: all of them had
tales to tell, many of them published here for the first time. The
portrait that emerges of Churchill is almost tangibly intimate. Here,
perhaps more than in any other book about him, is the character of
the man, untrammelled by formalities, as seen by those who were
with him at his most unguarded moments.

'This book, part intellectual autobiography, part coda to his monu-
mental Churchill biography, is required reading for Churchill
enthusiasts. It takes on all the pace of an adventure novel.'
                                ANDREW ROBERTS, *Literary Review*

'Any world statesman close to the end would be grateful for a
Martin Gilbert. What better way to meet your maker than in the
happy knowledge that a leading scholar is devoting his career to
tracking down, codifying and publishing every detail of your own?
Gilbert is a careful scholar with a proper respect for evidence, fact,
accuracy . . . . His primary concern is setting the record straight -
and in this entertaining and enjoyable book he explains how he sets
about it.'   BEN PIMLOTT, *Guardian*

ISBN: 0 00 637432 8

Harold Wilson

Ben Pimlott

'One of the great political biographies of the century.'
A. N. Wilson, *Evening Standard*

'The rehabilitation of Wilson has begun – and Ben Pimlott, the best British political biographer now writing, has made a hugely impressive job of it . . . His narrative of the young Wilson, from sickly boy scout to academic pupil of the formidable William Beveridge, and then to chirpy junior minister is quite outstanding – clear, thoughtful and gripping. This early part of the book is central to its larger achievement, since Pimlott shocks the reader out of basic anti-Wilson prejudice by demanding a human sympathy for him. The little, blinking, stubborn boy, hiding his hurt with cocky self-confidence, lives on as a permanent presence within the powerful politician . . . Some biographies enter the political discourse at once, thanks to their innate qualities and lucky timing. There are so many echoes of the Wilson years in the politics of today that this happy fate must surely belong to Pimlott's book. Wilson's soured relationship with the press (and the terrible problems it caused for him) – the conflict within him between national leadership and good party management – even the growing debate about national decline – are all suggestive and worth lingering over. As, indeed, are almost all of these 734 well-researched and finely written pages.'   Andrew Marr, *Independent*

'A masterly piece of political writing.'
Bernard Crick, *New Statesman*

'The narrative gallops along, sweeping the reader with it in a rush of excitement. A mass of complex detail is marshalled with the art that conceals art.'   David Marquand, *Times Literary Supplement*

'Fascinating . . . Pimlott the X-ray has produced another work of formidable penetration.'   Roy Jenkins, *Observer*

ISBN 0 00 637955 9

The Downing Street Years

Margaret Thatcher

The appearance of Margaret Thatcher's memoirs has been one of the most eagerly awaited publishing events in many years. As this book now shows, rarely has such a sense of anticipation been so amply justified.

No prime minister of modern times has sought to change Britain and its place in the world as radically as Margaret Thatcher, leader of the Conservative Party for fifteen years and prime minister for eleven and a half. In *The Downing Street Years* she sets out with characteristic forcefulness and conviction the reasons for her beliefs and how she sought to put them into action. She gives riveting accounts of the great and critical moments of her premiership – the Falklands War, the Miners' strike, the Brighton bomb, the Westland Affair and her three election victories. Her judgements of other world statesmen and her Cabinet colleagues are often brutally frank, her criticism devastating. The book ends with an account of her last days in power which is as gripping as anything in thriller fiction.

This is a work intensely revealing of the mind and personality of its author: her thoroughness, her passion for change, her tenacity and her astonishing determination are evident in every chapter of the book. The impression which emerges is, as one recent commentator put it, of a world-class battleship at full steam ahead.

0 00 638321 1

£9.99